IMAGES
of America

McNeil Island

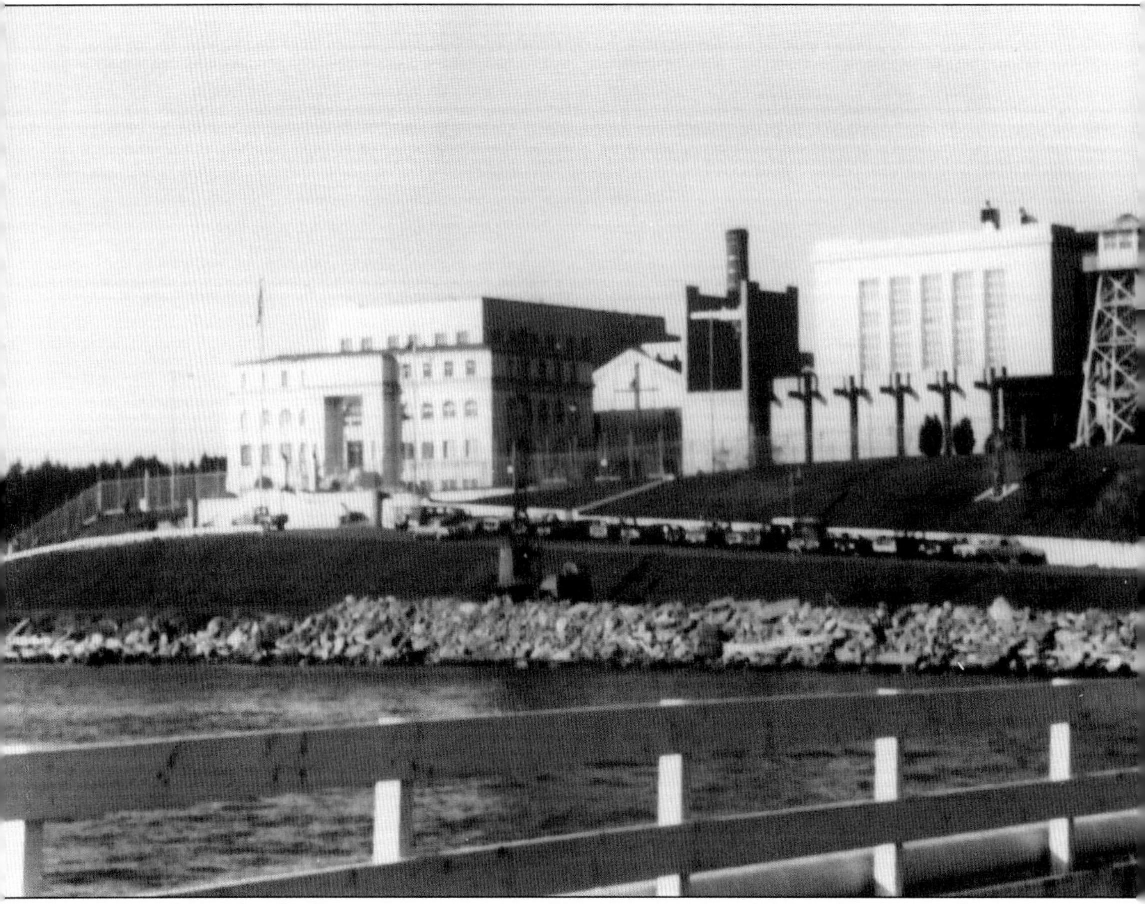

McNeil Island Federal Penitentiary is pictured here in 1980. From left to right are the administration building, Two House, Chapel of Mount Tahoma, and Three/Four House. Two House was designed by architect John Proctor, who then lived on McNeil. The administration building and Three/Four House were envisioned by the noted architectural firm of Heath, Gove, & Bell, which also did Paradise Lodge and a roster of notable buildings around Pierce County. Moritz Kundig created the award-winning chapel. In 1981, Washington State took over the facility, and it became McNeil Island Corrections Center (MICC). Three/Four House was demolished in 1995 and replaced with modern cell blocks. (Washington State Archives.)

On the Cover: Inmates enter the Magic Eye into the sally port in 1939. Three/Four House is on the right; both were designed by Heath, Gove, & Bell in the 1920s. John Proctor's 1907 Two House is on the left. (Courtesy of George and Faye Cripe.)

IMAGES
of America

McNEIL ISLAND

Ann Kane Burkly and
Steve W. Dunkelberger

ARCADIA
PUBLISHING

ISBN 978-1-4671-1628-2

Published by Arcadia Publishing
Charleston, South Carolina

Printed in the United States of America

Library of Congress Control Number: 2015953298

For all general information, please contact Arcadia Publishing:
Telephone 843-853-2070
Fax 843-853-0044
E-mail sales@arcadiapublishing.com
For customer service and orders:
Toll-Free 1-888-313-2665

Visit us on the Internet at www.arcadiapublishing.com

This book is dedicated to all the people who have loved McNeil Island over the years.

Contents

Acknowledgments

This book began on a 2012 boat ride to McNeil. I mentioned writing a book about McNeil's magnificence; Steve Dunkelberger, who came along with me, and Chris Moore, of the Washington Trust for Historic Preservation, suggested an Arcadia book, and here we are.

The book would not exist without the goodwill of all the people who valued McNeil enough to document her uniqueness. People kindly helped with research by photographing items, and many generously shared their scrapbooks, photographs, and their homes. Having lived on McNeil, I had items myself, and the most difficult part of the entire process was selecting photographs for publication. The willingness of those in corrections to open their homes to a stranger, connected only by our love of McNeil, validates my belief that only genuinely good people go into corrections.

Many agencies have been helpful in acquiring images, and we would not have the excellent ones we do without the assistance of the Washington Department of Corrections, which was very generous to this island brat. Jean Cammon Findlay and Anderson Island Historical Society friends Loren Else, the Cripes, and the Hawkes all shared goodwill and photographs from their collections. Rubado family descendants donated an invaluable photo album, and the Northwest Room of the Tacoma Public Library was helpful. The national and state archives provided many digitized records and prints, and we are thankful for their reserves and that our editor did not quit. I truly thank everyone who helped—you know who you are.

The most pleasurable part of making this book has been sharing old times and tall tales from across the eras of McNeil with island residents, staff, and even formerly incarcerated individuals. It was really heartwarming realizing that even those who had served time on McNeil thought well of her and their stay there. Nothing is more telling of the quality of staff and the tranquil influence of the island than those heartfelt admissions. Hopefully, the images selected for this book convey the singular specialness of McNeil, both as a community and as a uniquely storied prison.

INTRODUCTION

McNeil Island was such a magical place no book can truly do it justice. We have tried to show the fullness of life on the pristine island, which really made it the special place it was. In this history book, we cover McNeil's start, to the end of the Federal Bureau of Prisons (BOP) penitentiary era, with a mention of the former McNeil Island Corrections Center (MICC), and the Special Commitment Center (SCC) that still operates on the island. Surrounded by natural beauty on every side, McNeil's staff enjoyed a small-town feel instead of a prison atmosphere, and for the incarcerated, a more therapeutic feeling prevailed than at other prisons.

In 1841, cartographer Charles Wilkes named McNeil Island after William Henry McNeill, who was married to a Nishga chieftess and had captained the Hudson Bay Company steamers *Beaver*, *Llama*, and *Una*. McNeill had welcomed Wilkes to Puget Sound. In 1853, Oregon Trail pioneer Ezra Meeker settled on McNeil Island but sold the property in 1862. Meeker's homestead was where the present prison yard is located.

On January 22, 1867, Congress authorized the establishment of a territorial jail in the Washington Territory. On September 17, 1870, the federal government purchased 27.27 acres on McNeil Island for a federal prison, which officially opened in 1875. These 27 acres are the site of the main penitentiary complex today.

The original McNeil Island cell house was built in 1873. In November 1874, the penitentiary was placed under the direction of the US marshals. It was during Charles Hopkins's tenure that the prison opened on May 28, 1875. By the end of that year, the total prison population was nine.

In 1889, Washington was admitted to the Union. The first warden at McNeil Island Penitentiary was Gilbert L. Palmer in 1893. The total staff consisted of seven guards. Prior to closing in 2010, the custodial force of McNeil Island was approximately 411 for both the main facility and North Complex.

In 1891, the Three Prisons Act indirectly declared McNeil a federal penitentiary, but it was not until 1904, when Attorney General Philander C. Knox was placed in charge, that McNeil Island finally functioned fully as an official US prison. In 1927, an additional 67 acres were purchased for a prison farm to produce vegetables and fruit. Due to the need for water, another 1,618 acres were purchased in 1931. This brought the total prison acreage to 2,107, just less than half the island's 4,445 acres.

In 1934, the federal farm camp (North Complex) was completed, and by 1947, it had a population of 320 inmates. At one time, McNeil provided for itself by raising vegetables, fruit, pork, poultry, waterfowl, eggs, beef, and milk. The island packed beef for use by facilities throughout the state (approximately 70,000 pounds per week) at the meat processing plant, while the dairy supplied state schools with milk until private enterprise complained about government cost savings owing to lower prisoner labor cost.

Through the process of individual purchases and eminent domain, a fee simple title was granted to the US government for McNeil Island in 1936. The final transaction in 1940 involved 3.1 acres.

The entire island, roughly seven square miles, was now under federal control. Much development ensued, and in 1937, the damming of Eden Creek to create a sustainable water supply was begun; in 1944, Butterworth Lake was born. In 1948, construction began on the staff training center, which housed the resident's chapel, community center, and two-room schoolhouse. School was held for the first time in 1952–1953. A large pool complex with bathhouse and a caretakers' house were also added to the center's facilities. Continual improvements in prison property and inmate programs continued through the 1970s.

In 1976, the Federal Bureau of Prisons decided to shift to smaller institutions and began shutting down its federal penitentiary on McNeil Island. McNeil eventually became a federal prison camp, and former McNeil correctional officer Darrell Grey returned to McNeil as camp superintendent. Washington State's need for additional prison space prompted state officials to explore the possibility of acquiring the prison. However, in 1980, the Mariel Boatlift occurred, and McNeil was tapped to hold many of the refugees who came to America from Cuba. After the refugees were sorted, an agreement was reached between the states and the federal government, and in early 1981, McNeil began converting over to state operations. Some federal corrections staff transitioned to state positions after training new staff in procedures.

In 1981, the state signed a lease with the federal government granting the state use of the penitentiary. Later that year, the Washington Department of Corrections (DOC) began moving inmates into the newly renamed McNeil Island Corrections Center. Inmates were put to work fixing and improving the facility, which had not been maintained during the later years of federal operation. In 1984, the island was officially deeded to the state of Washington.

In 1990, the legislature appropriated $90 million to expand MICC, and by 1993, the DOC had built five new medium-security residential units, each housing 256 inmates, and a sixth segregation unit with 129 one-man cells. The original cell block was demolished and replaced in 1994 with an inmate services building housing a hospital, educational center, recreation room, hobby shop, music room, and gymnasium.

In 1993, the legislature established the 200-bed Work Ethic Camp at MICC, following in the honor camp's footsteps, one of only six in the nation. The balance of the island, 3,119 acres, was deeded to the Washington Department of Fish and Wildlife (DFW) for continuing use as a wildlife refuge. Wildlife agents are generally on the island once a week to monitor wildlife. Their boats also occasionally patrol the beaches. The land deeded for DOC use is in 24 separate parcels. Some parcels are about a hundred acres, and some are only two or three acres. For example, DOC land includes acreage for the minimum and medium facility complexes but almost none of the beaches or Butterworth Lake.

DOC is responsible for all island buildings, utilities, and roads. DFW is responsible for island wildlife. There are 52 island homes and a K-5 elementary school. A new deed to McNeil was issued in 1996 from the Department of Justice, which permitted construction of the new Work Ethic Camp. All other original deed covenants continued, such as maintaining the federal graveyard, public access limitations, and protection of wildlife. In 2001, the deed was modified to accommodate the Department of Social and Health Services' Special Commitment Center, which still operates on 87 acres of McNeil today.

On April 1, 2011, the oldest prison facility in the Northwest, the first federal penitentiary, and the last prison island in the nation marked the end of an era, closing its doors forever.

One

The Beginning

Puget Sound was formed around 13,000 years ago as the last ice age came to a crashing end, when a massive ice dam across what is now the Strait of Juan de Fuca suddenly broke loose, allowing billions of gallons of seawater from the Pacific Ocean to rush inland and mix with the ice and waters that had gathered in the lowlands between what are now the Olympic and Cascade mountain ranges.

The tumbling shards of ice crushed and battered the bedrock to create the rocky soil that makes it almost impossible to plant anything in backyard gardens to this day. The valley left by the flood is now at the bottom of Puget Sound. The high ground became islands that dot the waterway. McNeil is one of those.

The Puyallup, Nisqually, Steilacoom, Squaxin, and Fox Island tribes used the island as a rest stop during their trade and fishing trips around the waterway, at least after it was formed. Archaeological evidence shows that Native Americans camped on the island's shores and hillsides for short periods before continuing their travels.

It is perhaps no coincidence that Native American tribes in the Northwest have their own "Noah story" about a great flood, but their version has them collecting on a hill to avoid the rising waters rather than sailing on a boat that included two of every animal. Archeologists date Native American tools found in the area to 2,000 years before the creation of Puget Sound. It seems fitting that tribal folklore includes a tale of Native Americans gathering on a mountain on the southern edge of what is now the Chambers Bay Golf Course, a hillside that is now gone after years of industrial use.

This patch of earth and water, where McNeil Island was formed and later settled, is the focus of this book.

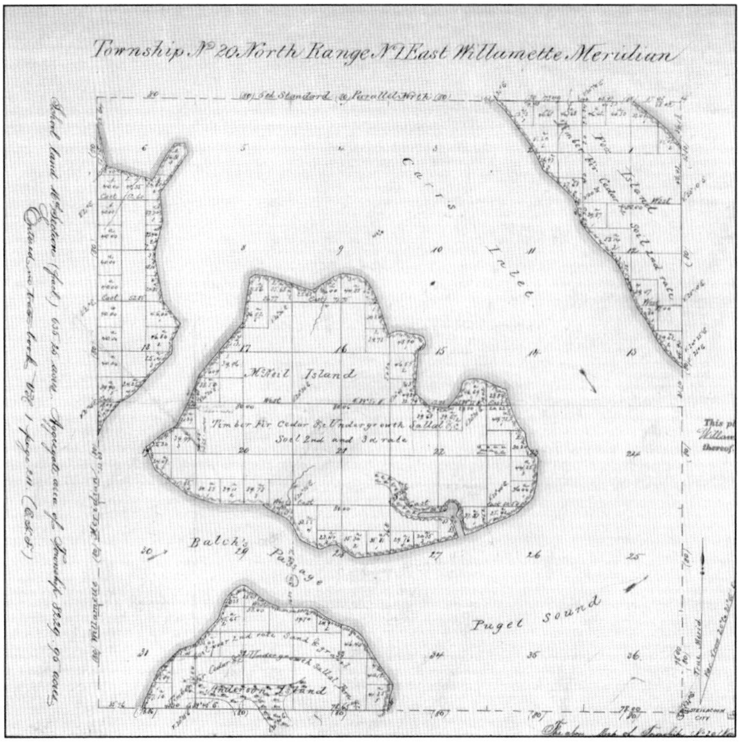

On this 1854 map, McNeil Island is in the middle of the Balch Passage to the south, Puget Sound to the east, and Carr Inlet to the north. Ezra Meeker's cabin was on the inlet on the southeastern side of McNeil. This area now houses Shop Row and the marine sheds. The slough was filled in as the prison grew. (Washington State Archives.)

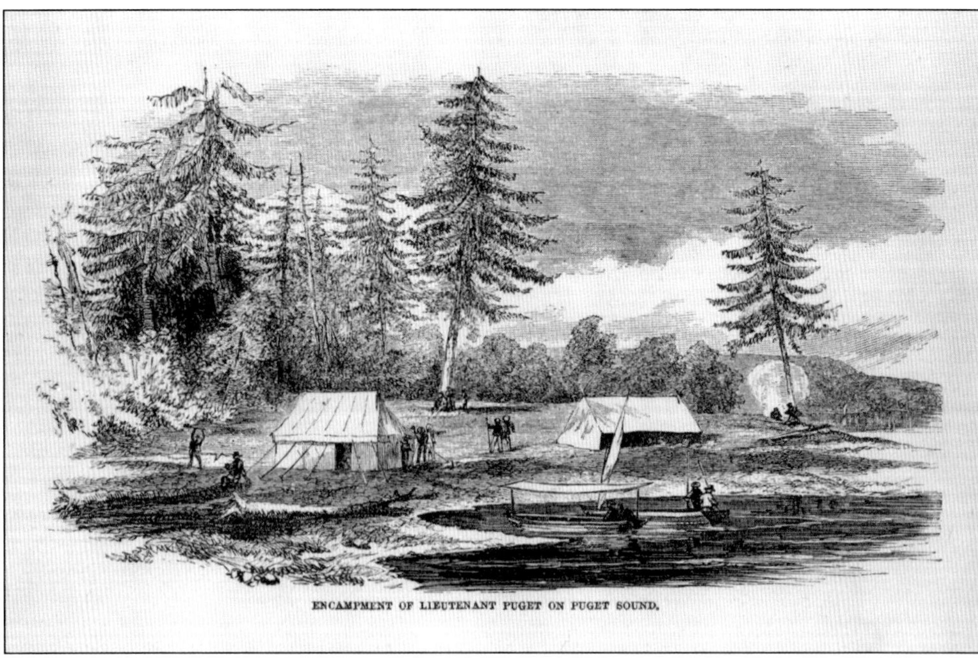

Lt. Peter Puget served aboard the HMS *Discovery* under the command of George Vancouver during a voyage of 1791–1792 to explore the South Pacific and the coast of North America for possible trade routes and resources. Puget served with such distinction during a trip aboard two rowing boats to map the southern reaches of the waterway that Vancouver named the entire sound after him. (Washington State Archives.)

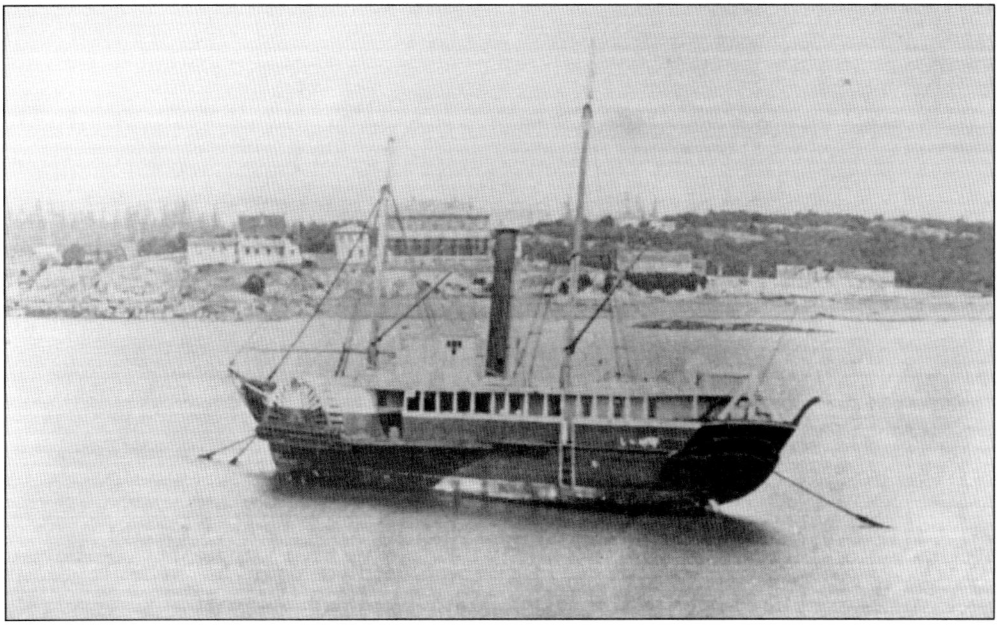

The *Beaver* was the first steamship to sail the West Coast from Canada to Oregon. She was captained by William Henry McNeill (note the two l's) between 1837 and 1851, who showed great hospitality to cartographer Charles Wilkes, who then named an island after McNeill. An American captaining a British ship was very unusual, which also played a role in Wilkes's naming of the island. The second "l" was lost to history. (Washington State Archives.)

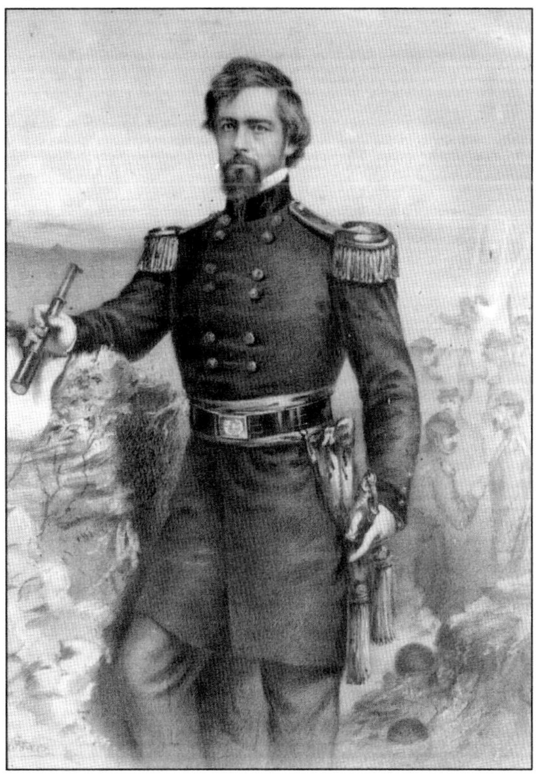

After serving with distinction during the Mexican-American War, Isaac Ingalls Stevens worked as a surveyor until he was appointed the first governor of the Washington Territory in 1853. He set out to survey the region in hopes of finding a railroad route from the East to the virgin coast of the Pacific Northwest thanks to the support of Pres. Franklin Pierce and Secretary of War (and future Confederate president) Jefferson Davis. Stevens would later serve in the US Congress and as a brigadier general in the Union army against his former secretary of war. He died during the Battle of Chantilly. (Washington State Archives.)

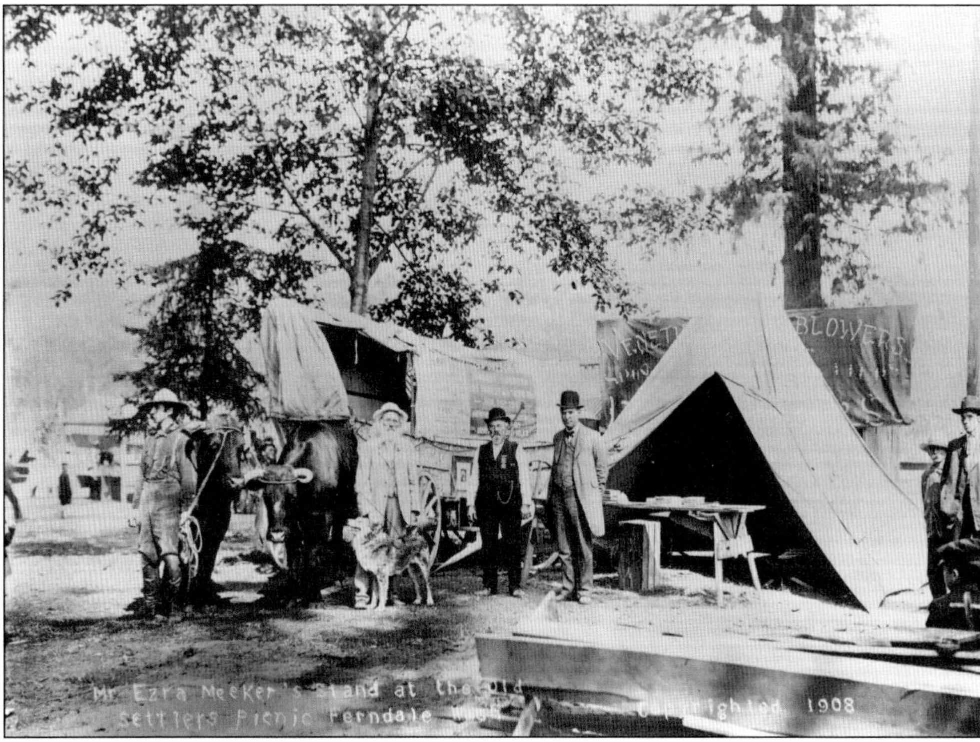

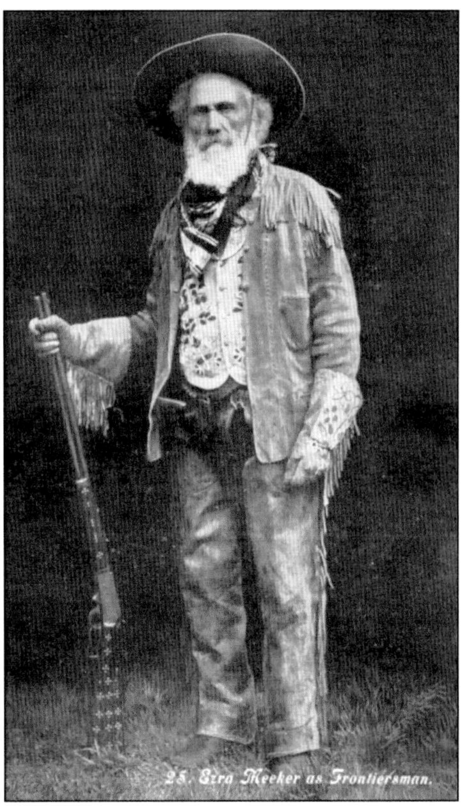

Ezra Meeker (center), seen at a 1908 settlers' picnic in Ferndale, is often pictured as an old man with a gray beard, but he was an original Oregon Trail pioneer who ended the trail on Puget Sound's McNeil Island. In June 1853—55 years before this photograph was taken—Meeker and his brother Oliver first settled on McNeil just opposite the town of Steilacoom. (Washington State Archives.)

After leaving McNeil Island, Ezra Meeker made his fortune as the "hop king" of Puyallup Valley. He served as Puyallup's first mayor and continually promoted Puget Sound to would-be settlers in the Wild West. Meeker retraced the route on promotional trips during the final decades of his life, making his last trip by airplane in 1924. (Washington State Archives.)

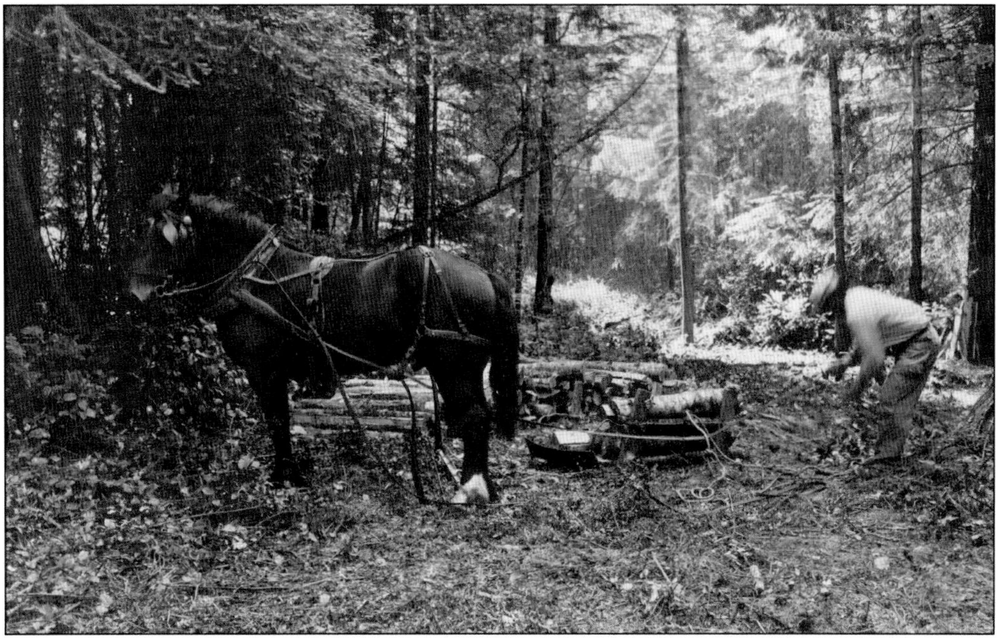

McNeil was virgin land when settlers arrived, forcing them to first clear their homestead to build a cabin, tack sheds, livestock pens, and vegetable gardens before establishing any sort of creature comforts like a school, church, or post office. Fir and oak trees milled onsite by the settlers made up their buildings, the ultimate in self-sustainability. (Washington State Archives.)

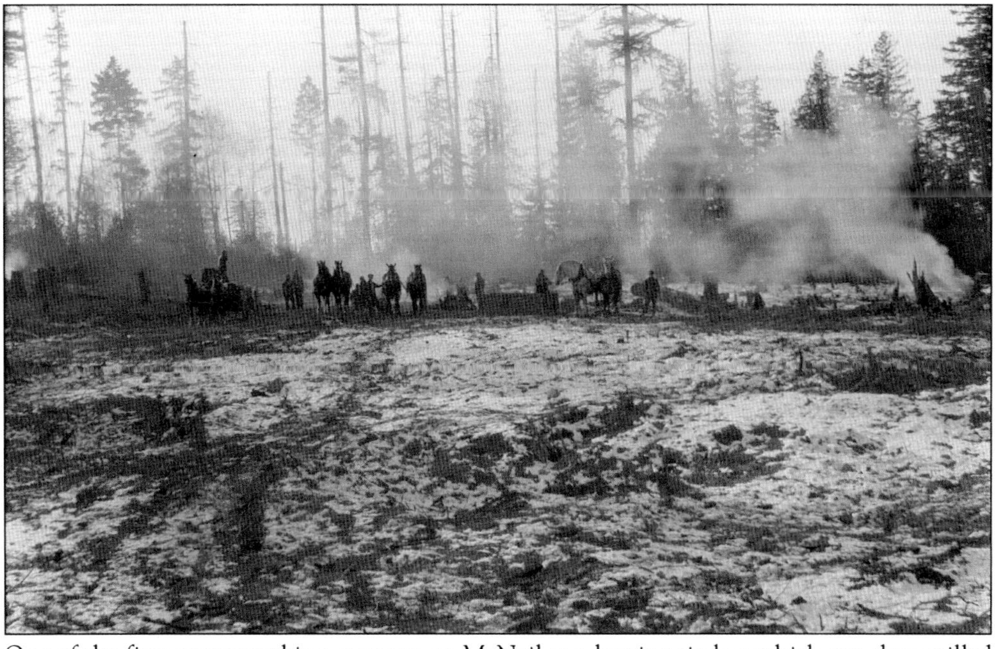

One of the first money-making ventures on McNeil was logging timber, which was then milled on the island or at nearby Anderson Island, or across the water in Steilacoom. The work meant long hours of backbreaking labor, a steady stream of horses to drag the logs to a collection point near the water, and the constant starting and monitoring of slash fires to burn off smaller limbs and branches. (Washington State Archives.)

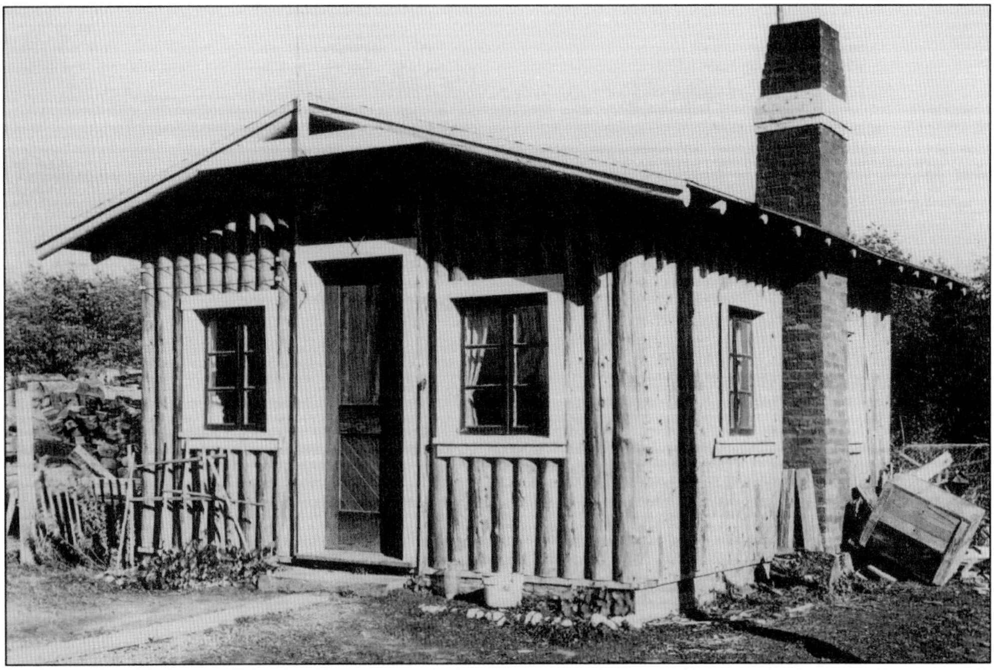

Some log cabins on the island were more elaborate than others, with some little more than wood-framed tents. Others, like this one with its brick chimney, benefited from access to the prison brickyard. This is similar to Ezra Meeker's cabin, sans his cat-and-clay chimney. Like Meeker's, it has a stone fireplace, glass windows, and a wooden floor. (Washington State Archives.)

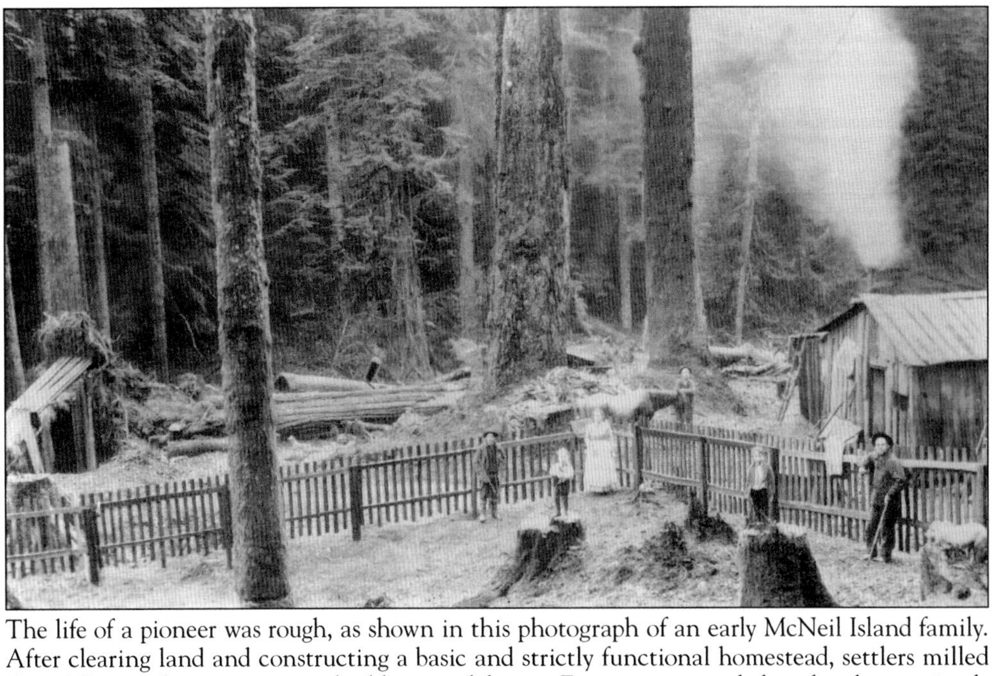

The life of a pioneer was rough, as shown in this photograph of an early McNeil Island family. After clearing land and constructing a basic and strictly functional homestead, settlers milled their fallen timber to construct buildings and fences. Fences were needed as they kept animals away from the residence and prevented livestock from wandering off and getting lost in the dense forest that blanketed the island. (Washington State Archives.)

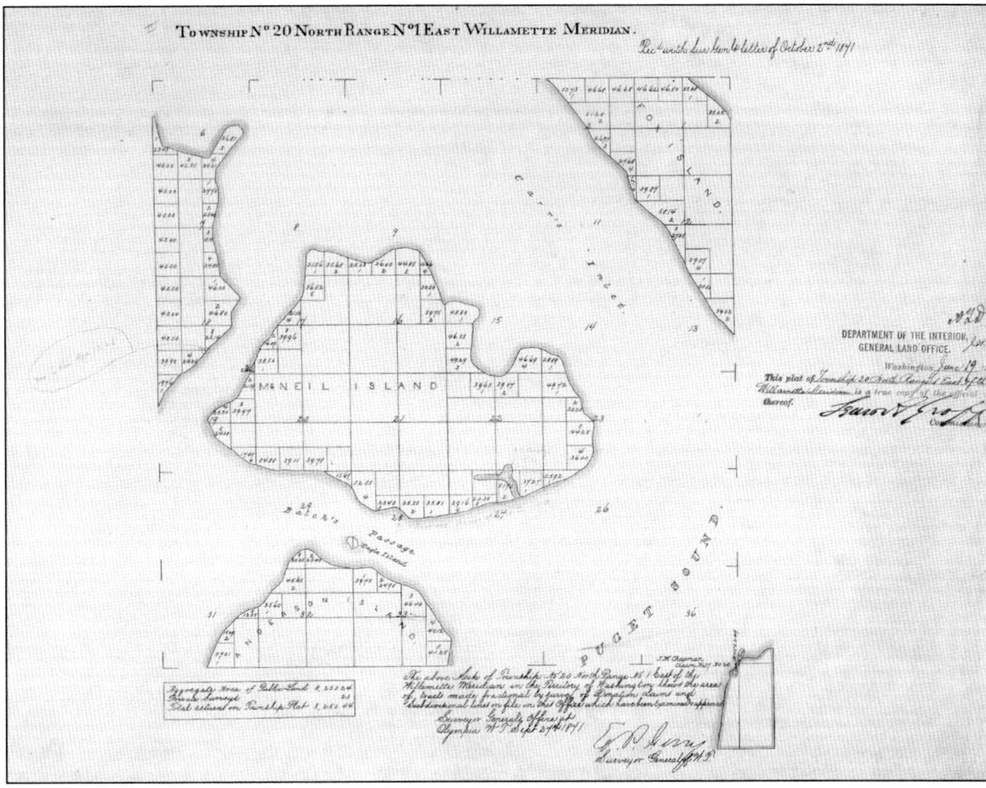

This map of the island from the 1890s includes survey notes from 1841 and 1871 to show that most of the waterfront parcels were claimed, while much of the interior remained available for purchase. Written in light pencil is a note pointing out the location of the penitentiary and the area reserved for use by the US government. (Washington State Archives.)

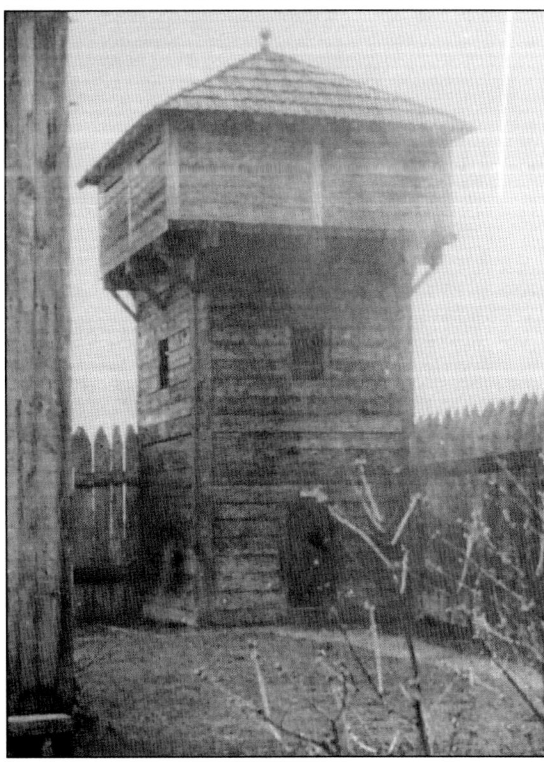

In 1875, the territorial jail was surrounded by a stockade fence and tower, built on the backs of inmates, as hard labor was part of early sentencing and was needed to run the prison. Under the Bureau of Prisons and then under state operation, a job was a reward, as the small amount of money earned went into the inmate's account, and time working was time outside the cells. (Washington State Archives.)

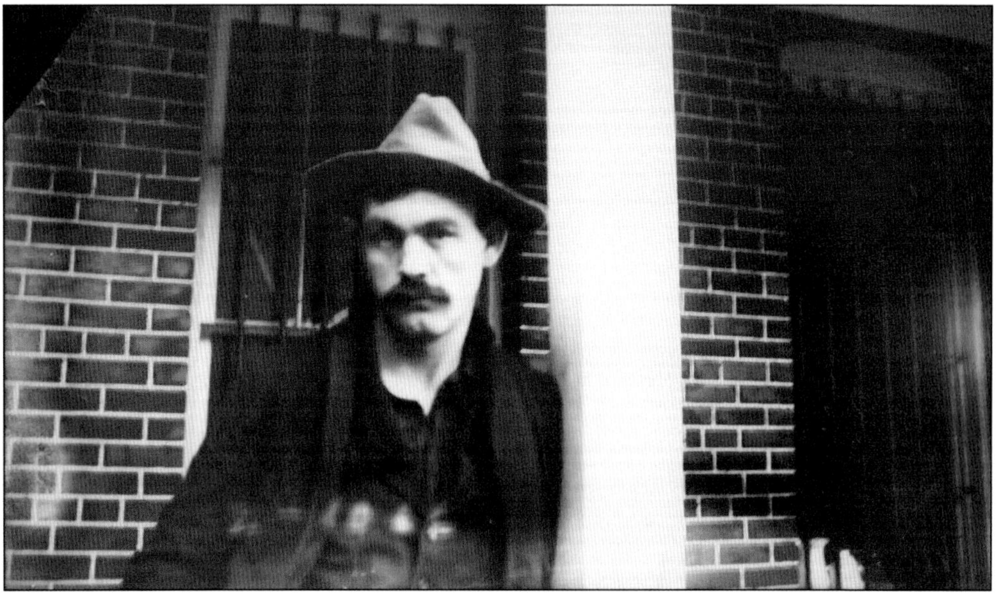

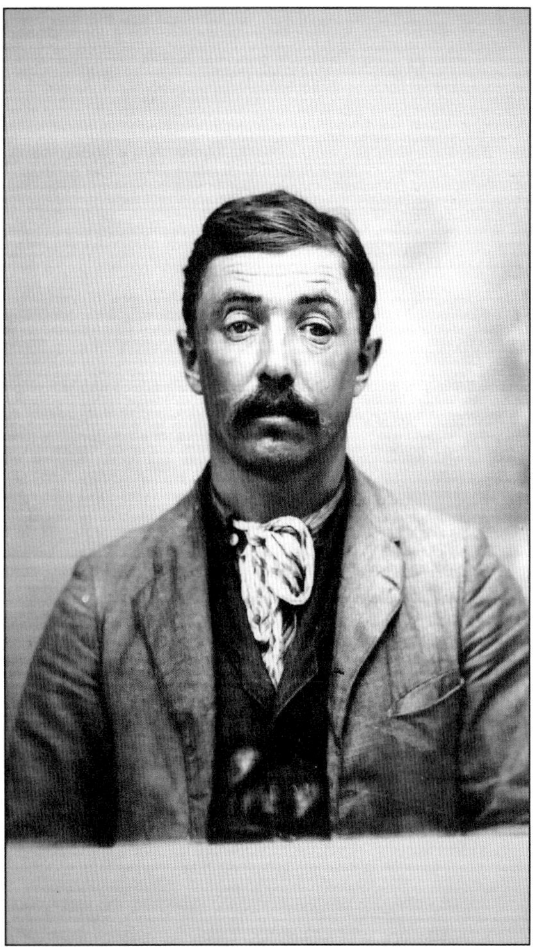

Abraham Gervais, 28, the first prisoner at McNeil territorial jail, was convicted of selling whiskey to Indians. He was to serve 20 months, according to the intake journal. Gervais was escorted by US marshal Edward Kearney, along with two other prisoners, as noted by the duty officer. They were noted in the log, issued their black and white uniforms, and immediately put to work grading the prison yard. (National Archives and Records Administration.)

Frank Lafontaisis, the second inmate at McNeil, was also convicted of liquor sales to Indians but was sentenced to 18 months. "Squaw men," as they were known, were white men who married into tribes, and they typically also supplied Indians with liquor, a crime with a sentence of up to two years of hard labor. McNeil's third inmate, John W. Hand, robbed a Fort Walla Walla store and served only one year. (National Archives and Records Administration.)

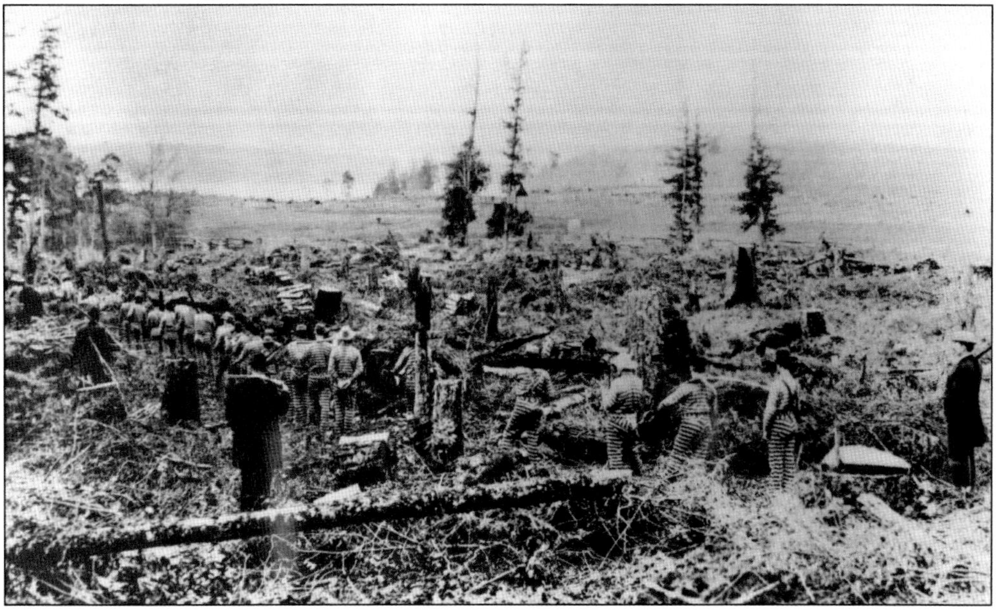

These inmates are clearing land guarded by warden Gilbert L. Palmer and his armed guards. Palmer served as warden from 1893 to 1901. Just as McNeil's first three prisoners did on opening day, Marshal Kearney wanted the men employed every day except Sunday, and his dictate continued forward, owing to necessity. McNeil functioned self-sufficiently, with staff and inmates providing most everything needed to survive, with minimal provisions sourced from the mainland. The first guards even rotated cooking their own meals. (Washington State Archives.)

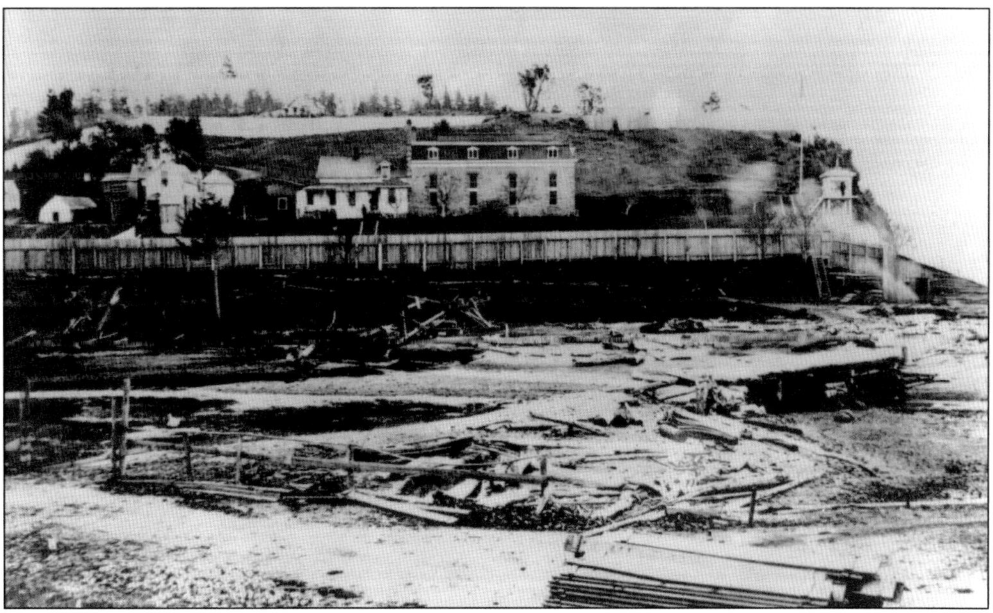

The masonry jail was constructed in 1873 and lacked staff space, a bath, and kitchen. It had just 48 small double cells. A needed addition delayed opening until 1875. Fire was a concern, with the kitchen made of wood. The area in the foreground was filled in 1904, and the new land now houses the marine office. The prison was made from what could be harvested and created on the island, including bricks, shingles, timbers, and firewood. (Washington State Archives.)

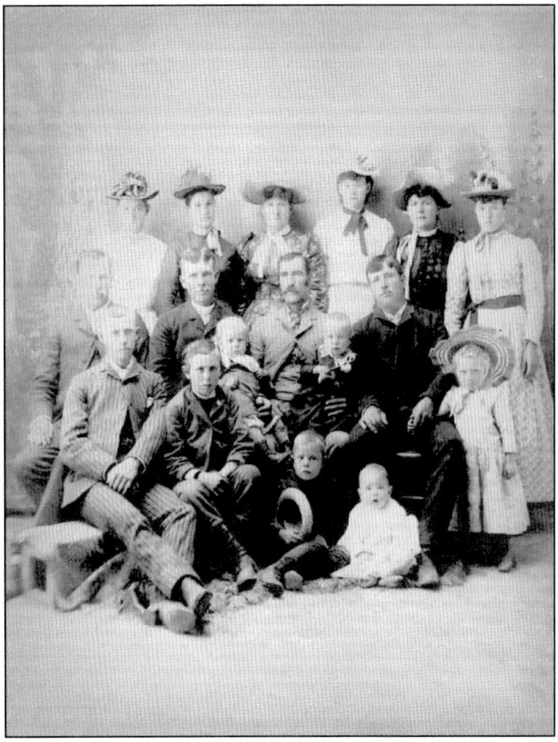

Carl and Ida Julin are pictured with their children. Carl Julin worked at McNeil's sawmill and brickyard starting in 1882. He bought a shack for $10 in 1884 and became a farmer who sold land. He also ran a post office and store. He was Gertrude's postmaster until his 1922 death. His children Esther and Charles followed as postmaster and shopkeeper, respectively, until the BOP bought out all residents in 1936. (Rick Anderson, Anderson Island Historical Society.)

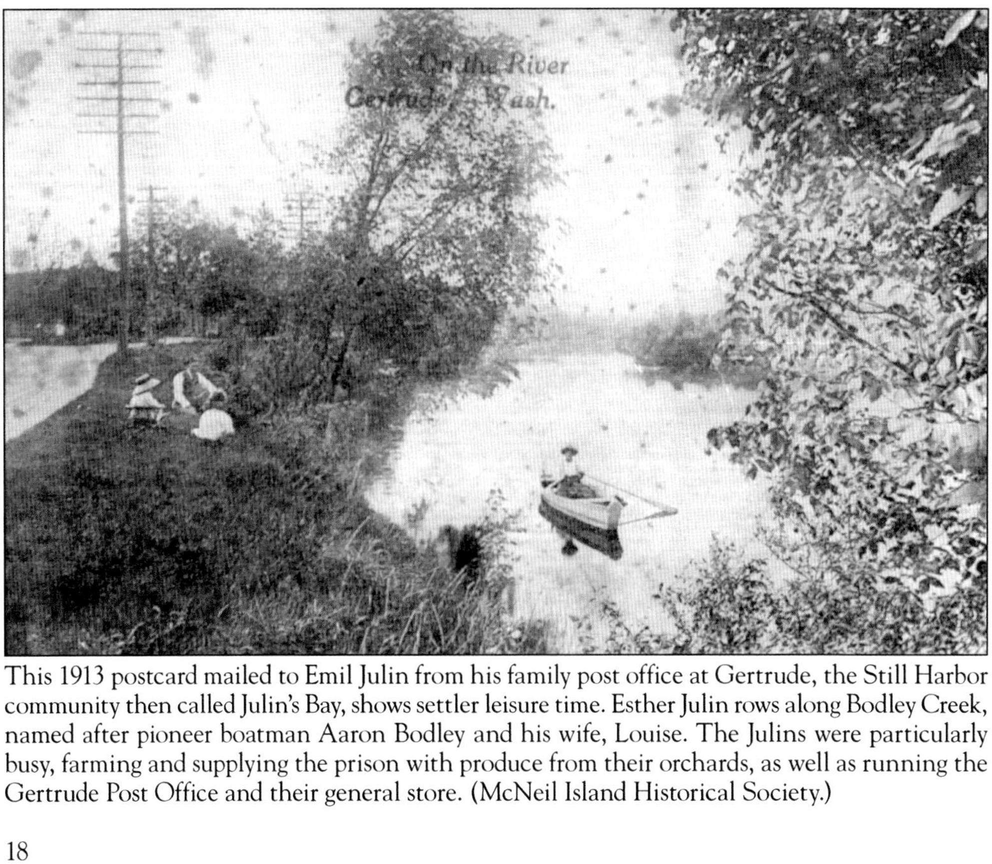

This 1913 postcard mailed to Emil Julin from his family post office at Gertrude, the Still Harbor community then called Julin's Bay, shows settler leisure time. Esther Julin rows along Bodley Creek, named after pioneer boatman Aaron Bodley and his wife, Louise. The Julins were particularly busy, farming and supplying the prison with produce from their orchards, as well as running the Gertrude Post Office and their general store. (McNeil Island Historical Society.)

Two

Settlers and Territorial Jail

McNeil gained its name in 1841, after a boat captain who worked for Fort Nisqually, a Hudson Bay Co. trading and farming post. Capt. William Henry McNeill was later credited with founding the city of Victoria, British Columbia. The island's name dropped the second "l" over time and was standardized to McNeil around the turn of the 20th century.

William Henry McNeill is best known in other parts of the world for his 1830 expedition from Boston to the Pacific Northwest around Cape Horn. He later became the chief factor at Fort Simpson in 1856 and retired in 1863 to live on Vancouver Island.

Another notable person linked to the island is pioneer Ezra Meeker, who homesteaded here with his brother Oliver in 1853 before founding Puyallup in 1862. Ezra and his wife and child lived on McNeil off and on for nine years before selling to F.A. McCarty. Ownership transferred a few times before falling to James Emmons Smith, who would later donate the plot of land for the jail. Other settlers who inhabited McNeil with Smith included John Swann, who logged and fished the local waters before the jail was built.

Other settlers included John Holm and James Ward, who sold lots to men like Charles Julin, who cleared roads, set up a post office, and gave his name to Julin's Bay, now called Still Harbor. McNeil became a thriving island with three communities: Bee, Gertrude, and Meridian. The island had three post offices, two schools, two churches, a brickyard, a general store, two lumber mills, boat building and rental facilities, and St. Ann's Home for unwed mothers. McNeil also had two cemeteries; the first was established for the prisoners, and the second was created in 1905 for the pioneers. Prior to 1905, pioneer dead were either buried on Anderson Island or in family plots on McNeil. The grave of Edwin Holm, an infant buried under four madrone trees on family land, is the only recognized pioneer grave on McNeil, as the residents of the pioneer cemetery were disinterred in 1936. The last madrone at Edwin's grave was felled on January 17, 2019. The site will be replanted from its cuttings.

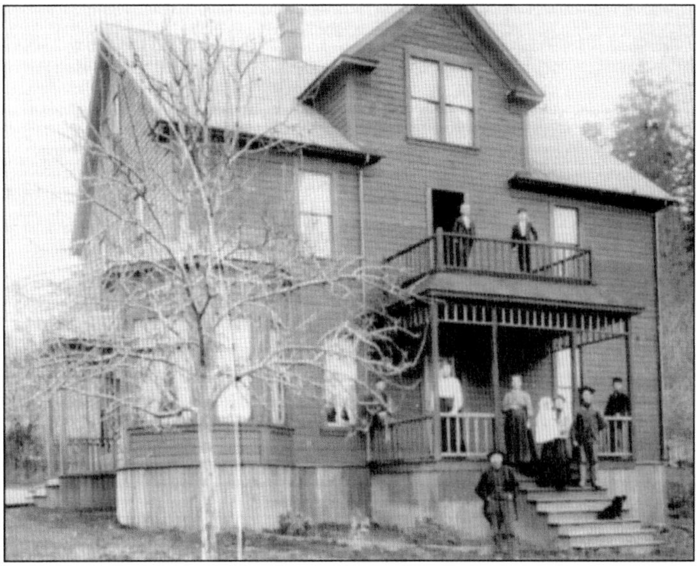

Carl Julin's first McNeil residence was a shanty he bought for $10. He prospered and moved up to this mansion to house his nine children. The Julins were one of the most active families on the island, hosting church services in their home prior to the Sunne church being built south of the prison near the current ferry slip. (Anderson Island Historical Society)

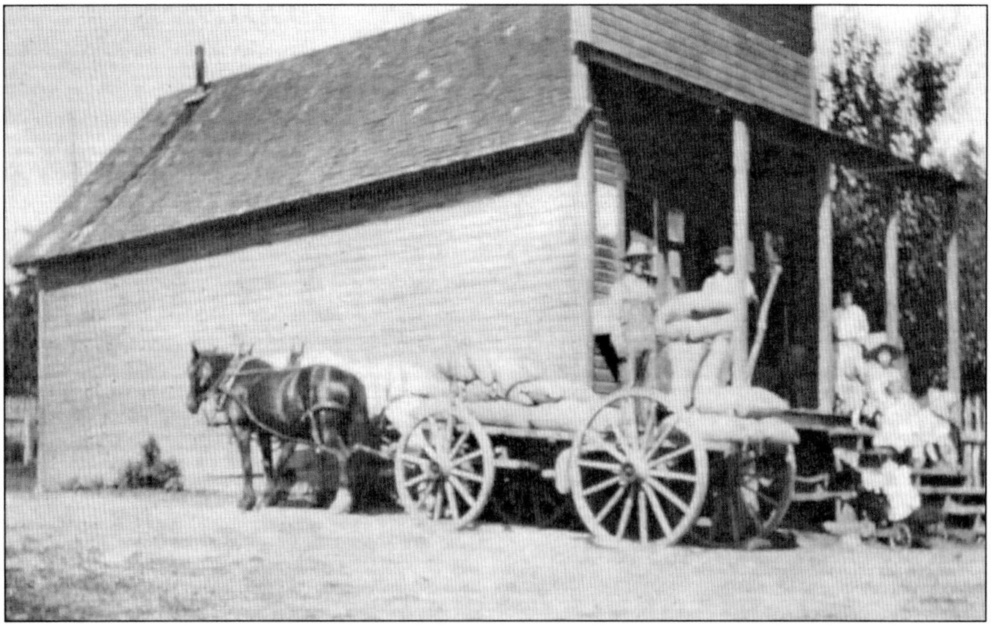

Julin's post office at Still Harbor was one of three on McNeil, with others at Meridian and Bee. Meridian opened first in 1890. Bee debuted in 1895, serving the prison and Anderson Island before closing in 1919. Carl Julin opened Gertrude's post office in 1900. His daughter Esther served as postmistress after him, from 1913 until her death in 1925. Son Charles then headed it until it closed in 1936. (Washington State Archives.)

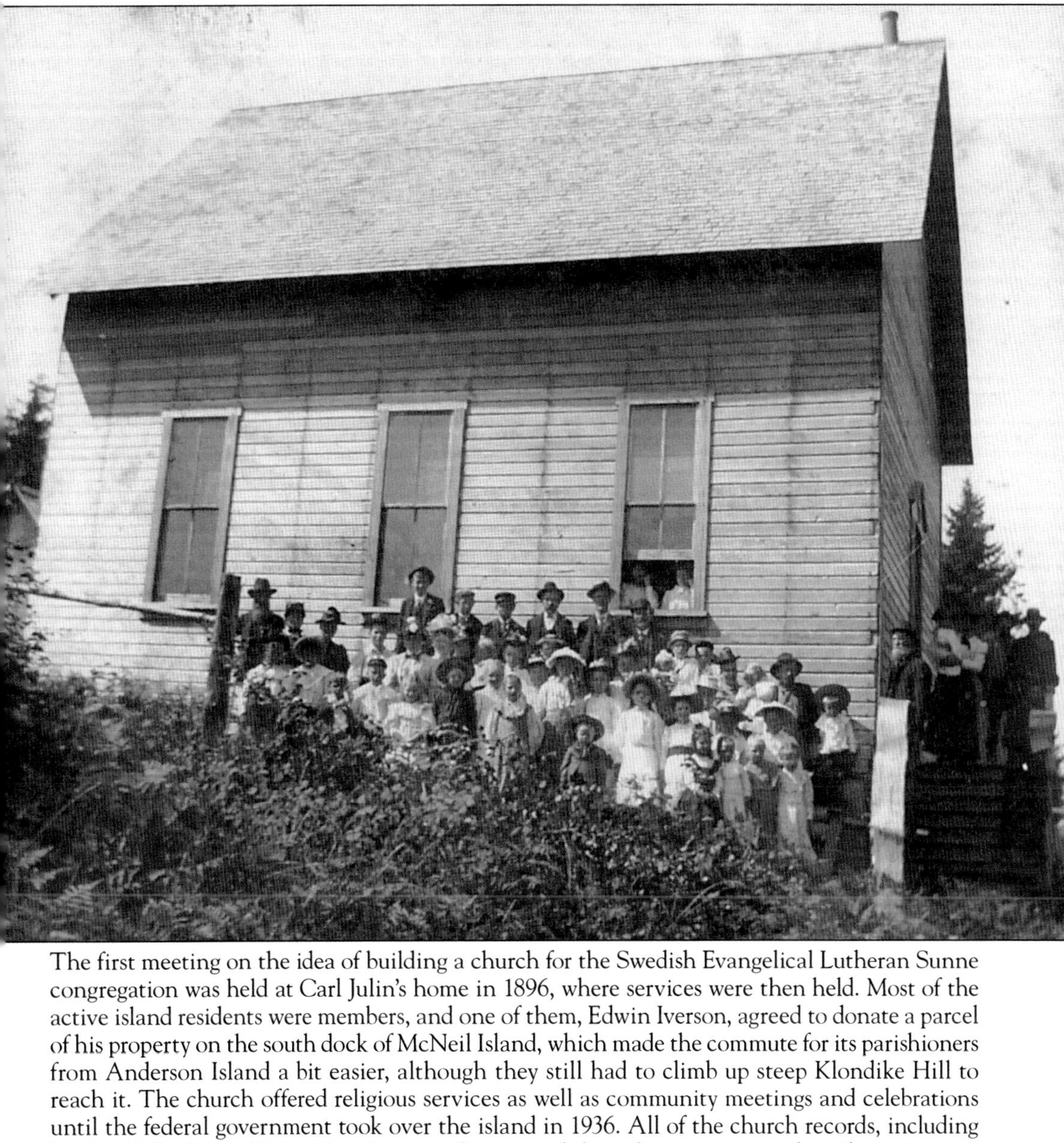

The first meeting on the idea of building a church for the Swedish Evangelical Lutheran Sunne congregation was held at Carl Julin's home in 1896, where services were then held. Most of the active island residents were members, and one of them, Edwin Iverson, agreed to donate a parcel of his property on the south dock of McNeil Island, which made the commute for its parishioners from Anderson Island a bit easier, although they still had to climb up steep Klondike Hill to reach it. The church offered religious services as well as community meetings and celebrations until the federal government took over the island in 1936. All of the church records, including birth and death certificates, baptism certificates, and those for marriages and confirmations are archived at Pacific Lutheran University. The church drew its name from Sunne, Sweden. (Jean Cammon Findlay.)

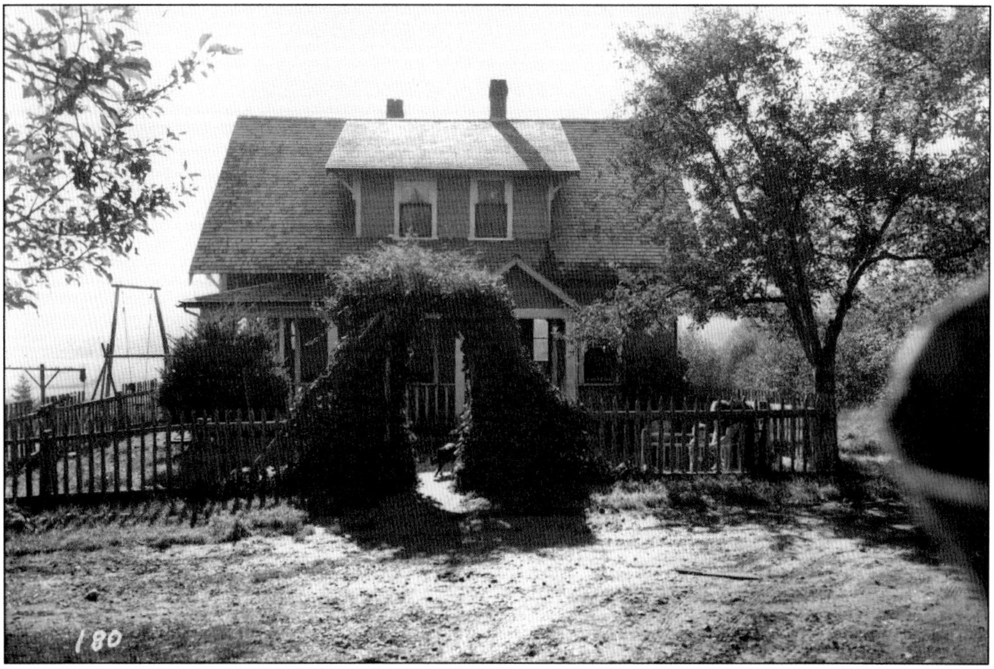

Caroline Ward at home with her child and cat. Jim Ward acquired his homesite on the bluff above the ferry slip in January 1886. His sons completed the home shown here about 1900, and it was inhabited by them until 1936 and then by staff families through 2001. The Ward home was demolished after the Nisqually earthquake, although its pinings were sound; another house is on the site now. (Washington State Archives.)

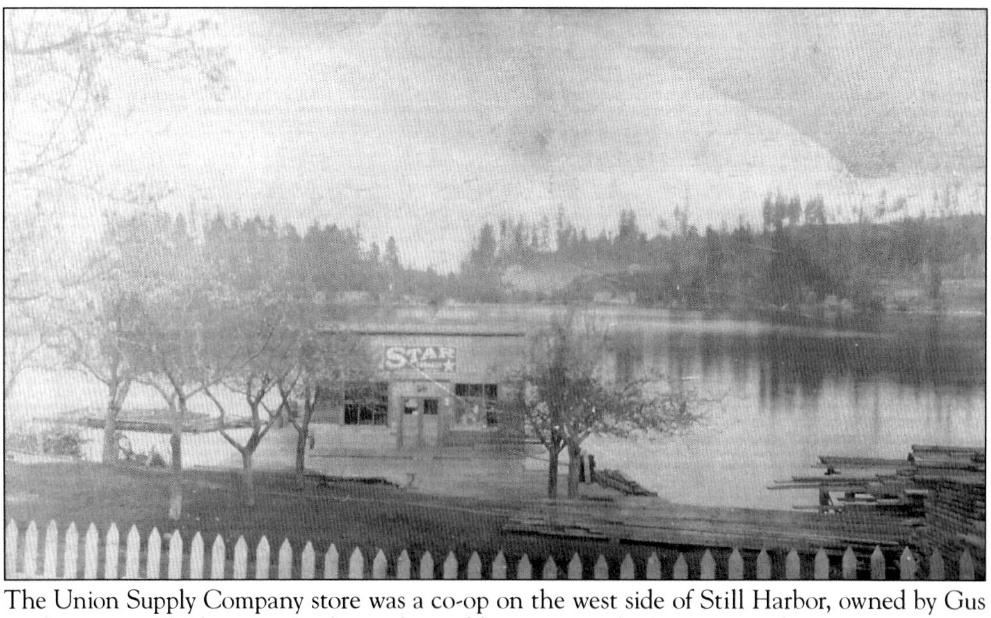

The Union Supply Company store was a co-op on the west side of Still Harbor, owned by Gus Carlson. It supplied provisions for settler and businesses. The Union Supply Company carried produce, as well as large quantities of tack, domestic goods, work clothing, machine parts, household and yard tools, and goods that both the settlers, sawmills, and boating companies, needed for operations, all deliverable by boat. (Washington State Archives.)

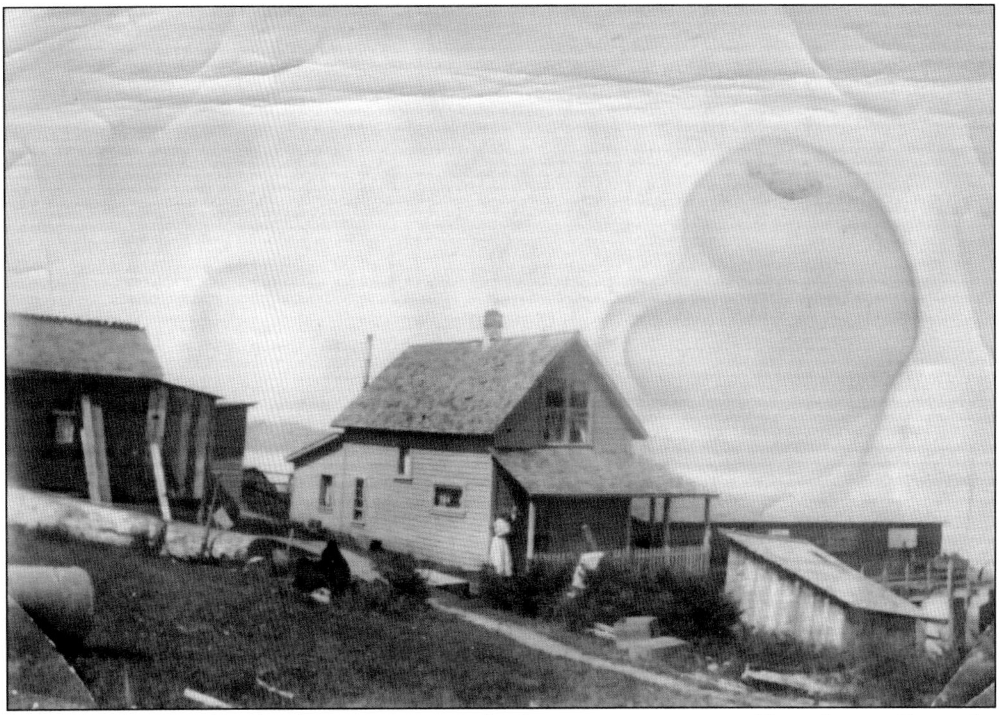

Oscar Cammon and his brother Martin started a shrimping company and boat shop at Gertrude. Oscar married Betsy "Bessie" Johnson of Anderson Island and lived at Still Harbor until they moved to Anderson Island, where they raised their family. Bessie later wrote *Island Memoir*, which chronicled the pioneer families of the sibling isles. She died in 1975 and is buried on Anderson along with her family. (Jean Cammon Findlay.)

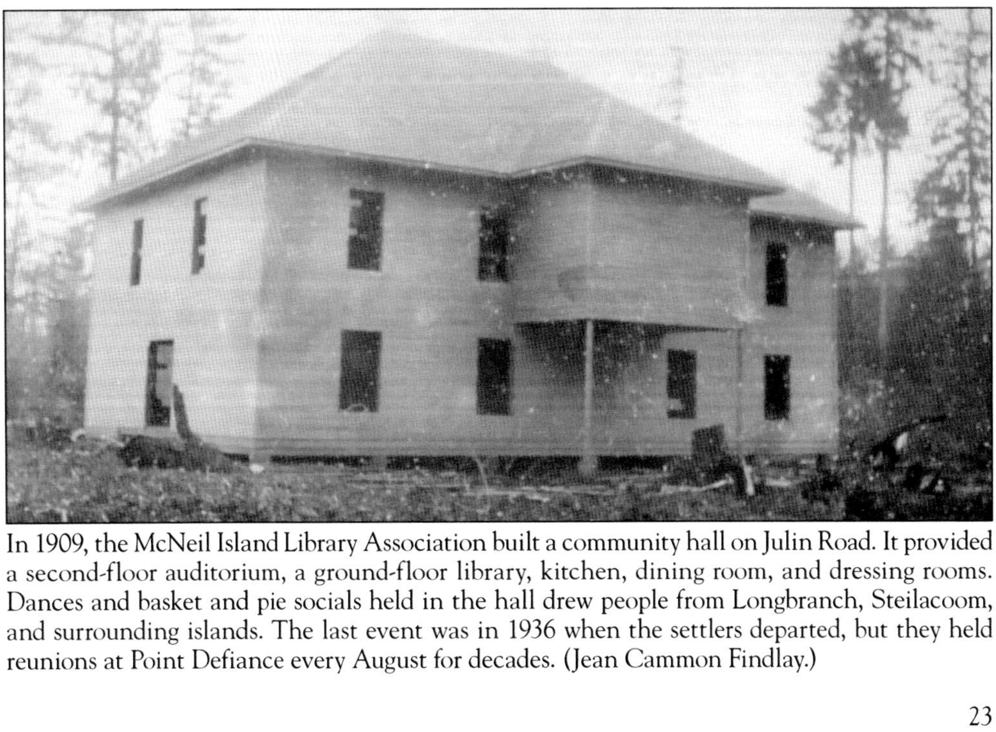

In 1909, the McNeil Island Library Association built a community hall on Julin Road. It provided a second-floor auditorium, a ground-floor library, kitchen, dining room, and dressing rooms. Dances and basket and pie socials held in the hall drew people from Longbranch, Steilacoom, and surrounding islands. The last event was in 1936 when the settlers departed, but they held reunions at Point Defiance every August for decades. (Jean Cammon Findlay.)

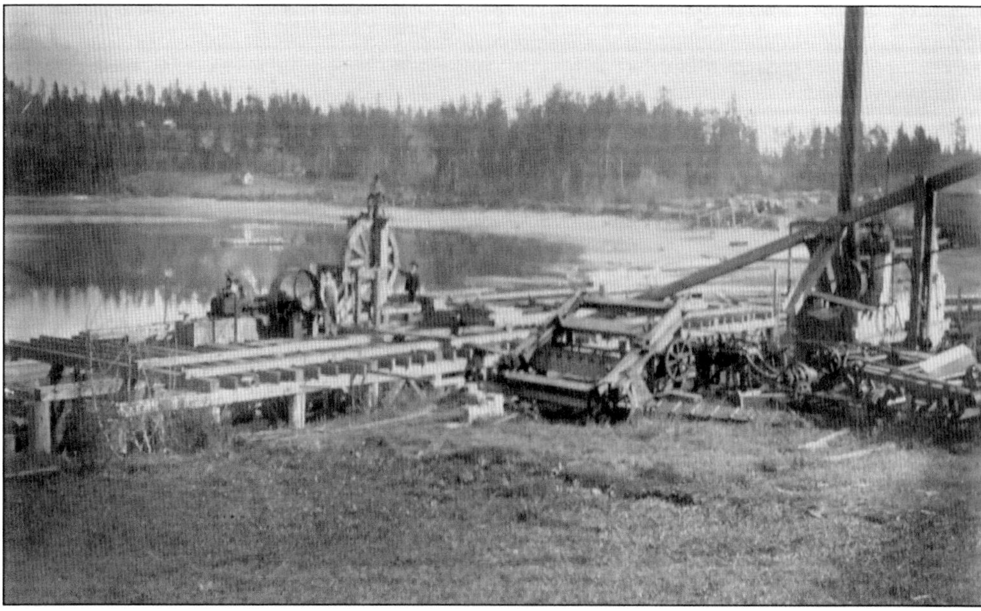

In the early 1900s, many residents made their living logging or milling McNeil's trees. Some used portable mills for cutting the timber into boards, while others were stationary. The largest of these was the Washington Lumber and Box Company, which began in 1908 when Herbert Williams, the Cammon brothers, and the Johnson brothers pooled resources. It changed hands several times until owner George Misener closed it in 1936. (Washington State Archives.)

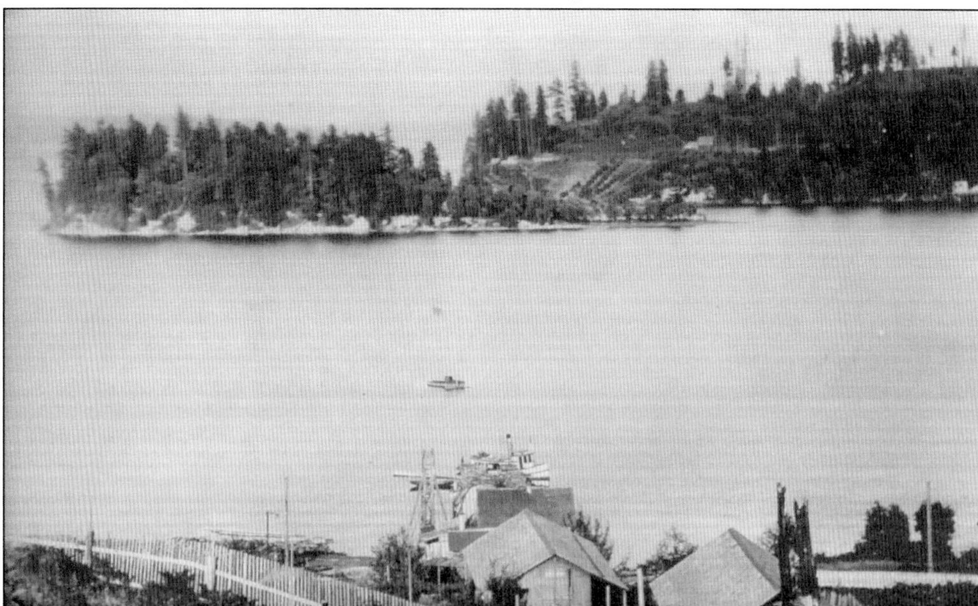

This October 15, 1914, Yoman, Washington, postcard of Still Harbor sent to Mrs. L.R. Mansfield (Augusta Johnson, Bessie Cammon's sister) details daily life: "Otto on Walter Larson's steamboat, Orlou, Carl and Gust fishing, Ben on the Killarney a month at Port Orchard, B & O are home . . . going to visit sister soon. Love from us all." The presumed writer is Oscar Cammon, since Otto and Ben were Bessie's brothers. (Jean Cammon Findlay.)

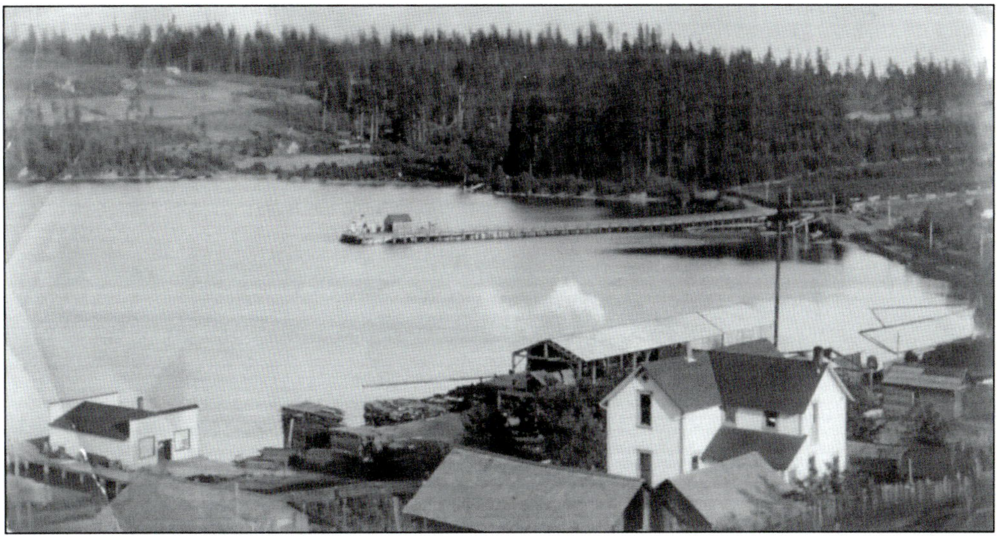

The Washington Lumber and Box Manufacturing Company, the largest sawmill on McNeil Island, sat on the island's northwest, or leeward side, at Still Harbor. The sawmill can be seen along the bottom of this c. 1910 photograph. The long pier was needed to load boards onto ships at low tide, when the water at the pier's end only reached a depth of nine feet. (Washington State Archives.)

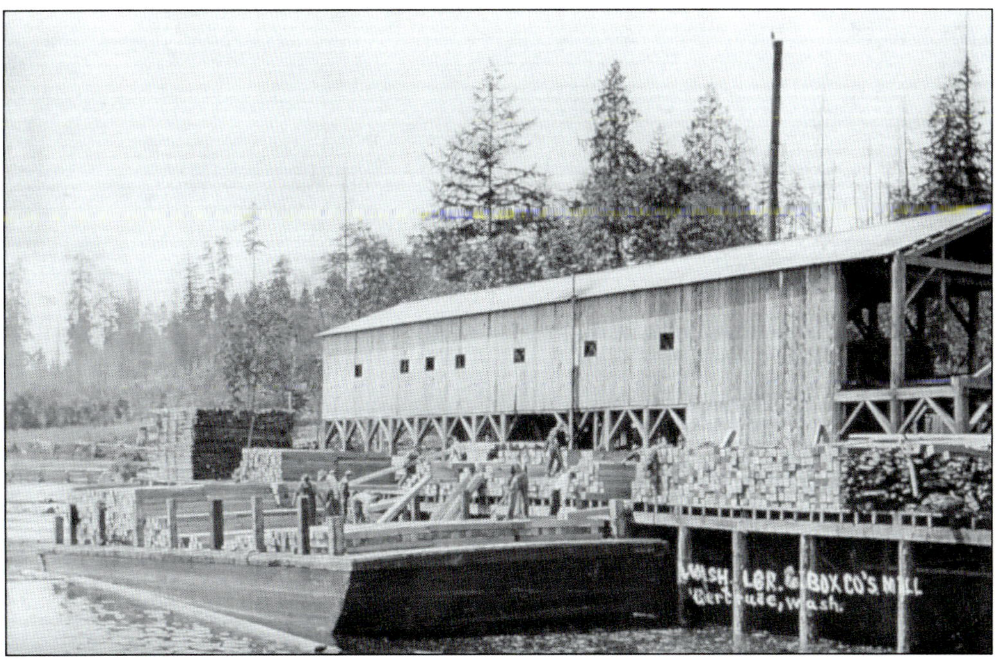

Employees of Washington Lumber and Box Manufacturing Company had hard jobs felling and dragging trees for cutting. They then loaded the sawn lumber onto skiffs for awaiting ships. This image shows Gertrude Island, which housed St. Ann's Home for unwed mothers, located off the northwest corner of McNeil. The island was named after Gertrude Duntze, a relative of Capt. John Dutnze, who explored the island in 1846. (Washington State Archives.)

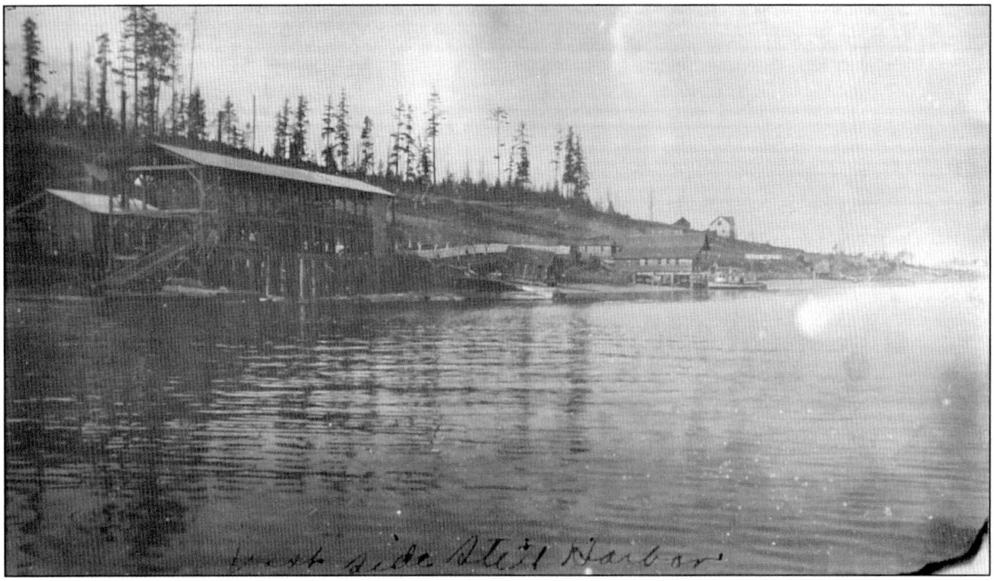

The Cammon brothers' boat shop at Still Harbor is seen here in 1911. The brothers began their fleet with the *Zillah*, which proved too small and prompted the 1903 purchase of the *Anna B.* The name came from Martin Cammon's girlfriend Anna Butsch, who lived on McNeil. Oscar had a daughter named Anna, although she was born four years after the brothers bought the boat. (Washington State Archives.)

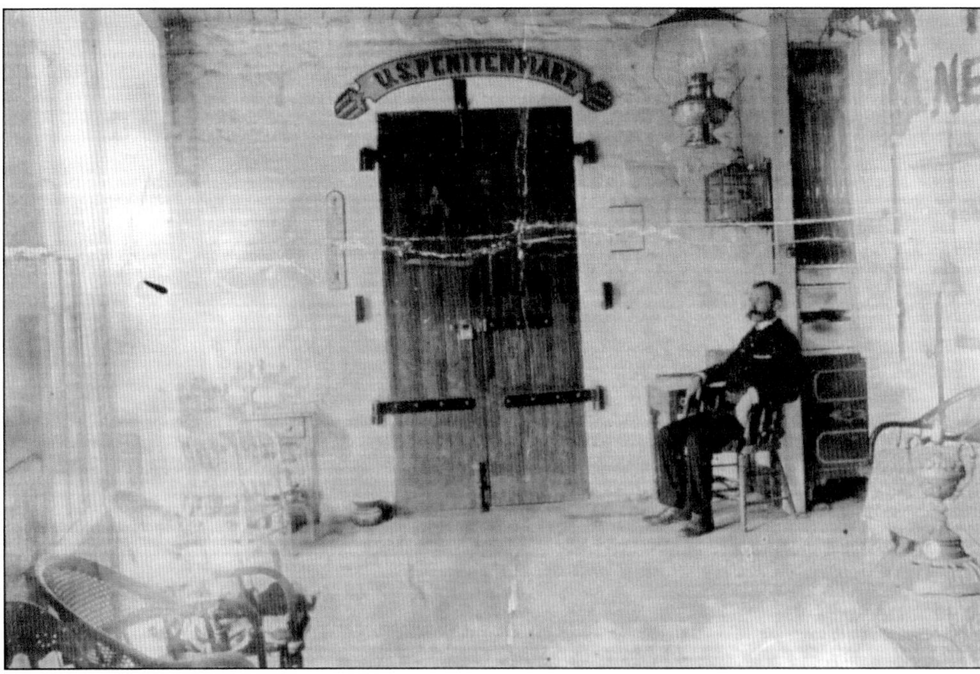

Deputy warden Robert Longmire rests in the guards' quarters, before the only door into the prison, in 1900. The Three Prisons Act of 1891 designated McNeil a penitentiary while Leavenworth and Atlanta were being developed. They are both in use today, but McNeil was the first US penitentiary and the only one that grew by need, not design. Despite its humble beginnings, McNeil became the prototype for US prisons. (Washington State Archives.)

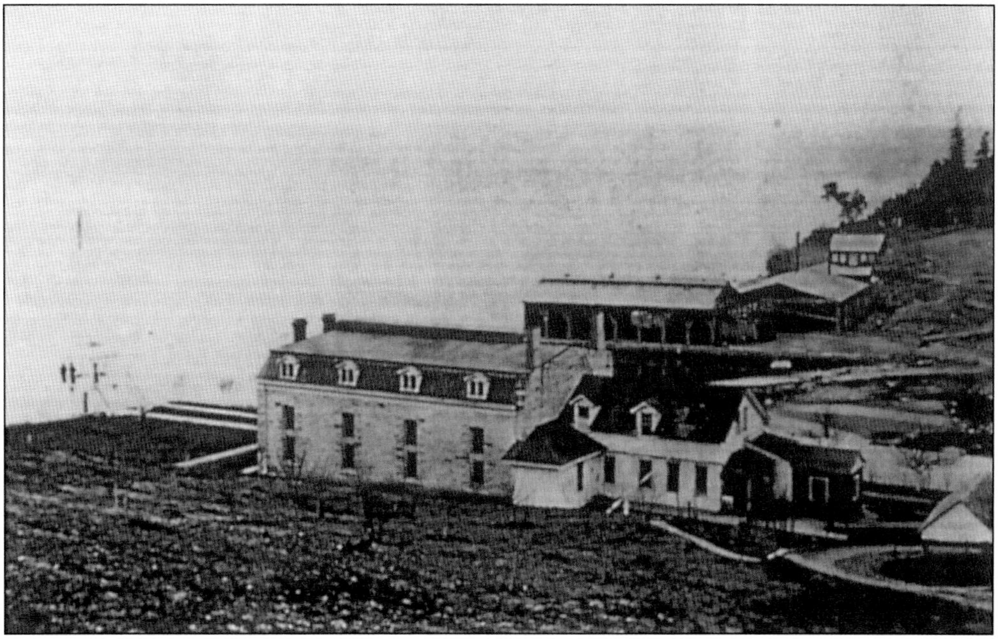

Any unescorted inmate found where this 1909 photograph was taken would have been in trouble, since the hill overlooking the prison was a staff-only area. The original brick prison and kitchen addition are at center, while the background shows the brickyard and a view of Balch Passage with Anderson Island in the distance. (National Archives and Records Administration.)

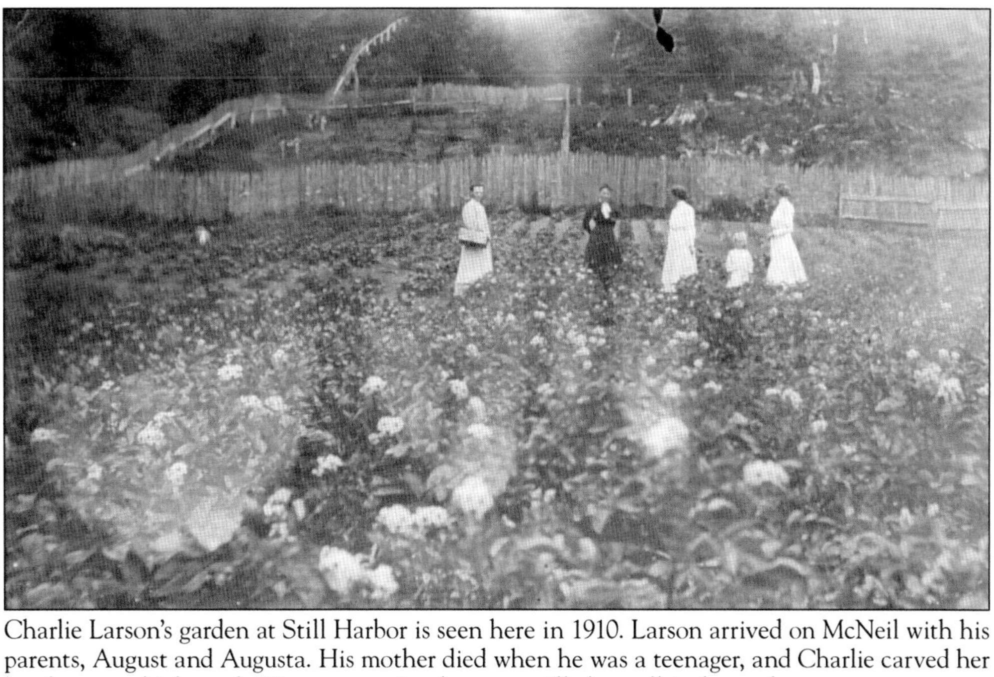

Charlie Larson's garden at Still Harbor is seen here in 1910. Larson arrived on McNeil with his parents, August and Augusta. His mother died when he was a teenager, and Charlie carved her headstone, which read, "You never miss the water till the well is dry and you never miss your mother till she's gone." His garden was raided of tubers by 12 escaped prisoners, who put the vegetable tops back to hide their crime. (Jean Cammon Findlay.)

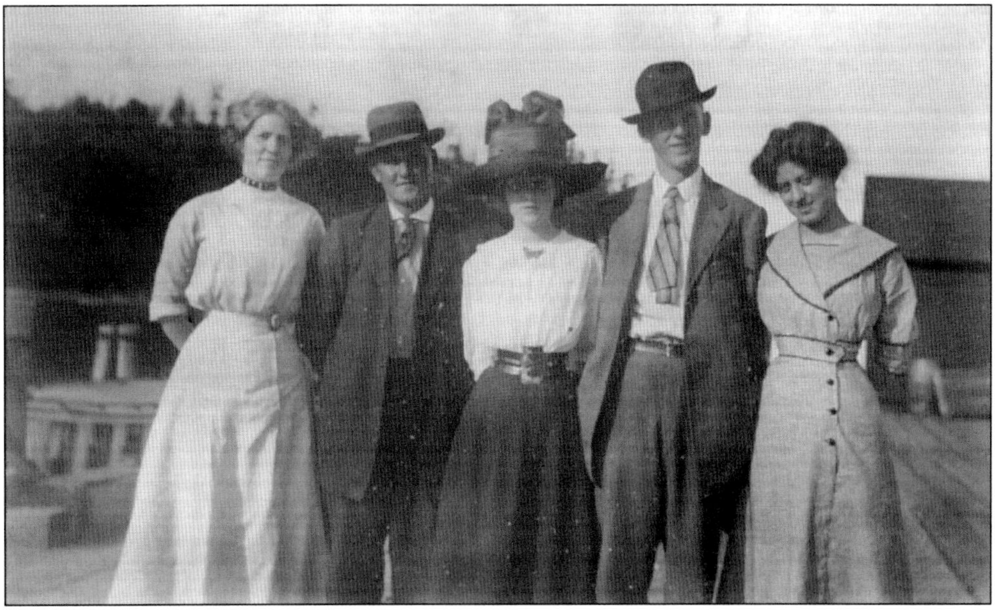

This is a private mailing card with, from left to right, Elvia Miller, Victor Brolin (who built his family's home on Anderson Island), unidentified, John Anderson, and Ella Dinetz. The families were cousins and friends and went back and forth between Anderson and McNeil—a very typical arrangement between the sister islands. (Jean Cammon Findlay.)

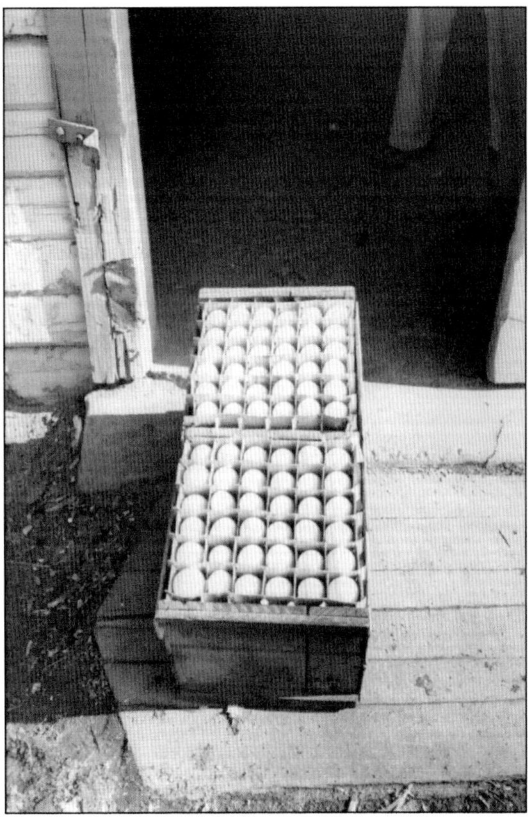

These 30 dozen eggs, on the farm barn threshold, were collected by inmates for use by the prison and for outside sales. The crate reads, "Washington Co-op Egg & Poultry Assn of New York packed by Washington Egg & Poultry Co-Operative Association Seattle, WA Thirty Dozen Eggs." The honor farm facilitated self-sufficiency for McNeil's prison and was a great source of revenue until private business competition complaints put an end to the farm's outside sales. (Washington State Archives.)

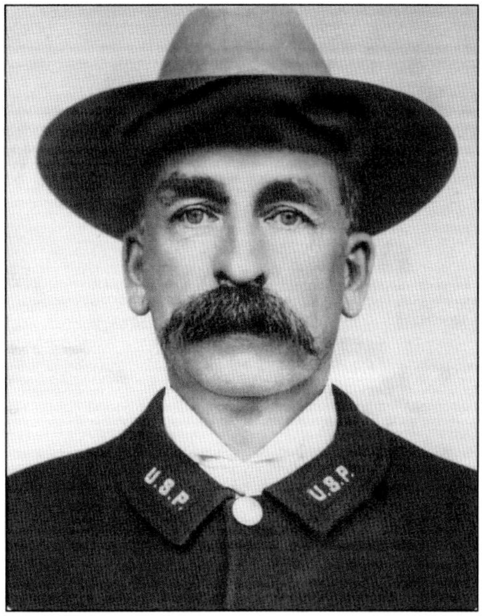

Gilbert Palmer, the first warden of McNeil Island Penitentiary, served from 1893 to 1901. Prisoners under Warden Palmer had to clear land for agricultural and industrial purposes since they ate what they grew and sold their surplus to pay for foods they couldn't produce on McNeil. In 1891, the Three Prisons Act declared the territorial jail a federal penitentiary, and operations were turned over to the US attorney general. (Washington State Archives.)

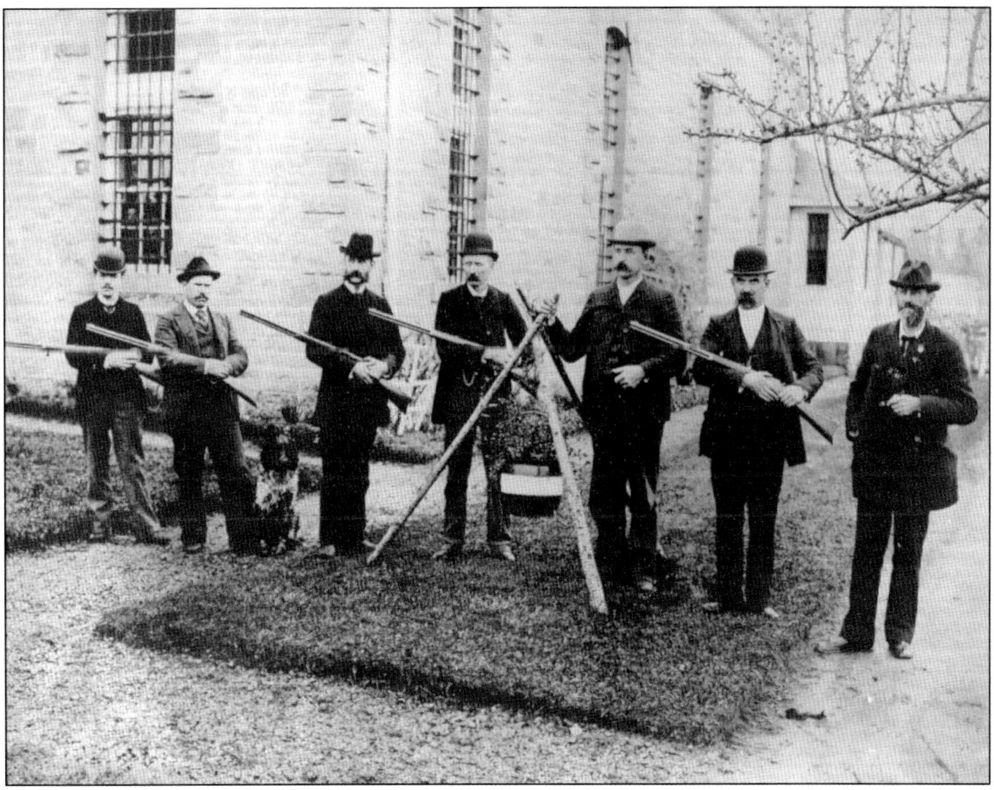

The entire staff showed up for this 1895 photograph. From left to right are Robert Troutman, John Drake, Warden Gilbert Palmer, John Devion, Deputy Warden Robert Longmire, Frank Moner, and H.E Palmer, Warden Palmer's son. They wore their own clothing, but the government provided them rifles they were required to carry. They sourced and prepared their own food and did their own laundry, working seven days a week with a day off each month. (Washington State Archives.)

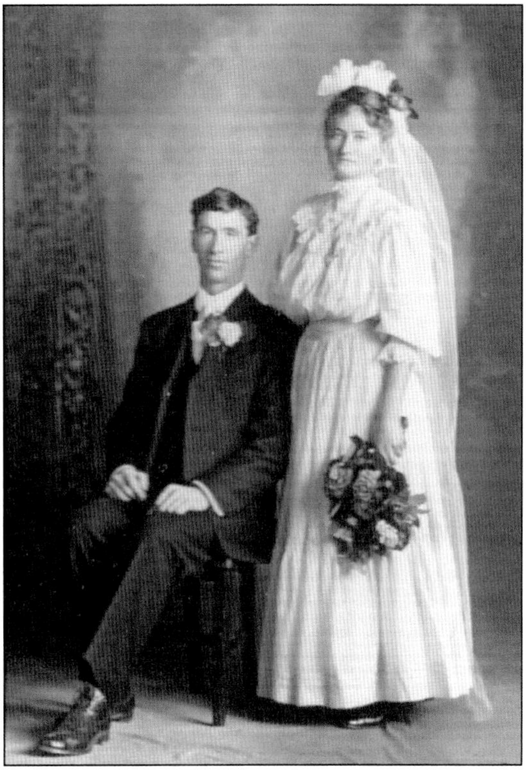

Emma Cammon was born in North Dakota on January 20, 1886. She married Gustave "Gus" T. Carlson on May 26, 1909. They lived on McNeil before moving and opening Carlson's general store on Oro Bay. Gus immigrated from Sweden, and is listed in the 1900 census living on McNeil Island with his father, Carl G. Peterson, and his brother and sister Oscar Carlson and Lizzie Peterson. Lizzie was sister-in-law to Emma and Gus Carlson's sister. (Jean Cammon Findlay.)

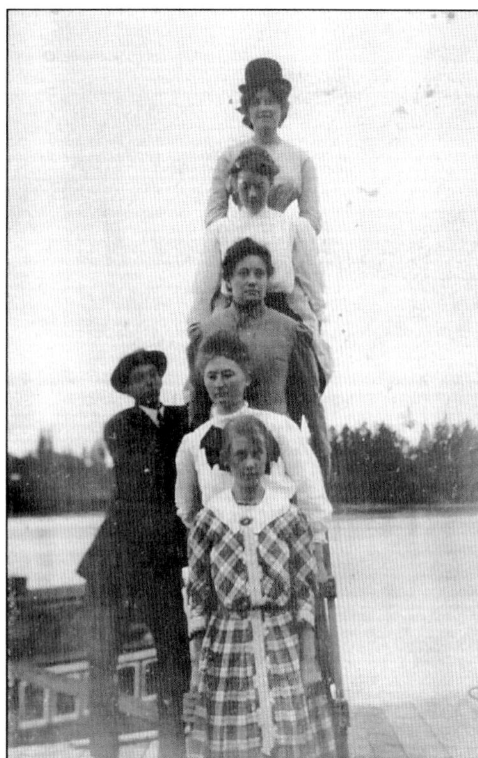

This c. 1905 private mailing card shows a group of fun-loving young people. From the top are Ella Dinetz, Bessie Johnson Cammon, Agusta Dinetz, Emma Carlson, and Augusta "Gussie" Dinetz. Ben Johnson steadies the ladder at Still Harbor. Get-togethers like these were a common event in the vibrant and close-knit Gertrude community on McNeil Island. (Jean Cammon Findlay.)

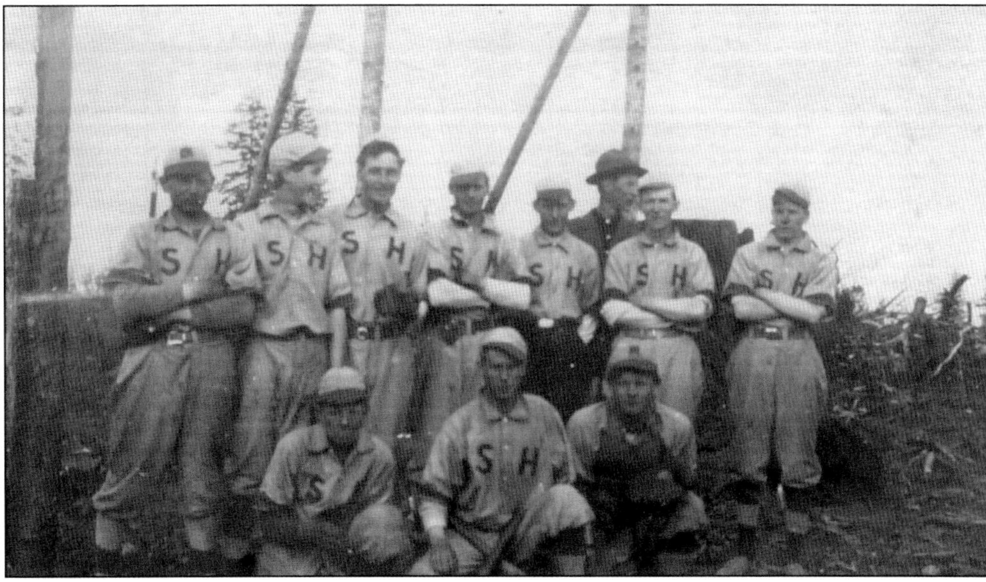

Members of the Still Harbor baseball team included, from left to right, (first row) Jim Corey, Henry Hannum, and Ed Michaelson; (second row, standing) Clarence Michaelson, Francis Nelson, John Moard, Art Anderson, Martin Moard, coach Hador Miller, Carl Carlson, and Art Larson. Clarence and Ed Michaelson were brothers, and grandmother Bessie Cammon's nephews by marriage. Coach Hador Miller had a farm at Still Harbor where he had lived for many years, but he moved away after marriage. (Jean Cammon Findlay.)

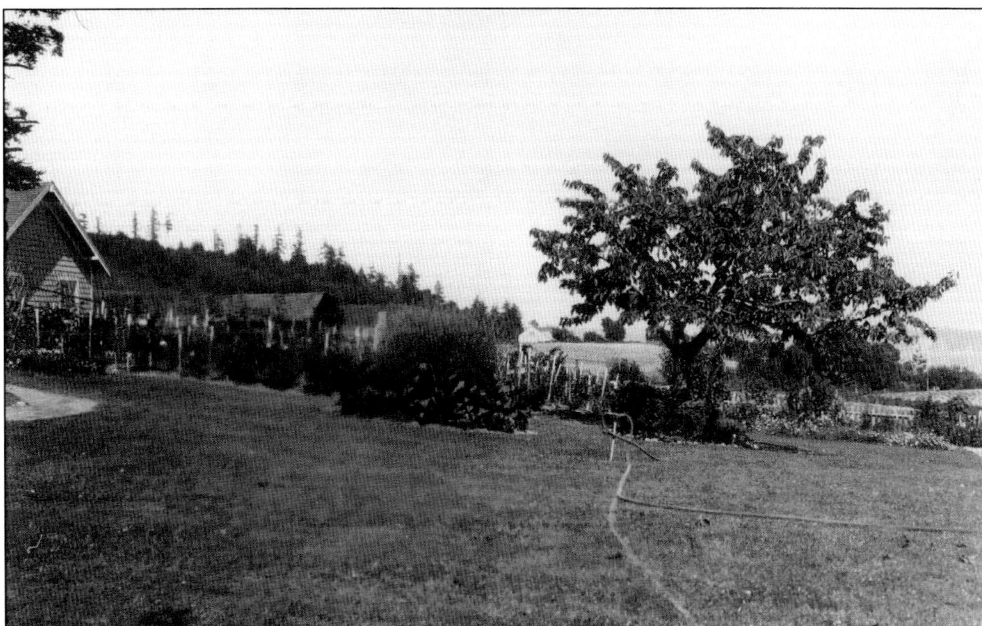

This settler home was sold to the prison and became the chaplain's house. The lush grounds provided respite from the demands of spiritual care to the inmates. Previously, chaplains only visited on Sundays. McNeil had constant clerical care until the chaplain resigned in a 1922 scandal. The original warden's home, 501, is in the background; it also had magnificent landscaping, common to McNeil homes through the BOP years. (Washington State Archives.)

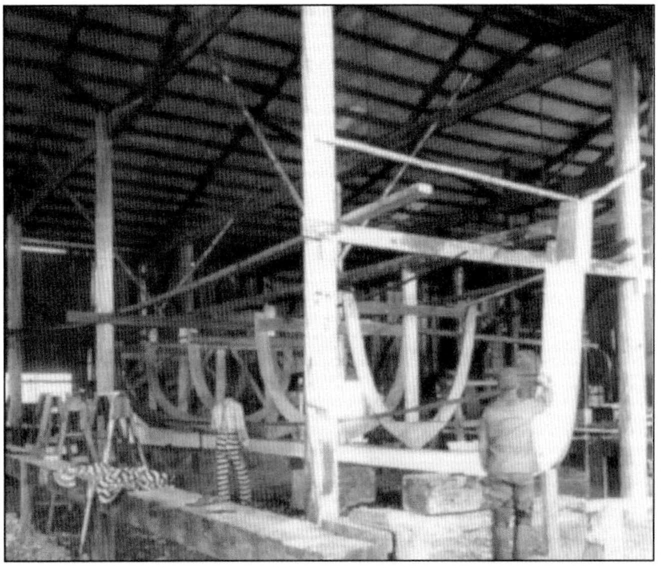

Inmates work on the construction of a large boat in 1909, possibly under the supervision of Steilacoom resident Neil Henly, the man not in a prison uniform leaning against the hull on the right. He was a guard at the prison until his boat building skills were put into practice and he became the marine foreman. He remained in charge of boat building at McNeil for many years. (National Archives and Records Administration.)

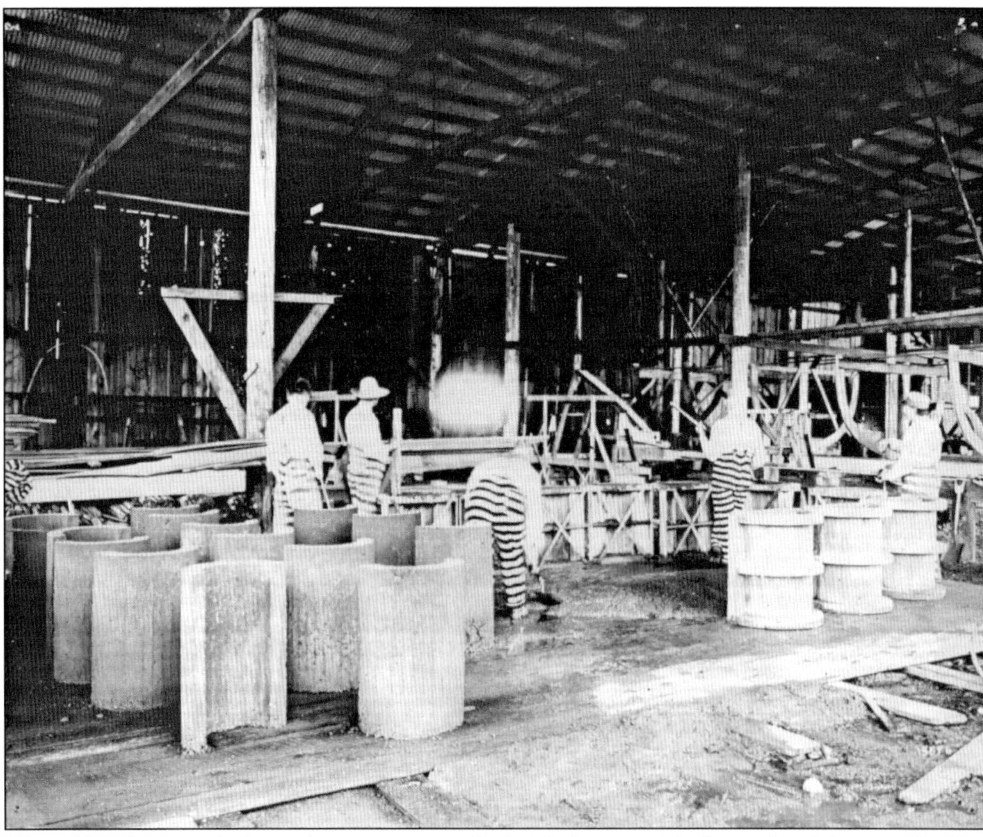

This 1899 photograph shows five inmates in the brick factory with the tools of their trade. One is dredging the channel with a shovel. Their striped pants and white shirts were standard prison uniforms, no matter the weather. The brickyard was next to the marine shed and repair operations, seen along the right. Sewer pipes were fabricated in the brickyard, as well as other needed items. (National Archives and Records Administration.)

Warden O.P. Halligan's tenure from 1904 to 1919, McNeil's longest, saw much growth. Notable additions were a hospital and the baseball field. Halligan's 1913 annual report notes, "The prisoners manifesting true American spirit . . . in this weekly diversion." Roy Gardner escaped during a game in 1921, but one of his accomplices was shot dead by tower guards. Halligan's two bull terriers roamed the island while he used his Irish charm on lady visitors. (Washington State Archives.)

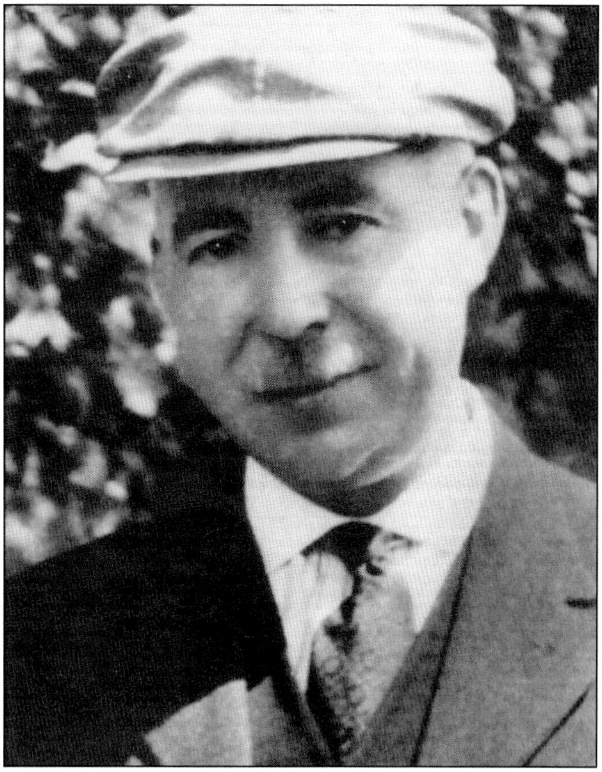

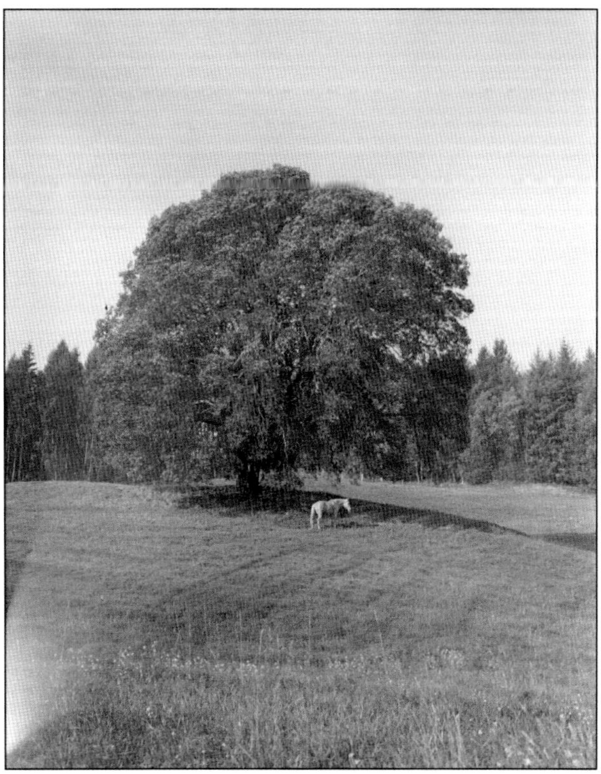

In 1910, John Holm's horse stands beneath the four madrone trees surrounding the grave of his infant son, Edwin William, who was buried in August 1895. His gravesite was memorialized by Jack Henderson in *The Four Trees*, which eloquently conveys the dignity evidenced on McNeil by inmates and staff. Holm's burial is officially the only settler remains on the island, and it is still respected to this day. The last tree was felled on January 17, 2019, but the site will be replanted from its cuttings. (Washington State Archives.)

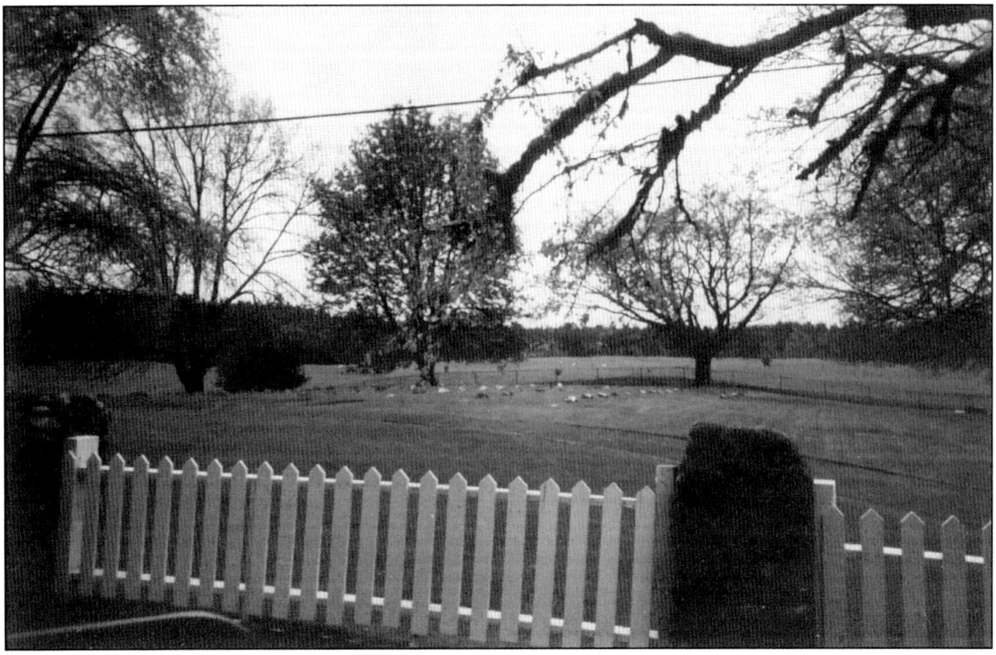

Originally, prisoners were buried by the jail, although escapees were buried where they fell. As the pen grew, land was appropriated near where the SCC is today, and burials were moved to the new Hillcrest cemetery in 1904. It holds 125 numbered markers, along with name markers from 1962 until 1972, when Joseph Dial was the last interment. A trustee school bus driver was one of the later burials. (McNeil Island Historical Society.)

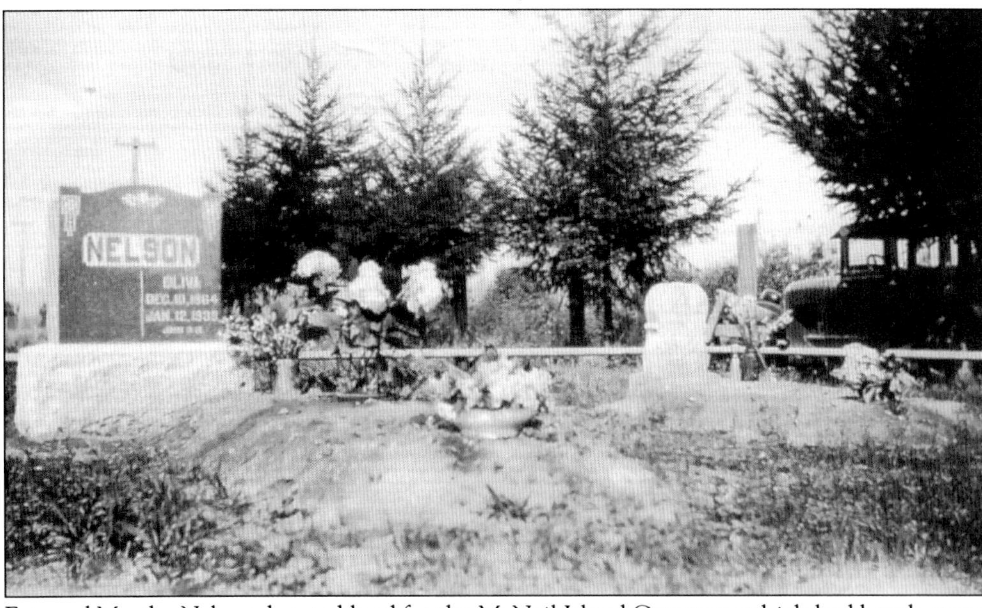

Eric and Martha Nyberg donated land for the McNeil Island Cemetery, which had beach gravel paths and a central open-air chapel. Christian Tangen was the first burial, in October 1905, and his son Carl the second, in November. In 1937, the Bureau of Prisons moved the bodies of 86 pioneers off the island to cemeteries of the families' choice. Many were reburied on Anderson, with several at Trinity Church in Parkland. (Jean Cammon Findlay.)

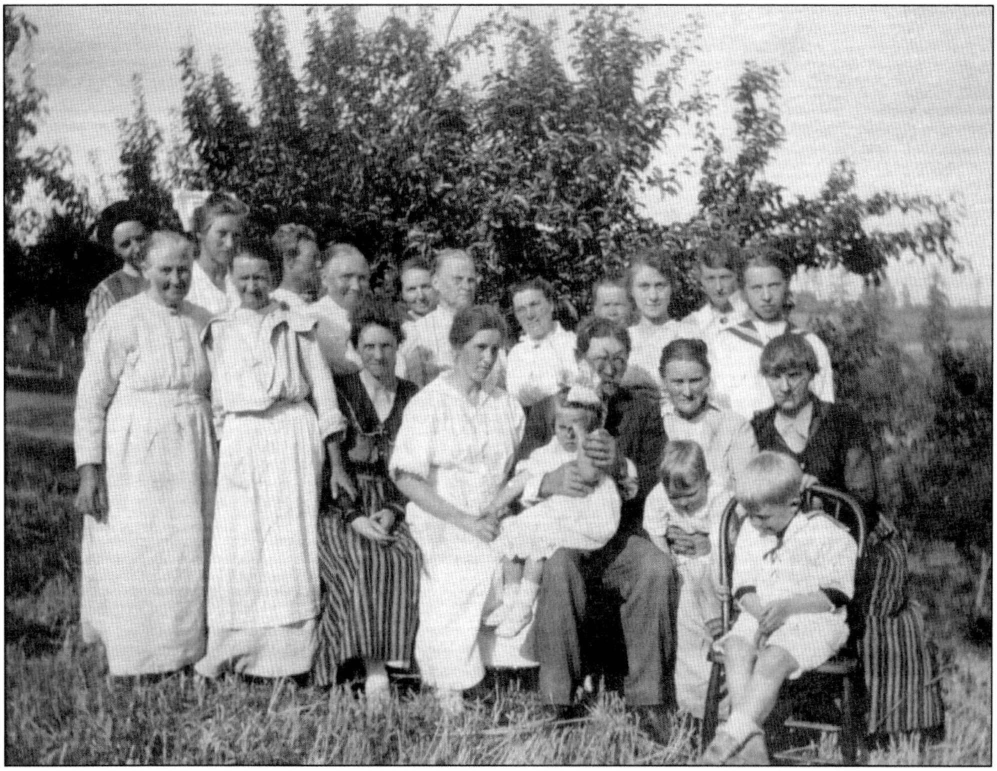

Norwegian-born Marie Fadum (seated left of center in black dress) came to the island via Greenbush, Minnesota, to be with her daughter Anna, who homesteaded with her husband, Ole Anderson, on McNeil just opposite Anderson Island. Fadum was a widow and came with her other daughters Cora and Tilda, who settled on Anderson Island. They were quickly followed by her eldest daughters Ella and Hannah, who arrived in 1908. (Jean Cammon Findlay.)

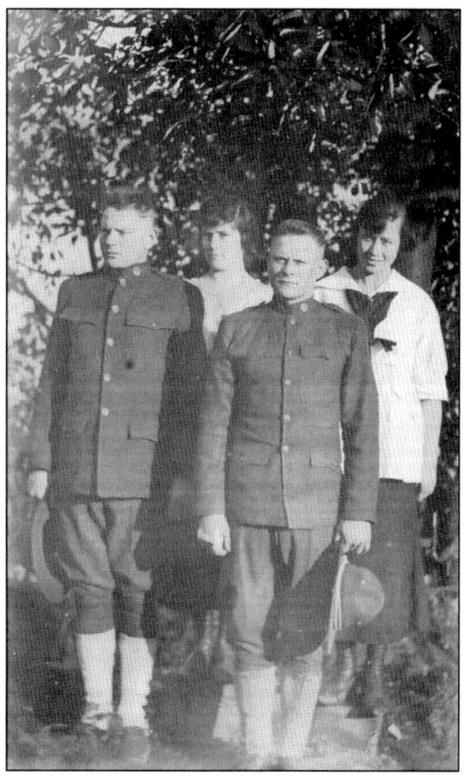

Seen here from left to right are Edward, Helene, Clarence, and Berthe, four of Henry and Elizabeth Michaelson's eleven children. They reached McNeil in the 1890s from Wisconsin. The children were counted on McNeil's 1917 census, aside from Oscar, 16, who died in 1915. Edward and Clarence served in World War I. Helene and Berthe, a year apart, cared for their baby brother Harold, who was born a week before their mother died in April 1916. (Jean Cammon Findlay.)

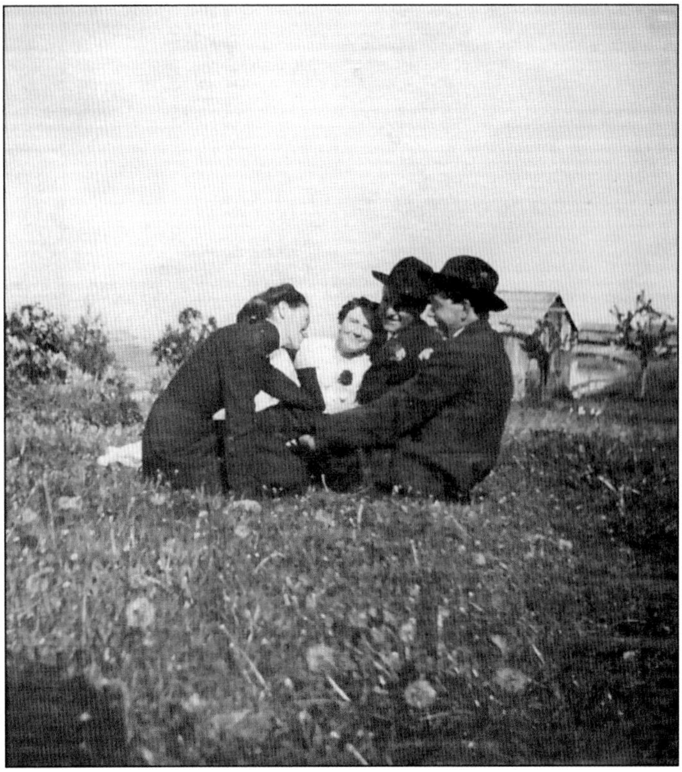

Pictured is a happy gathering of McNeil and Anderson residents. From left to right are Karoline Elizabeth "Lizzie" Kammen (later Americanized from Swedish to Cammon), married to Henry Michaelson, with a home on McNeil Island; Mrs. Reed; Victor Brolin; and Ben Johnson. This photograph was taken in 1904 by the old apple shed. Ben Johnson was a younger brother to Betsey "Bessie" Johnson Cammon. (Jean Cammon Findlay.)

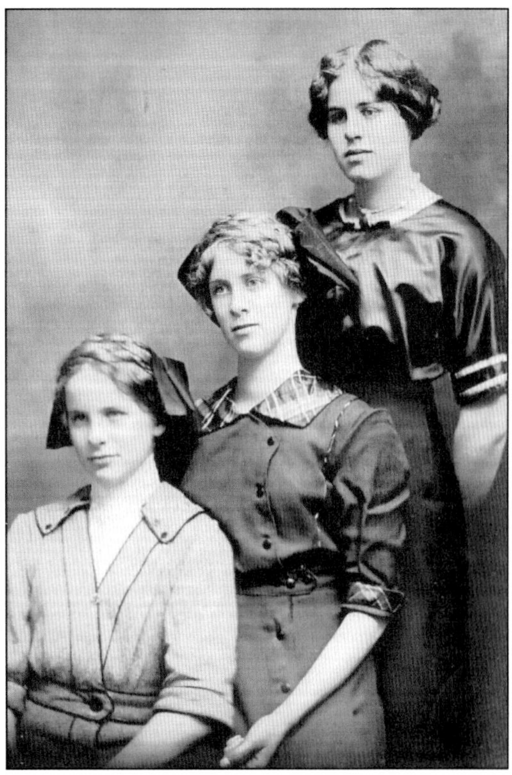

From left to right, Edith, Evangeline, and Edna Ostling lived on Anderson, visiting McNeil often, which was so common that a joint island Utopian Club existed, and the 1900 census considered both islands as one. They are the daughters of islanders Carl Ostling and Louise Ekenstam Ostling, who had come to the island with her parents, brothers, and sisters in 1877. They would have four children: three girls and one boy, Allan. (Jean Cammon Findlay.)

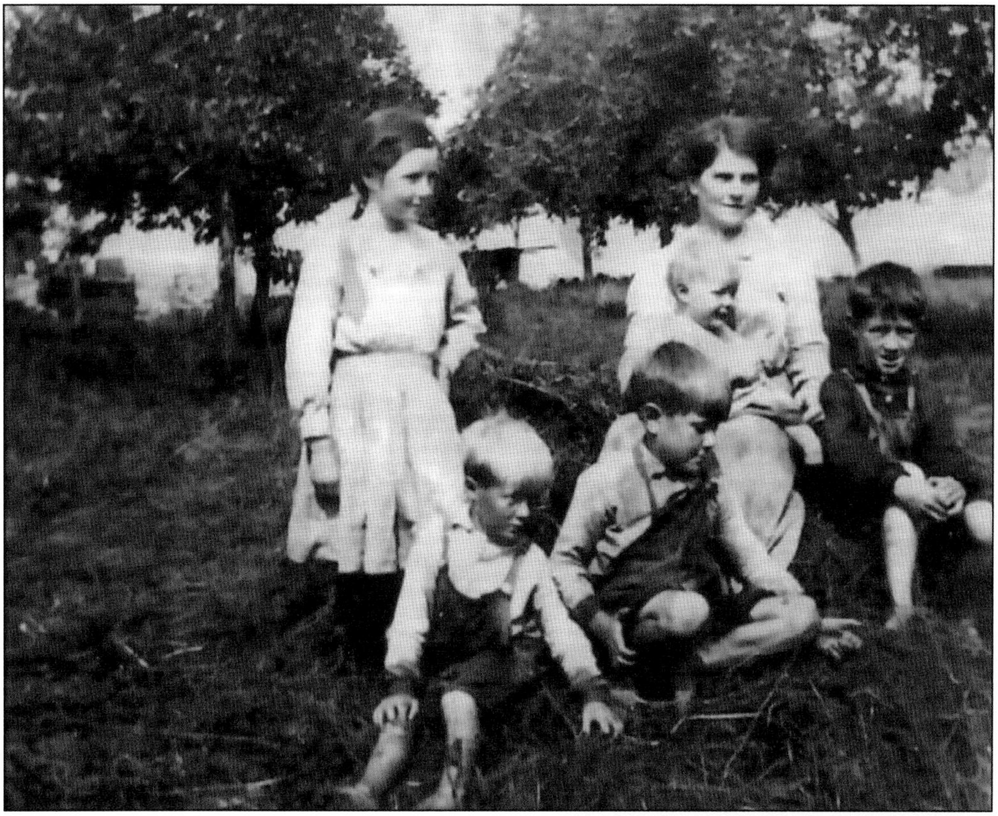

Edith Luhr and her children (from left to right) Gladys, Frank, Chet, Bill, and Thelma are pictured in 1910 at their Luhr Creek home, site of an old Native American camp. Father John farmed, sold produce, and made moonshine from a still the feds never found. He canoed the sound yodeling, advertising his wares. The family moved off McNeil in 1936, but son Frank became a boatman, and Bill owned Bill's boat rentals at Luhr Beach. (Luhr-Johnson families.)

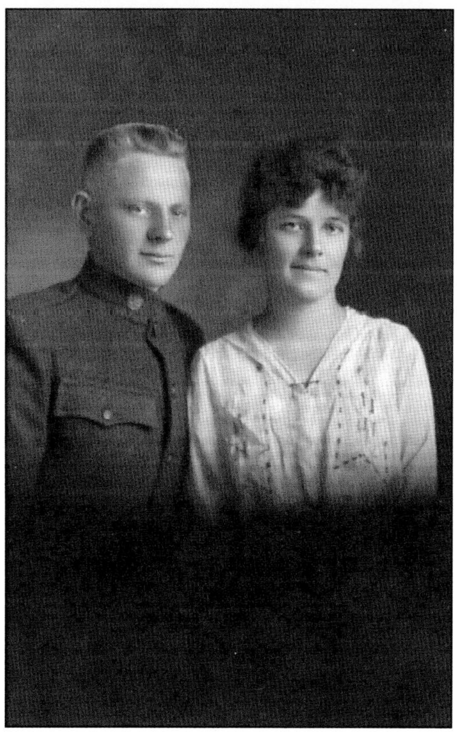

Clarence Michaelson married Marjorie Waldron in 1918 after he returned from World War I. He signed his name Mikelson on the marriage license. Martin, Oscar, and Karoline "Lizzie" Cammon lived on McNeil and were the three surviving children of their father's second marriage to Bertha Hansdatter. Hans Kammen's third marriage, to Inger Johnson, produced five children: Adolph, Emma, Clara, Minnie, and Alice. Clara died at age 20 in 1907. (Jean Cammon Findlay.)

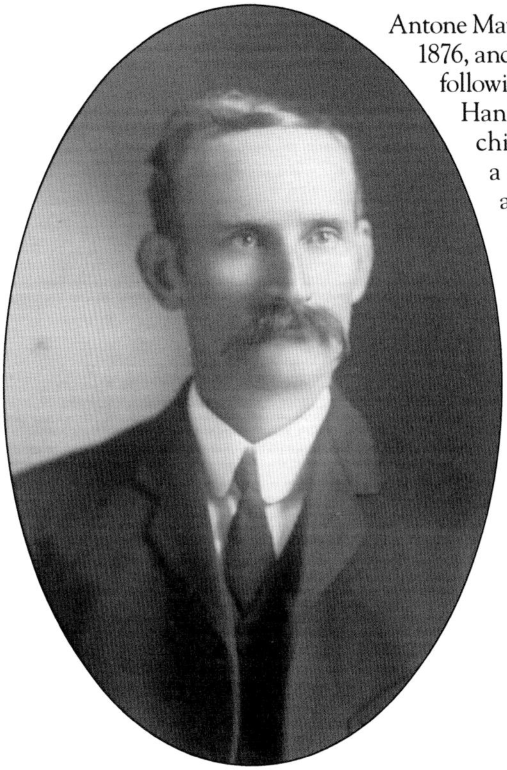

Antone Matinus "Martin" (Kemmen) Cammon was born in 1876, and his second wife, Berthe Kammen, died in 1880 following the birth of Josef Emil, who died as an infant. Hans then married Inger Marie and had five more children. Martin and his brother Oscar operated a store on Still Harbor before trying their hand at shrimping. Martin never married and died in 1957. (Jean Cammon Findlay.)

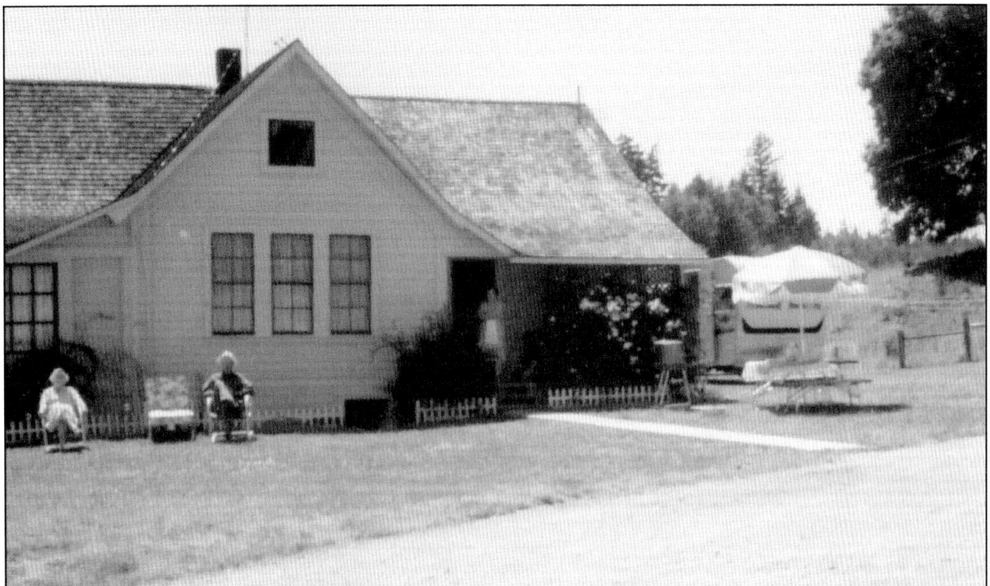

John Holm settled on McNeil in 1882 and built this home for his wife, Petra, in 1888. They raised three daughters—Alice, Elma, and Jennie—and their infant son Edwin is buried on the property under four madrone trees. After the BOP took over in 1936, inmate crews refused to cut the trees. Staff families such as the Wiseharts, pictured here in the late 1950s, lived in the house. (Courtesy of David Wisehart.)

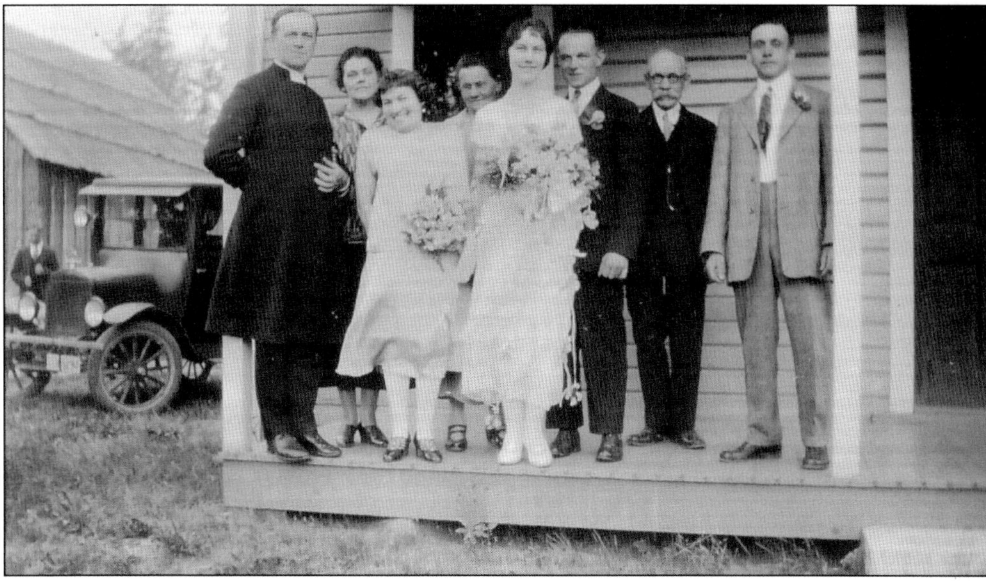

Olga Nelson and Max Guernsey's wedding took place on June 1, 1925, at the Nelson home on McNeil Island. The marriage certificate lists the Lutheran pastor (far left) as Ernest C. Bloomquist. No one else is identified in the photograph, but one of the witnesses was Gus Tangen and another was Violet Seaburg. They are likely at far right and second from left, while the parents were relegated to the back row. (Jean Cammon Findlay.)

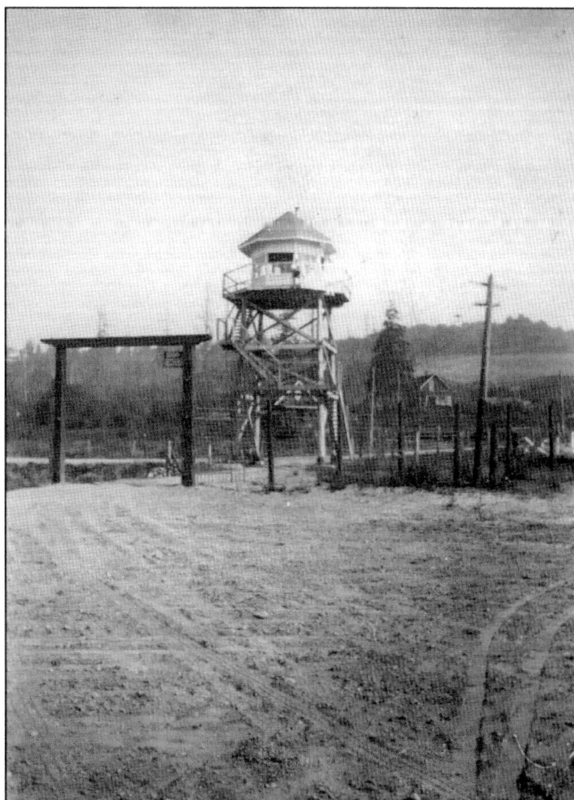

This 1928 guard tower overlooked the rear entrance of the penitentiary, near settler homes, as seen in the background. Homes and land near the early prison were purchased, and a farm ringed the pen by 1900. In 1927, as the prison expanded, farm operations moved to the southwest of McNeil. A sign on the gate instructed cars to slow down so as not to disturb the livestock. (Washington State Archives.)

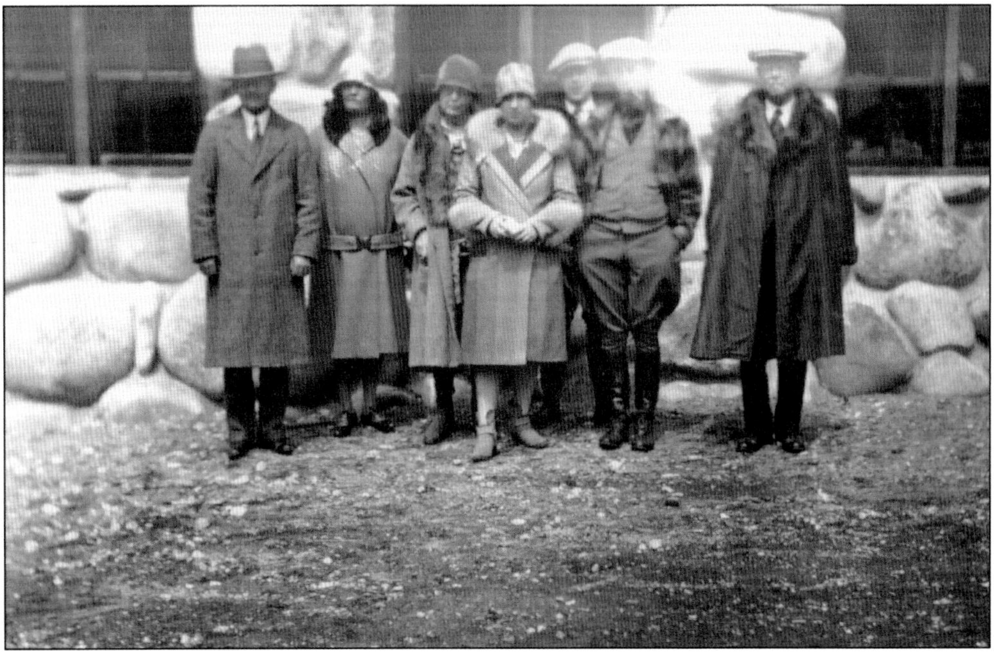

Socialite Fench W. Archer, at far right in a fur collar, and his wife, Dora, third from left, are pictured with a group of influential visitors from Seattle as they tour the prison prior to Fench being appointed McNeil's fifth warden in 1922. Archer's connections brought heightened awareness for McNeil and much-improved conditions for staff and inmates alike. (Washington State Archives.)

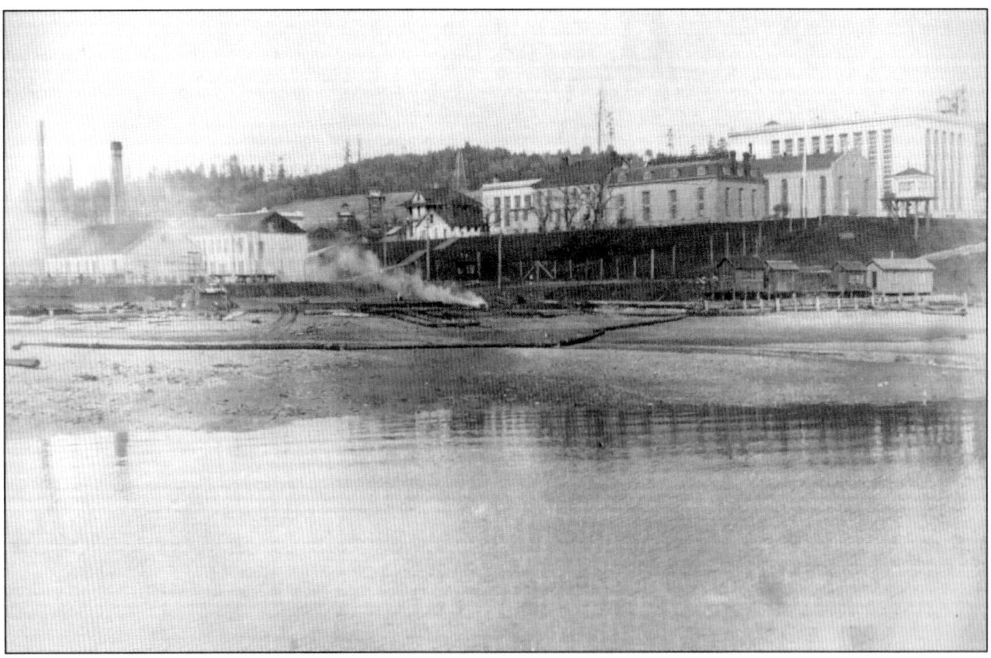

McNeil Island Penitentiary is pictured in 1920. The mudflats at left are what was left of the slough that was filled in in 1904 during Warden Halligan's tenure. The 1912 marine sheds are still in place at far right below the cliff housing the main institution. At center is the original prison with Two House, and Three/Four House is past it to the right. (Washington State Archives.)

Three

Penitentiary

The Three Prisons Act of 1891 turned the territorial jail on McNeil Island into a US penitentiary, but corrections and island life continued as it had. There was some influx of funding, and better oversight, but McNeil remained primarily on its own. A surge of development occurred owing to a post-1889 inmate population increase, due to laws enacted by the new State of Washington. Growth as a nation caused an uptick in punishable crimes, and McNeil met the demands for the West Coast, including Alaska.

Meanwhile, varying lives intermixed, as island residents worked at the pen part time and full time over four decades. That overlap, with island residents seeing prisoners daily, and perhaps working alongside them, forged McNeil's tendency toward treating cons with decency. There was discipline via a swift kick, and punishments such as inmates being dosed with castor oil and handcuffed to their cell bars for hours, followed by isolation and rations of bread and water—a standard practice of the era. However, the old strict rules, such as silence, were done away with, and the striped uniforms disappeared in 1914. McNeil Island continued to function as a small town would, with the added element of living and working alongside a prison and prisoners. This surprisingly congenial state of affairs continued until 1936, when the original settlers were bought out by the federal government. After that, any island resident was either a full-time employee or staff family member, so the unique mix of resident and inmate interaction, although changed, continued through the years. That, coupled with the beautiful view of Mt. Rainier between the Cascades and the Olympic mountain ranges and, for most staff, the relaxing boat ride to and from work, created a soothing atmosphere. McNeil experienced far fewer incidents (and murders) than any other institution throughout the years, as both a federal penitentiary and a state corrections facility.

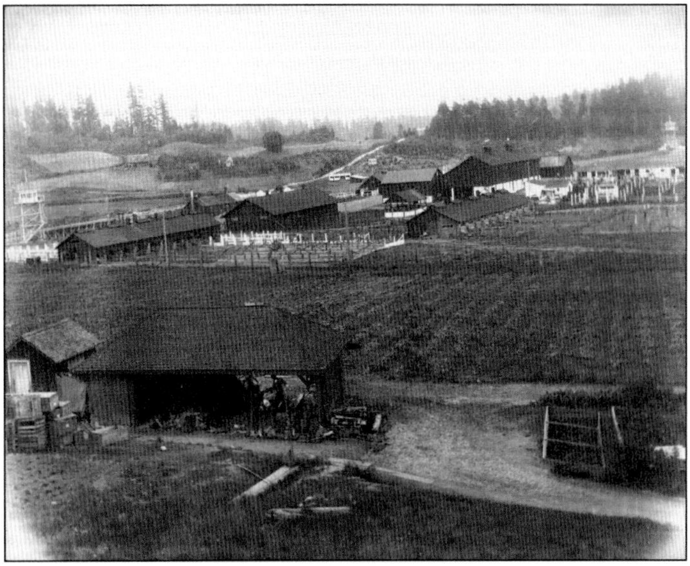

The prison farm is pictured in 1921, sitting on Apfel flats, where the fire station is today. The four madrone trees sit on the hill beside the road up Center Hill. The prisoner count was at 535, up from 11 in 1875. In Warden Maloney's three-year term, the population had doubled. These few fields and barns had to feed nearly 600 men. Costs became prohibitive, and the government sought more land. (Washington State Archives.)

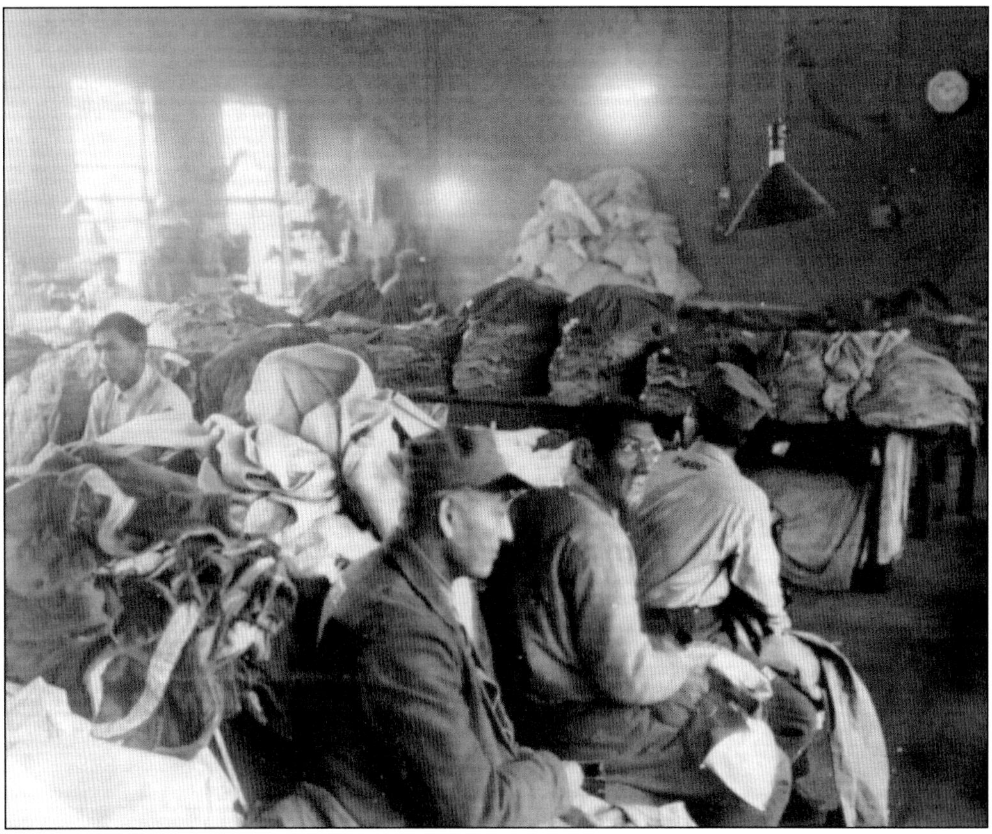

Prisoners work in the laundry around 1920. In 1875, the guards and inmates did their laundry in a tub of water heated over a fire. The laundry was hard work made better by teamwork. Asian or Native American prisoners often worked there together. Working in the laundry had its perks: anyone who wanted revenge could have it, through too much starch or shrinking. (Washington State Archives.)

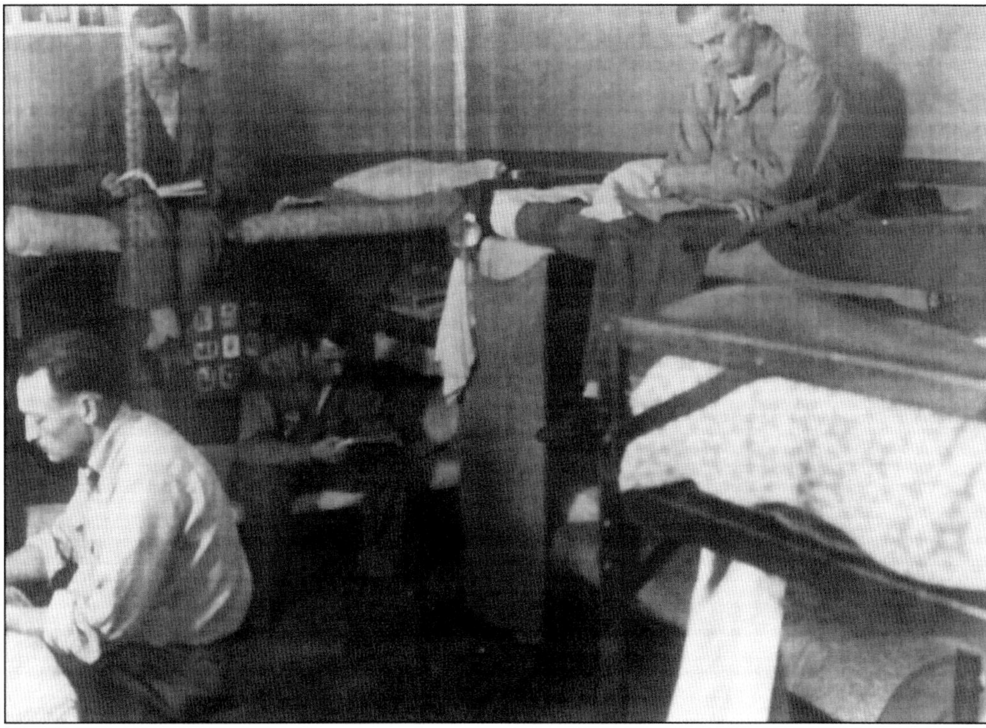

Inmates occupy time by reading in the first cell house in this image, which shows the crowded conditions. By 1920, six men were housed in cells meant for two. Overcrowding was a problem that would continue for years at McNeil, as the count grew due to convictions for narcotic sales, income tax fraud, and mail fraud. (Washington State Archives.)

Inmates clear land by hand in 1915. Two large draft horses stand ready to haul timbers away in a wagon left of center. The men all wear jackets and caps to fight the chill as they work chopping wood and burning debris. A new poultry house is at center near an outhouse and outbuilding amidst various sheds, stumps, fires, and log piles. (Washington State Archives.)

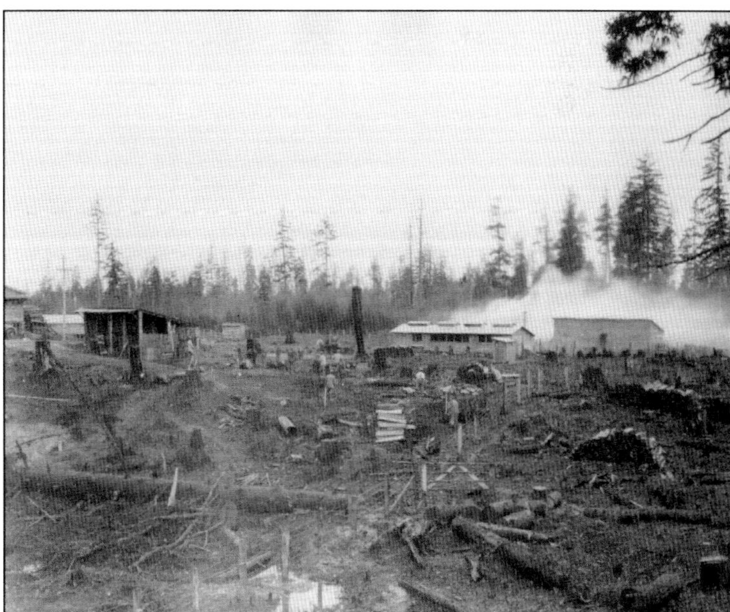

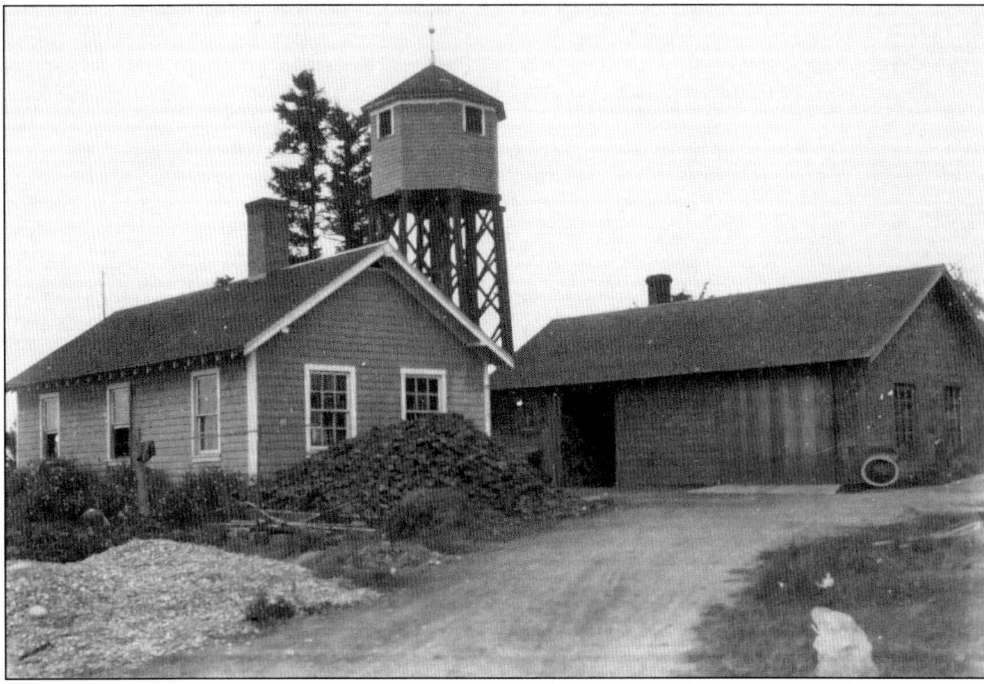

This settler house and outbuilding were bought by the prison and converted to farm buildings when the farm was near the main institution. The buildings sat under the guard tower on the bluff at the right rear of the main institution, near where the first warden's house sat, looking out over the prison. (Washington State Archives.)

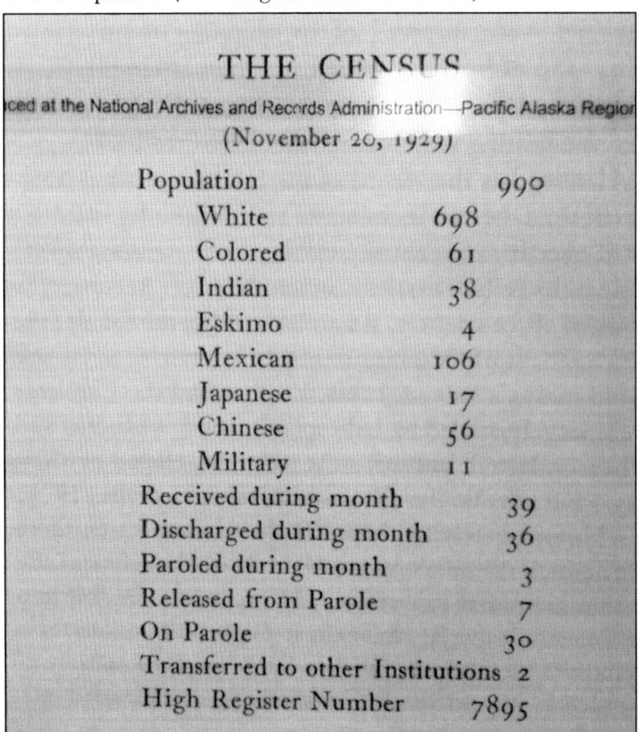

THE CENSUS

(November 20, 1929)

Population		990
White	698	
Colored	61	
Indian	38	
Eskimo	4	
Mexican	106	
Japanese	17	
Chinese	56	
Military	11	
Received during month		39
Discharged during month		36
Paroled during month		3
Released from Parole		7
On Parole		30
Transferred to other Institutions		2
High Register Number		7895

This census count from the November 20, 1929, *Island Lantern* shows the mainly homogeneous population that, thanks to Prohibition, had nearly doubled. Fench Archer became warden in 1922 and commissioned Heath, Gove, & Bell to design Three House to combat crowding. Of steel and concrete construction, it had 40 five-man cells, but with the count so high, another row of bunks was added, to hold 10 men total. (National Archives and Records Administration–Pacific Alaska Region.)

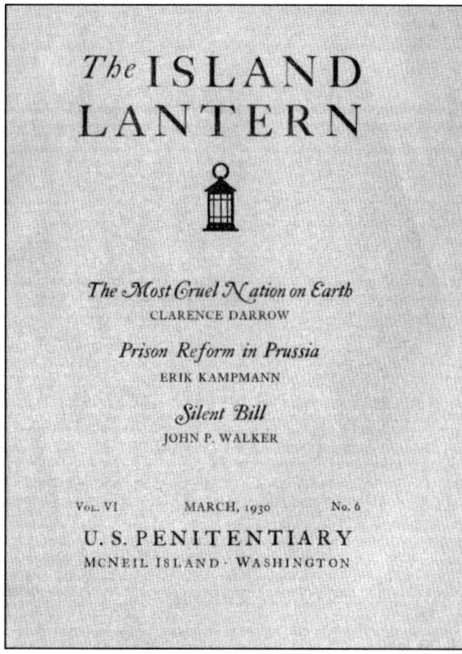

The ISLAND LANTERN

The Most Cruel Nation on Earth
CLARENCE DARROW

Prison Reform in Prussia
ERIK KAMPMANN

Silent Bill
JOHN P. WALKER

VOL. VI MARCH, 1930 No. 6

U. S. PENITENTIARY
MCNEIL ISLAND · WASHINGTON

The Island Lantern began in 1924 when inmate con man Fred Peters convinced Warden Archer to allow a prison press. The inmates pooled meager resources, and Archer solicited a donated press and supplies from the community, which readily helped. From humble beginnings, the *Lantern* became an award-winning publication with a global circulation that informed inmates and clientele about conditions and provided thought-provoking commentary. Clarence Darrow was one of many illustrious contributors. (McNeil Island Historical Society.)

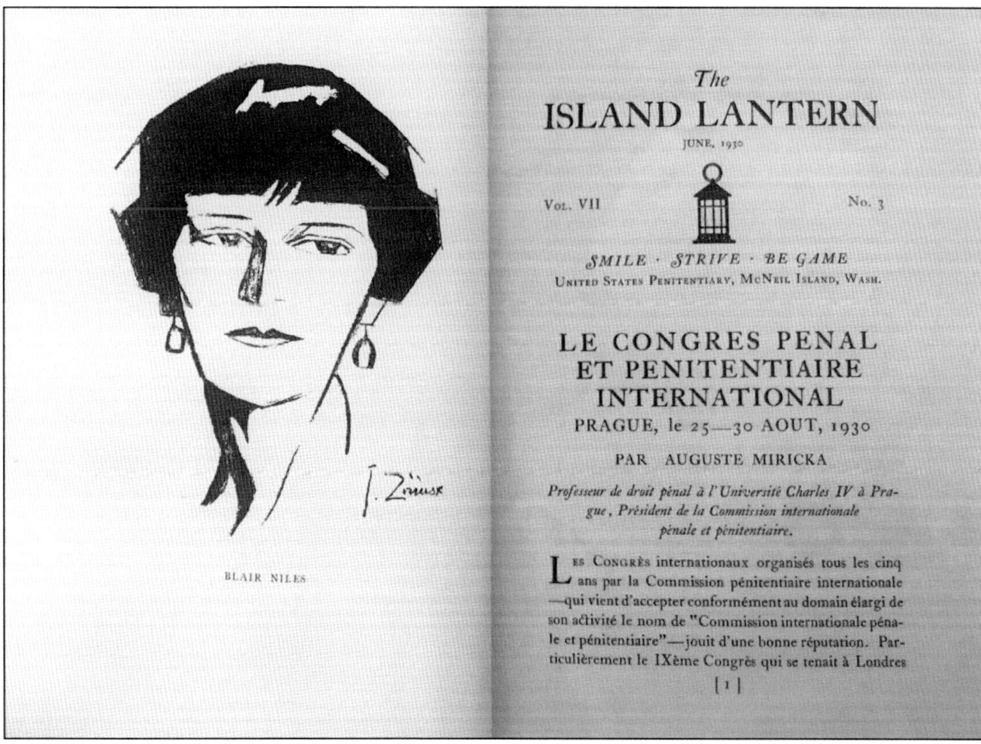

BLAIR NILES

The
ISLAND LANTERN
JUNE, 1930

VOL. VII No. 3

SMILE · STRIVE · BE GAME
UNITED STATES PENITENTIARY, MCNEIL ISLAND, WASH.

LE CONGRES PENAL
ET PENITENTIAIRE
INTERNATIONAL
PRAGUE, le 25—30 AOUT, 1930

PAR AUGUSTE MIRICKA

Professeur de droit pénal à l'Université Charles IV à Prague, Président de la Commission internationale pénale et pénitentiaire.

LES CONGRÈS internationaux organisés tous les cinq ans par la Commission pénitentiaire internationale —qui vient d'accepter conformément au domain élargi de son activité le nom de "Commission internationale pénale et pénitentiaire"—jouit d'une bonne réputation. Particulièrement le IXème Congrès qui se tenait à Londres

[1]

Fred Peters was a Canadian, so he published a special French edition of *The Island Lantern* for its debut at the International Penal and Penitentiary Congress in Prague in August 1930. There was also an English version, and many prominent penal experts contributed, such as Stanford Bates, director of the US Bureau of Prisons, and Dr. Mary B. Harris, director of the first women's federal prison. (McNeil Island Historical Society.)

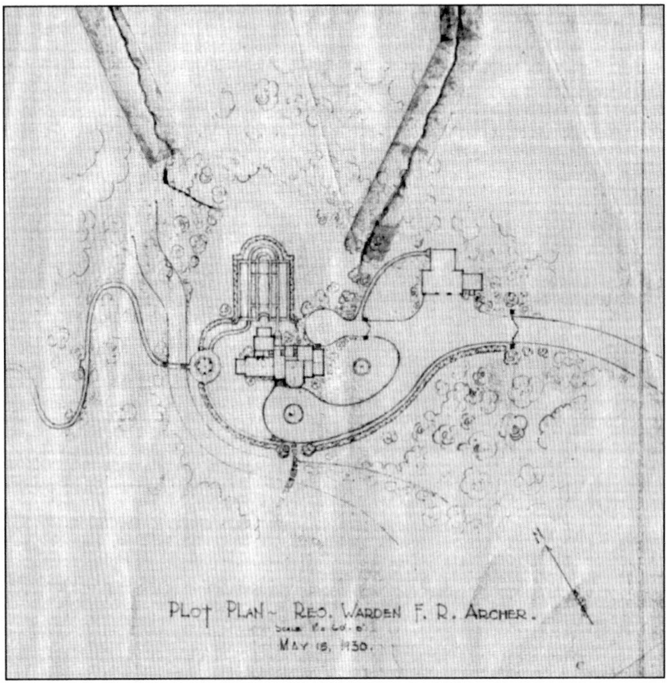

This plan, sketched by an inmate draftsman working with Heath, Gove, & Bell, the design firm selected for Warden Archer's house in 1930, illustrates extensive abundantly planted grounds, as Dora Archer and architect George Gove loved flowers and gardening. Low stone walls bordered tiered gardens with a water feature that fed a stream beside fruit trees and an arbor. The inmate gained a valuable reference and contacts for post-prison work. (Washington State Department of Corrections.)

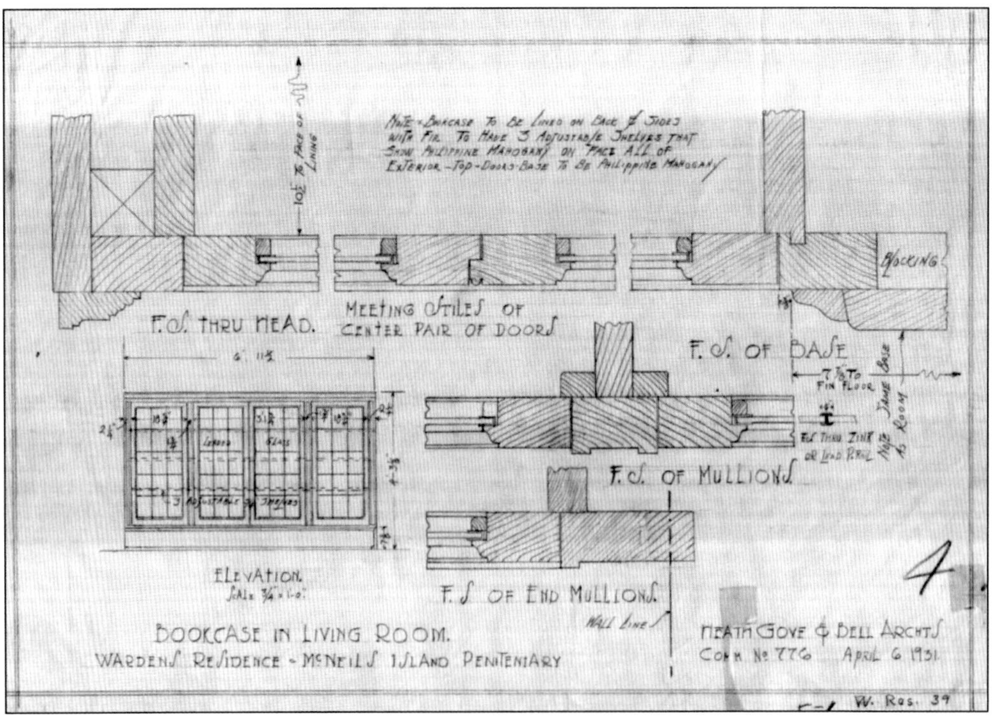

This is a detailed 1931 blueprint of mullioned bookcases for Warden Archer's home by Heath, Gove, & Bell. George Gove was the communicating architect for the prison, so he did most of the designs. Inmate craftsmen used these blueprints as they did the work onsite and at the prison. Working for such a prestigious firm was invaluable experience for the inmates. Jobs were prized because of the benefit to post-prison employment. (Washington State Department of Corrections.)

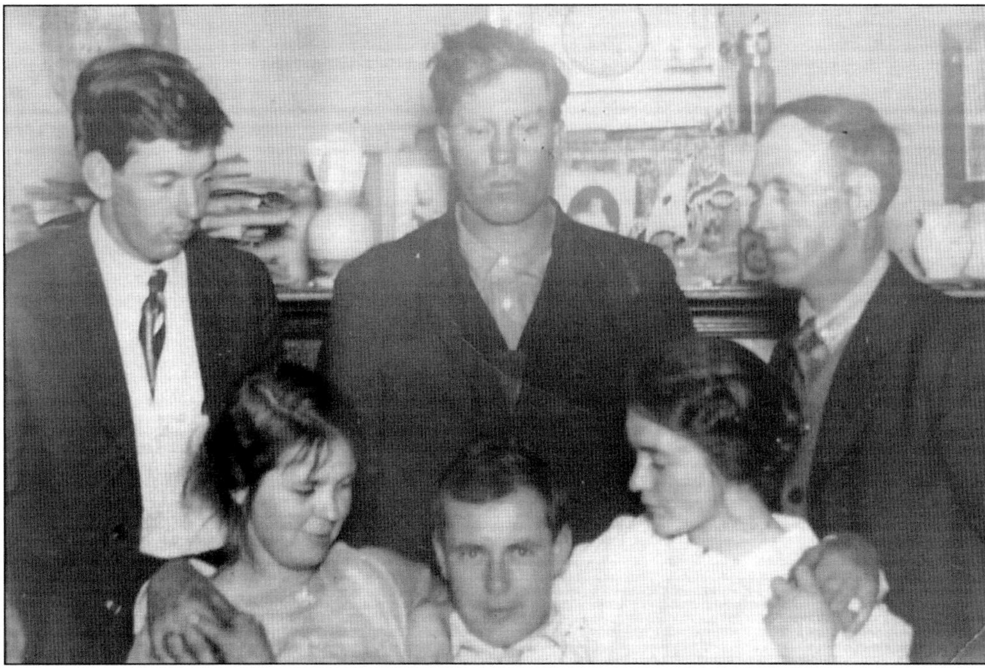

Pictured at the Cammon home in Still Harbor are, from left to right, (first row) Mrs. Harper, Ben Hannem, and Irene Westrom; (second row, standing) Ben Johnson, Mr. Harper, and Charley Johnson, who settled on Anderson in 1893. Ben Hannem moved to McNeil with his parents, Bernt and Berit, around 1900 and stayed until the BOP took over in 1936; Irene Westrom was the daughter of Selma and Albert Westrom, who lost his hand at the Washington Lumber and Box Company. All were from very involved island families. (Jean Cammon Findlay.)

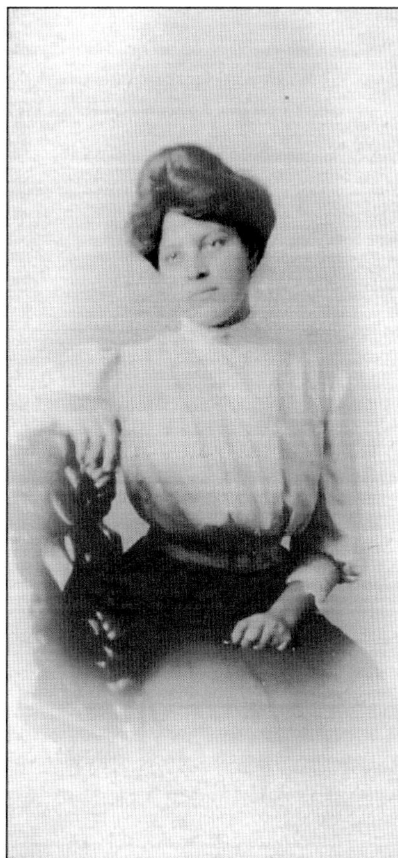

Alma Larson's mother, Agusta, died when Alma was six, but she could not attend the funeral on Anderson island (McNeil had no cemetery then) because she was too young to make the crossing during the storms that day. Alma spent her childhood with her siblings, tending house and preparing vegetables for market or playing with the Julin or Nelson children. She later married into the Mansfield family and moved to Seattle, where she died in 1968. (Jean Cammon Findlay.)

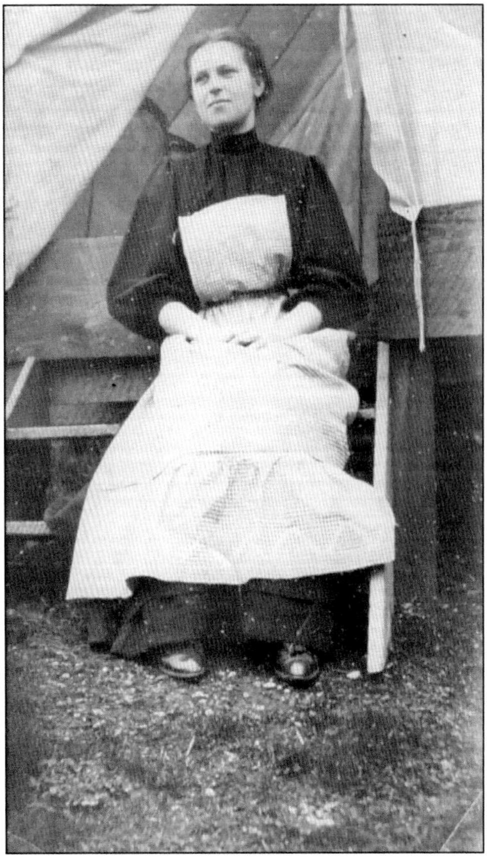

Hilfrid Swanson is seen here at Still Harbor. She was born in 1890, and in 1916 married John R. Pace, who died in 1972; she would die a year later. It took a special type of person to live on an island where everything had to be either made or brought in on a boat from the mainland. (Jean Cammon Findlay.)

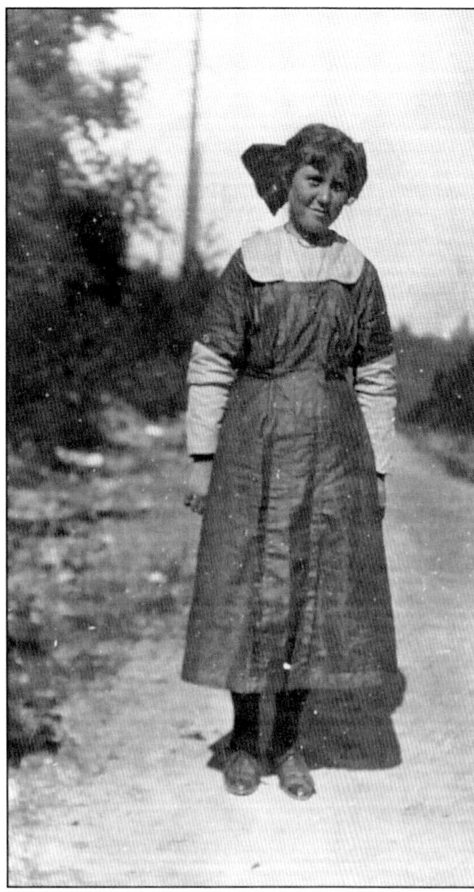

Didi Taylor is pictured here at Still Harbor. Didi was Agnes (Parr) Burg's sister. The Parrs ran the Parr Brothers Lumber Company on McNeil's southwest end until it burned in 1926. The island's vast forests fed the various mills on the island and brought paychecks to its residents. A brothel at a home on four corners provided services for the west end millworkers. (Jean Cammon Findlay.)

Irene Westrom grew up on McNeil Island with her family, living a life where everyone knew everyone else and gathered in community centers and churches for socials and committees, either on Anderson or McNeil Island, since everyone had access to a boat and that was the fastest way to get around. (Jean Cammon Findlay.)

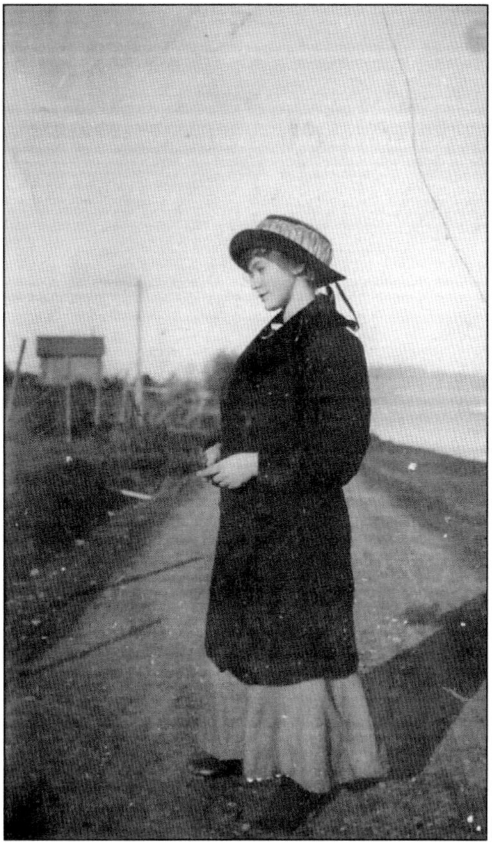

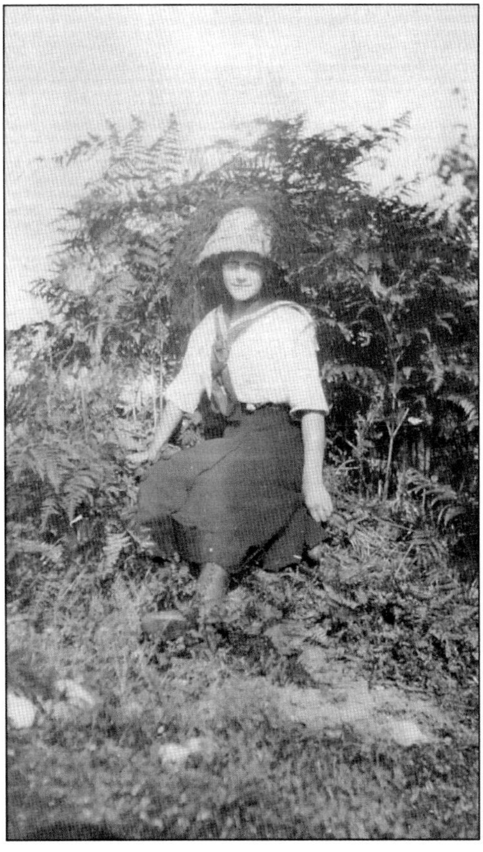

Beulah Hannum, as most children on McNeil Island, spent much of her free time fishing, sewing her own clothes, or socializing with friends from school when not tending to family chores. Of course, everything also included either walks through the woods, riding a horse, or boating between islands. (Jean Cammon Findlay.)

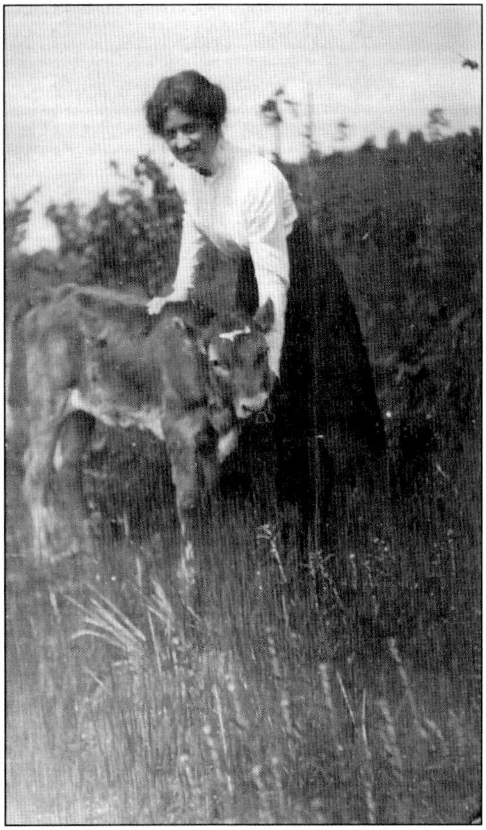

In the early 1900s, Ella Dinetz was the girlfriend of Martin Cammon of Still Harbor and Anderson Island, who took this photograph. Most of the McNeil Island families tended at least a small farm and a collection of animals during the early days because hard currency was often difficult to come by. (Jean Cammon Findlay.)

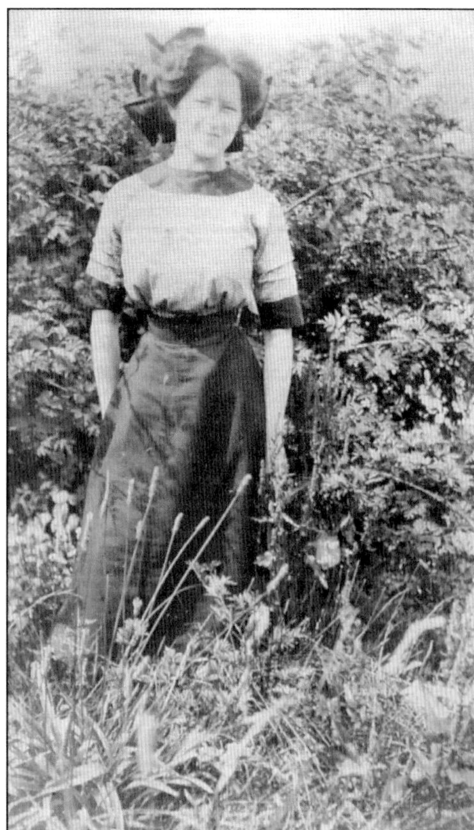

Hannah Sherwood of Still Harbor is dressed in her Sunday best for church and an afternoon with her beau, since that was the only time anyone had spare time away from work, school, or chores. Leisure time was spent on walks or lounging on the beach. (Jean Cammon Findlay.)

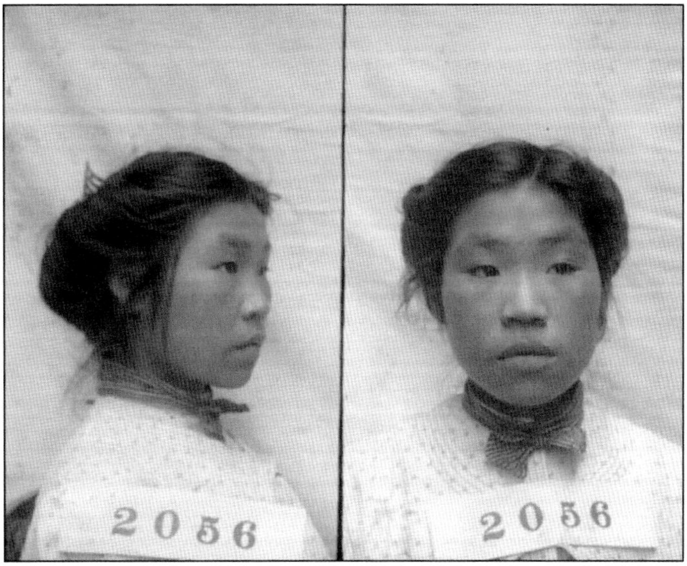

Carrie Sang-sing, prisoner No. 2056, arrived at McNeil Penitentiary in 1911. Females were imprisoned only occasionally, as other avenues were tried first since there were no separate facilities for them. Sang-sing and others were initially housed in the guards' quarters. This unfortunate situation lasted for several years until the hospital was built, and then women were held there. (National Archives and Records Administration.)

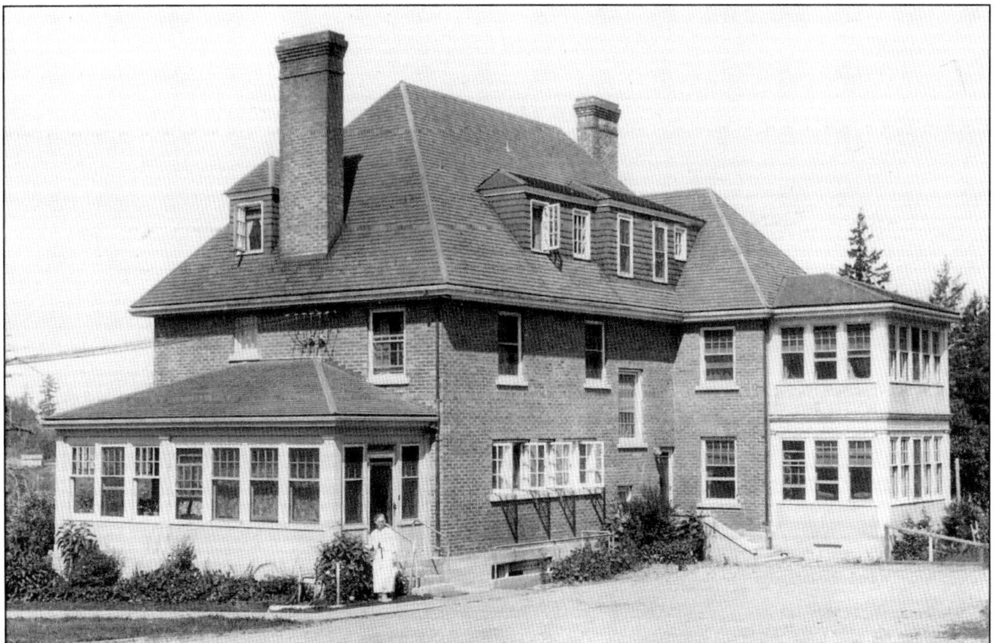

In 1932, Warden Archer's wife, Dora, stands at the back door of their new home overlooking the prison. Built by inmate laborers under the direction of skilled craftsmen, most building materials were sourced on McNeil, although Philippine mahogany was shipped in for the interior bookcases, china cabinets, and wainscoting. Its French Eclectic design suited the country estate style popular in the era and befitted a rural island manse. (Washington State Archives.)

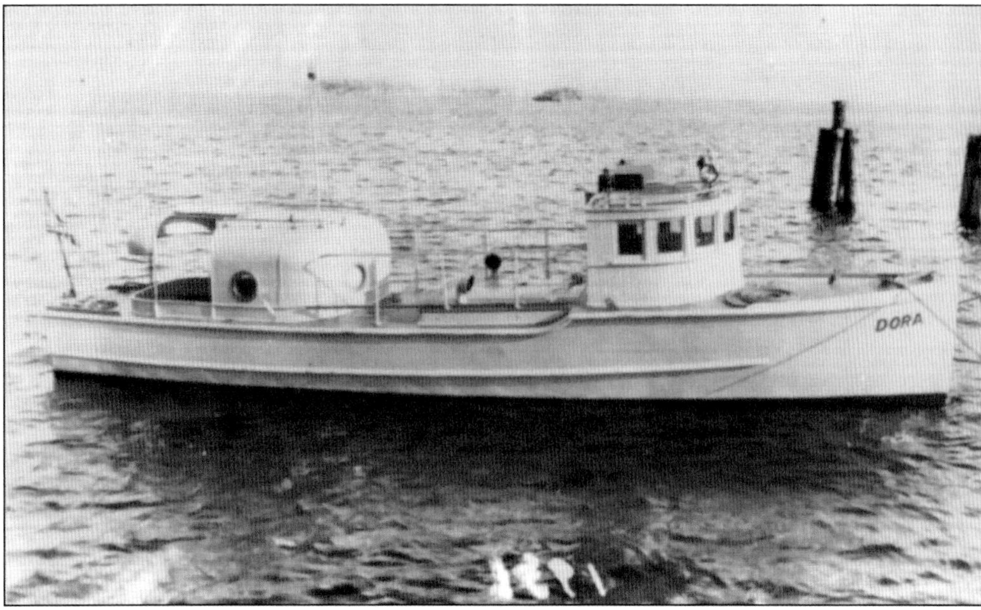

The *Dora*, named for Warden Archer's wife by her adoring fanbase of staff and prisoners alike, was a former Navy launch acquired by inmate Fred Peters in 1931 negotiations, where he overshadowed the prison dignitary he had chauffeured so much that Navy brass assumed he was the person in charge. Although another example of Peters exerting his graft skills, it worked out well for McNeil's fleet. (Washington State Archives.)

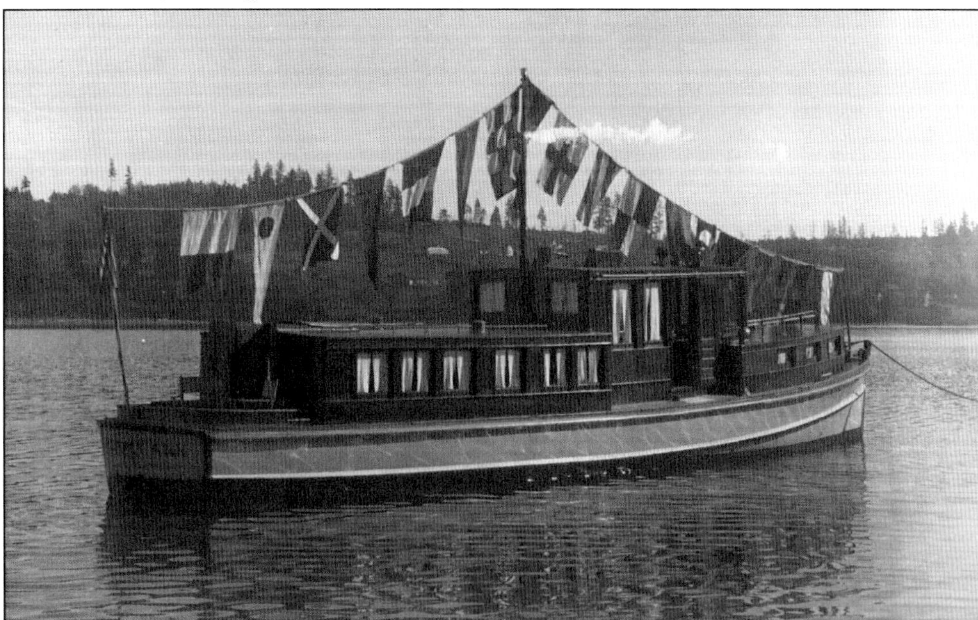

The *Margaret Ann* was part of the Mosquito Fleet that sailed the sound, connecting islands with the mainland and each other. Her tug chassis with an up cabin was a versatile and well-utilized design, as seen in the storied *John G. Sargent*, built by inmates at McNeil in 1909. Boats were used for business, whether hauling logs or selling groceries, and for pleasure, but prison boats were all business. (Washington State Archives.)

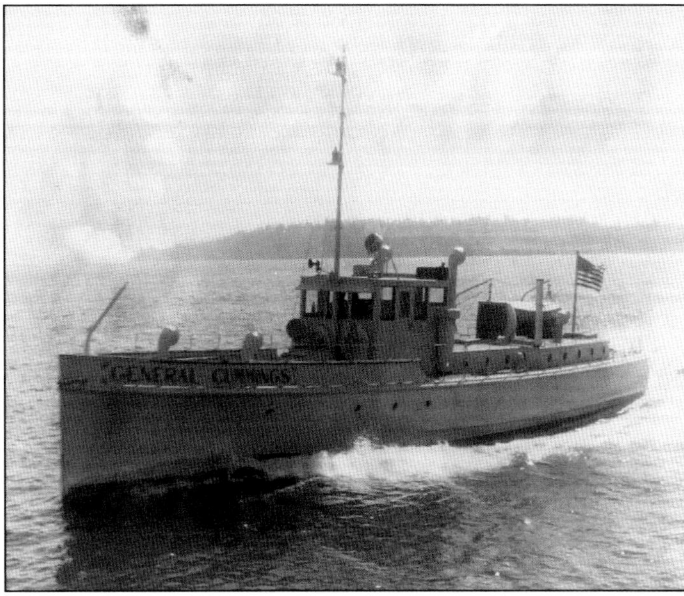

The *General Cummings* was another former military boat used by the prison to transport inmates and staff to and from the mainland during the BOP years. McNeil had an extensive fleet, with usually five to seven boats at any time. The fleet usually had a barge, two tugs (with one being a fireboat), two patrol boats, and three launches, and shared a car ferry with Anderson and Ketron Islands. (Washington State Archives.)

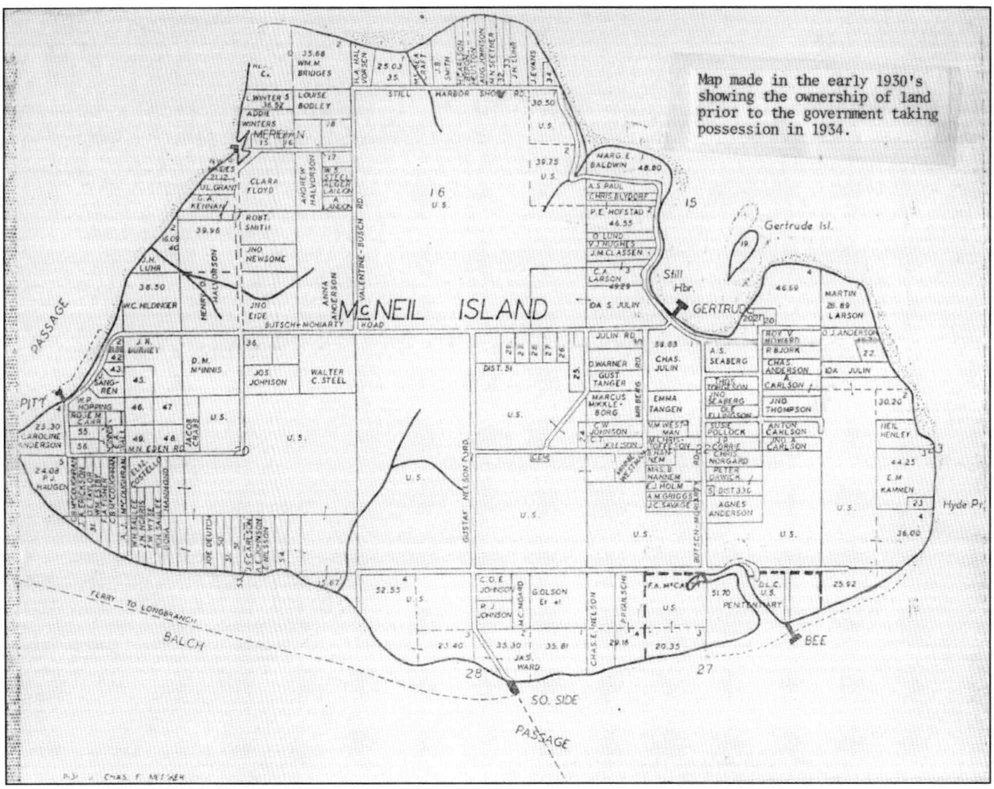

This early 1930s McNeil map shows settler properties prior to the government buyout. Most owned waterfront property, but it was the Great Depression, and the majority of islanders, with a few exceptions, requested the government agent negotiate for them so they could be bought out and acquire much-needed cash. Isolated on McNeil, the prison was their only client, so they had become disadvantaged in a buyers' market. (Courtesy of Sue Zukowski.)

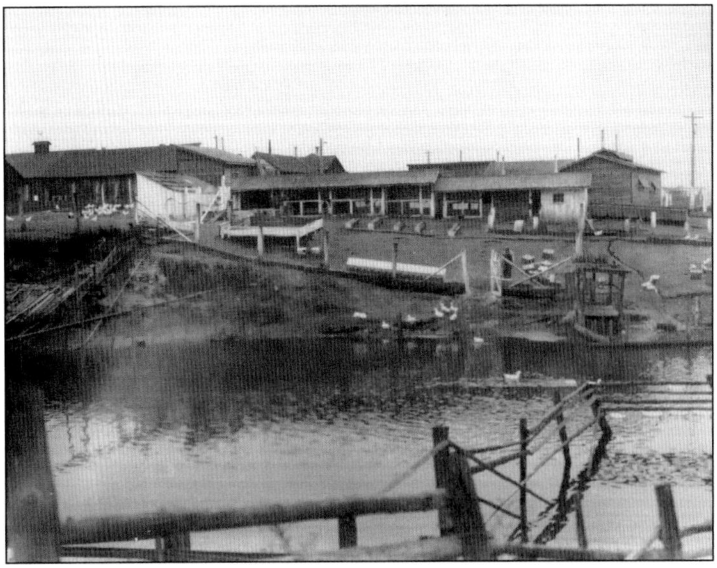

The honor farm poultry pens are seen here in 1930, with the flocks being tended to by an inmate trustee. The camp at the honor farm was approved and built under Warden Archer and eventually came to hold 328 men, although typically the number was in the mid-200s, as being a trustee at the farm was an earned privilege. (Washington State Archives.)

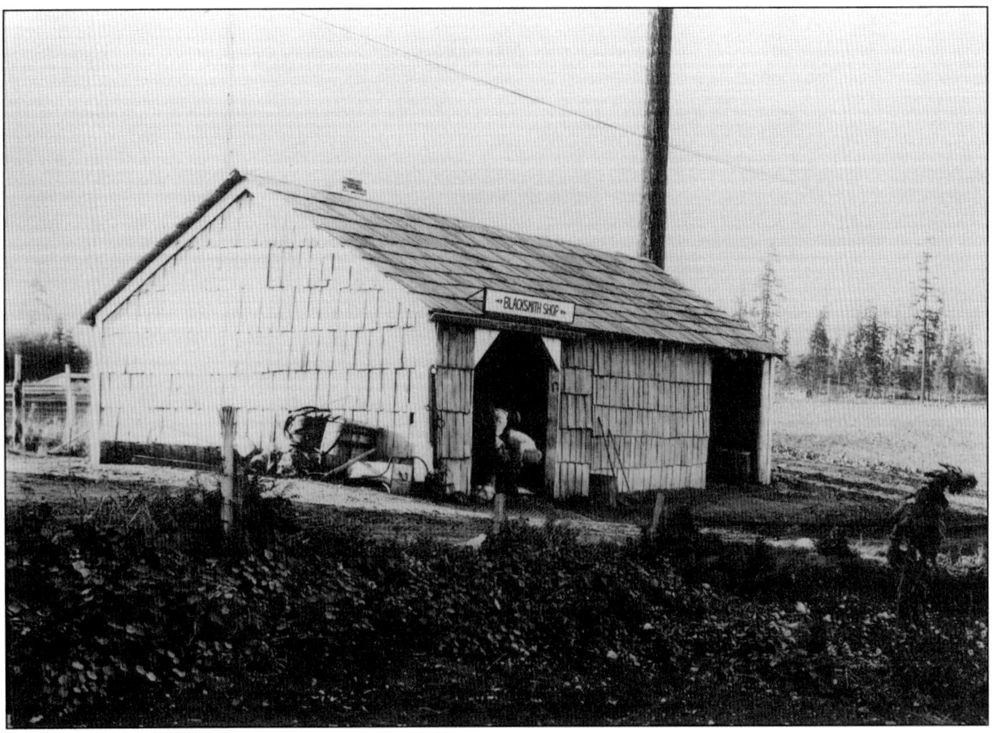

This blacksmith shop was crucial on McNeil Island, as horses were required for many tasks in daily island life. Both the settlers and the prison had blacksmith shops. The prison smithy also turned out beautiful andirons and other fanciful wrought iron as requested by the firm of Heath, Gove, & Bell for various prison projects, such as details at the warden's house. (Washington State Department of Corrections.)

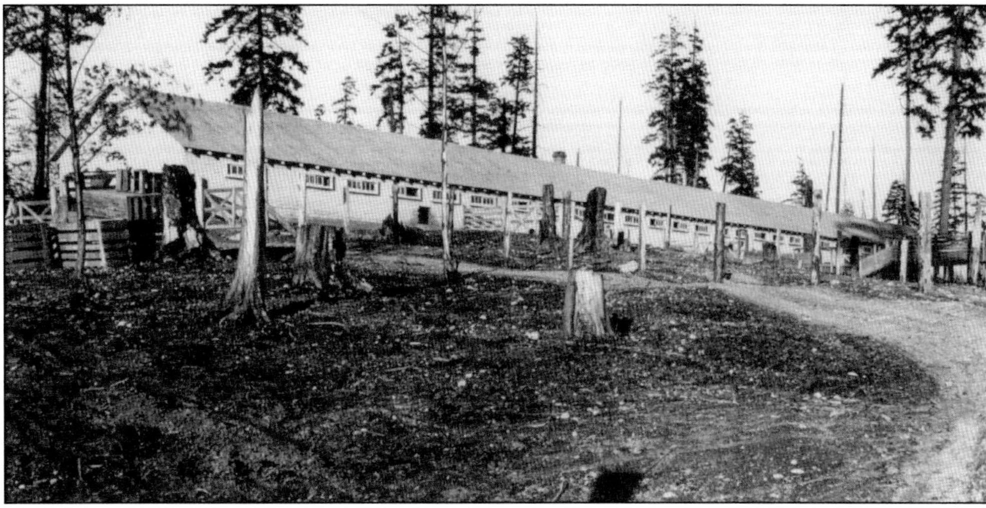

The McNeil piggery is pictured in the 1930s. Feeding the inmates was always a daunting task since the prison was located on an island. A key principle of penology is keeping prisoners happy by serving good food, as that is all they really have to look forward to each day. Bacon had to be on the menu, along with ham; conscientious trustees saw to it that they were. (Washington State Department of Corrections.)

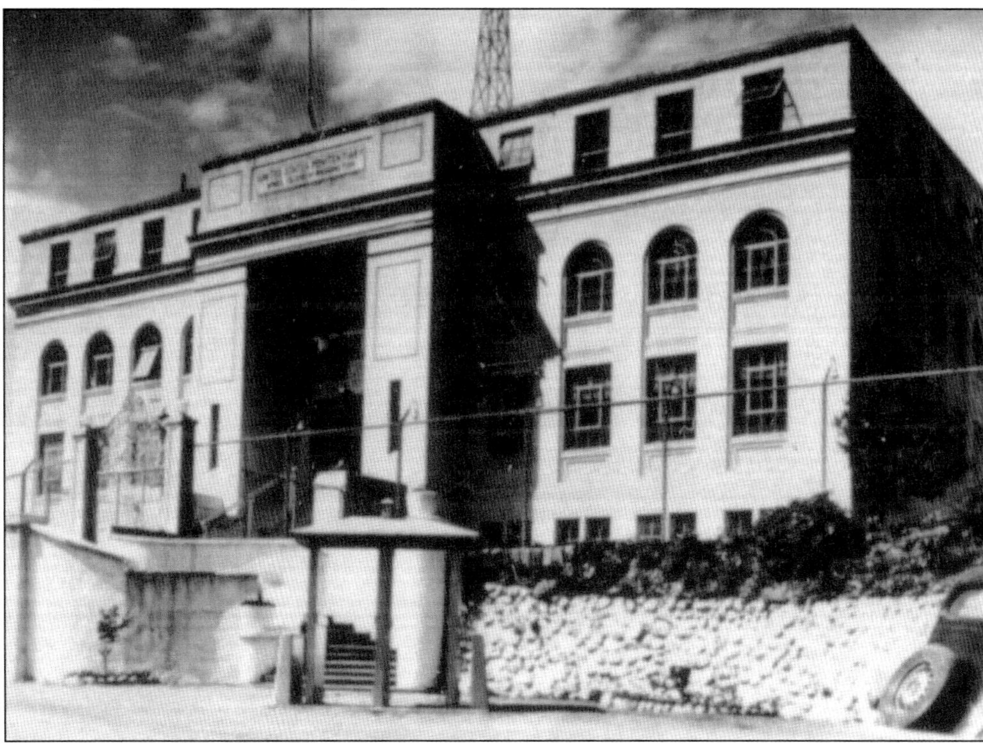

The facade of the administration building, designed by Heath, Gove, & Bell, featured clean lines, a commanding recessed entrance accentuated by stately columns, and gracefully arched windows, all set behind magnificently detailed wrought iron gates. It was constructed by skilled inmate craftsmen and laborers. The 1928 building possesses an unsurpassed view of Mt. Rainier and the south sound. (Washington State Department of Corrections.)

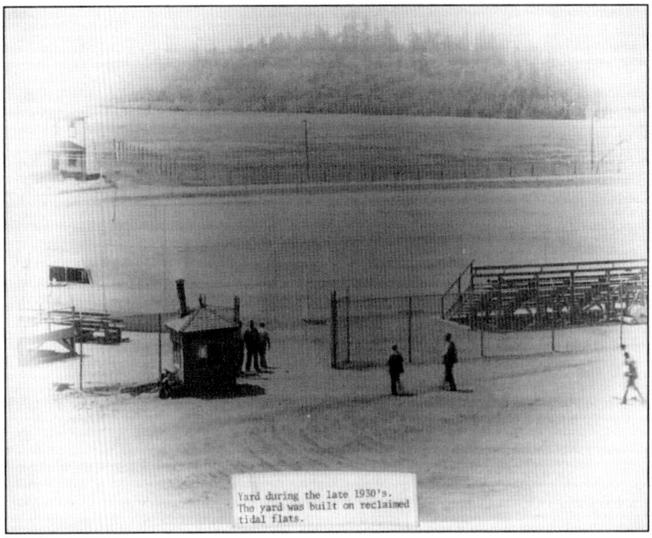

McNeil's big yard had the best view in the prison system and was renowned by staff and inmates. Reclaimed from tidal flats under Warden Halligan, the yard held many ball games over the decades, usually between inmates and civilians. Numerous local school kids can say they played ball on the yard with convicts. The interaction was good for both of them. (Washington State Department of Corrections.)

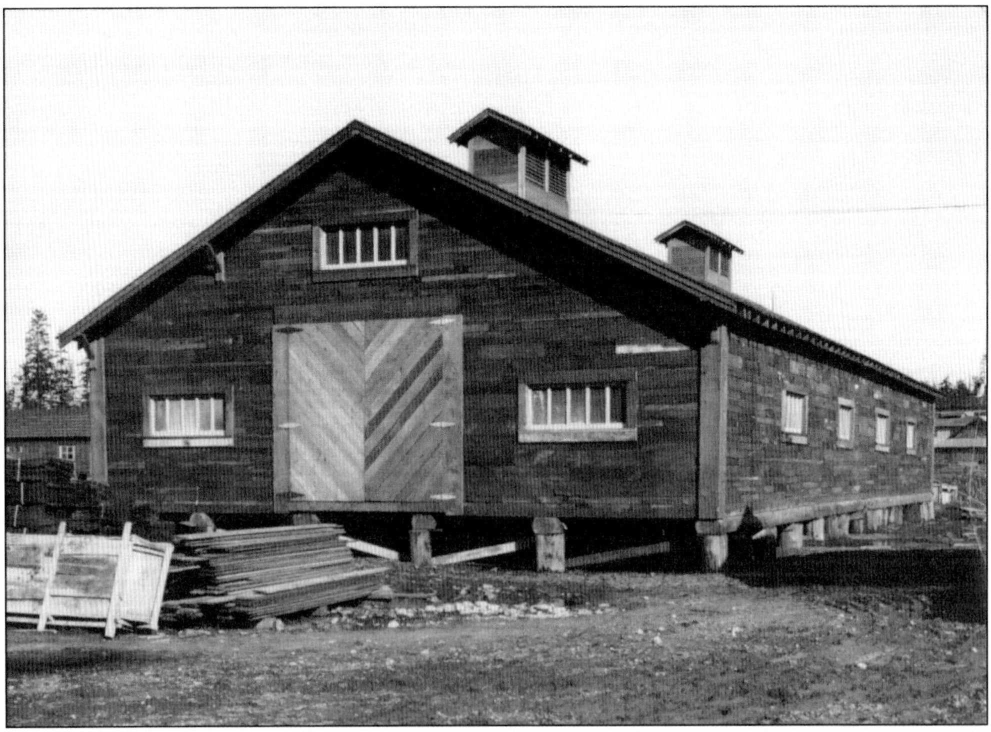

The beautifully constructed barns at the prison farm were designed by Heath, Gove, & Bell, and are similar to outbuildings the firm designed at both Paradise Lodge on Mt. Rainier and at nearby Ft. Steilacoom and Western State Hospital. Wood and materials for the barns were procured and processed on McNeil by inmate teams working under inmate foremen. This was all part of the rehabilitation plan of helping them repatriate into society. (Washington State Department of Corrections.)

The practicality of island life matched well with the frugality of government spending on prison operations, with many of the former settler homes finding new life as prison offices or houses. This home, for example, went from housing a family to being the administrative hub for the camp farm. (Washington State Archives.)

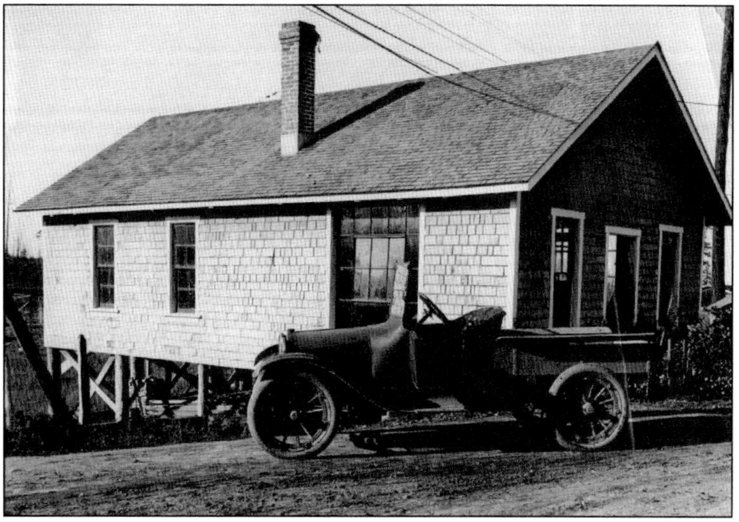

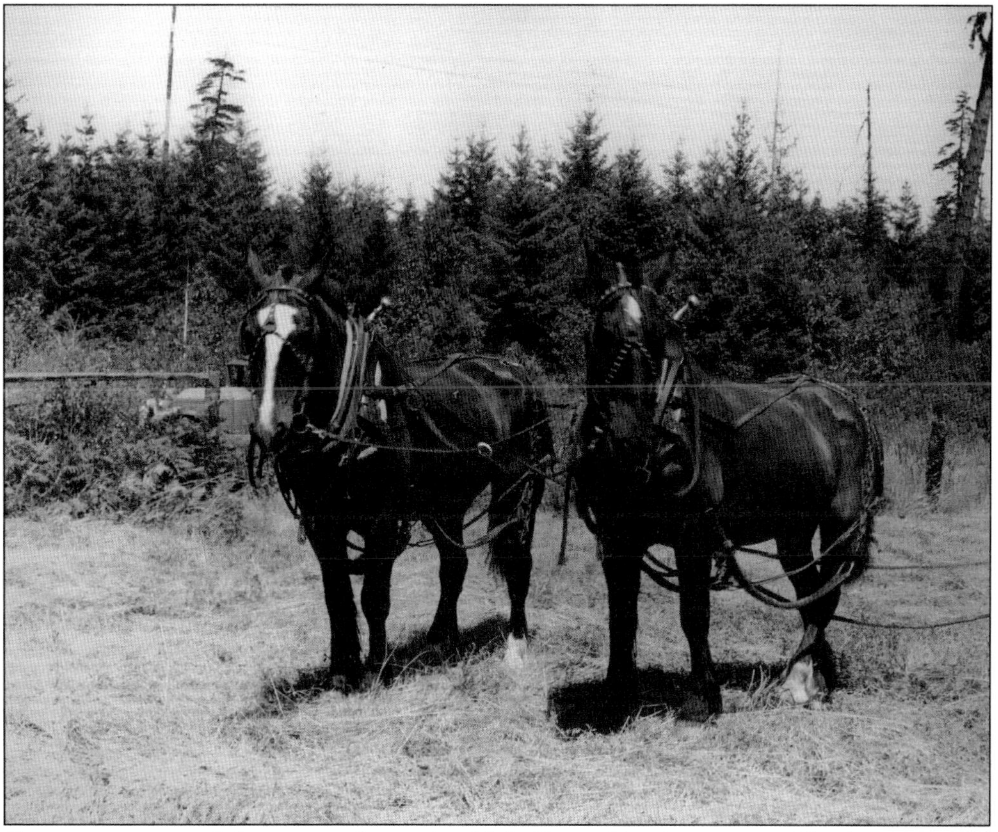

Horses were required for many tasks in island life. Teams like this were used by the prison and settlers for convenient travel, plowing fields, drawing heavy wagons, and removing tree stumps. As the honor farm expanded, horses were used by staff and inmate foremen to check on fencing and work details and by inmate cowboys who herded McNeil's 500 head of Angus and Hereford cattle. (Washington State Archives.)

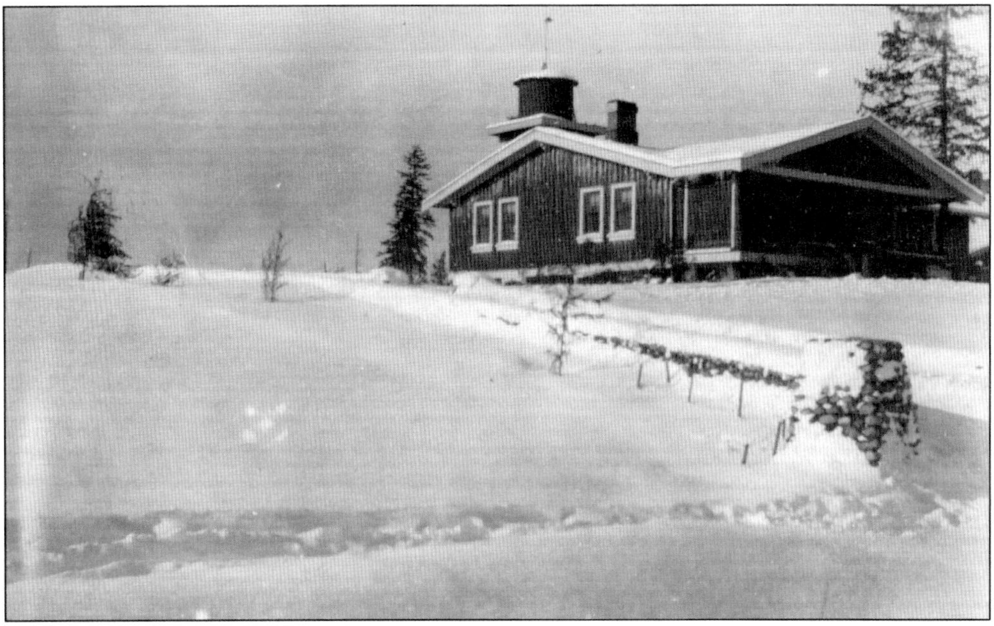

McNeil's first schoolhouse opened in 1891 at Section 16 near A.V. Savage's homestead, off Butsch-Moriarty Road. School District 51 started in 1888, but classes were held in settler homes. Savage's home sat across the stone wall of what became the prisoners' Hillcrest Cemetery. After the district sold its 27 acres to the government, which also acquired Savage's additional 40 acres, all the property became part of the honor farm. (Washington State Archives.)

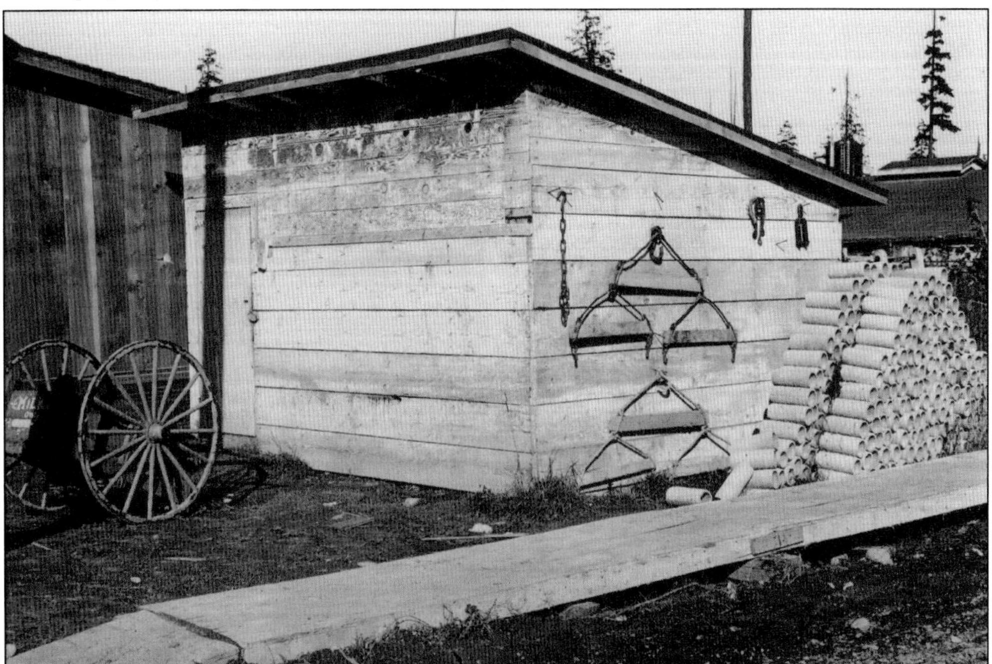

A former pioneer's storage building became the tack shed at the camp farm, where horses were used by prisoners to sow and harvest crops used in the prison kitchen as a way to control costs and provide activities and income for inmates. (Washington State Archives.)

This 1910 plat of Still Harbor on McNeil Island shows that most of the landowners had smaller waterfront properties, while larger inland tracts were owned by farmers such as Charles Julin, who came to McNeil in 1882, and bought lots at lower prices. Julin increased his wealth by parceling off some of his land and reselling it to newcomers. Still Harbor was once a thriving community of boatmen and loggers. (Washington Department of Corrections.)

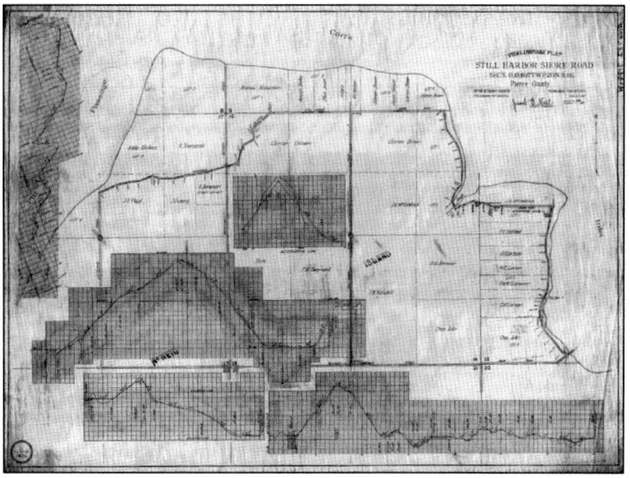

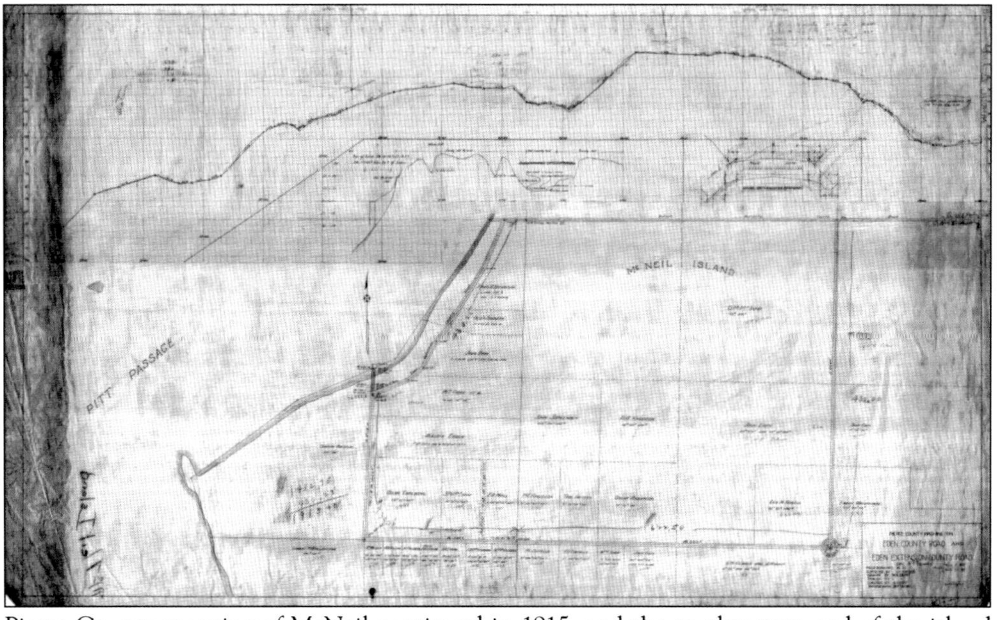

Pierce County mapping of McNeil continued in 1915, and the southeastern end of the island was documented. This plat mentions Eden County Road because the original large landowner was John Eden, who had just a small waterfront parcel on this chart. Eden Creek is named after him as well, and his 1890s home still stands beside it, having been occupied by state prison staff until closure in 2011. (Washington Department of Corrections.)

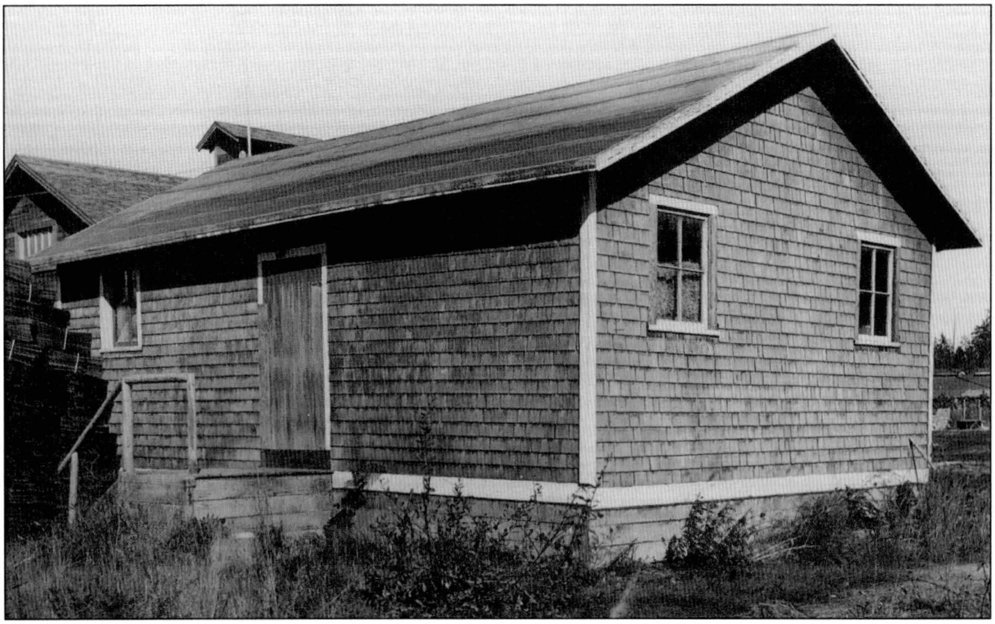

Of course, not every former settler's home was needed to house guards or offices, but nothing was ever wasted. This house, for example, was simply converted to a hay barn at the honor farm, where it was used for decades. Anything that could be reused was recycled or repurposed until it simply had nothing else to give. (Washington State Archives.)

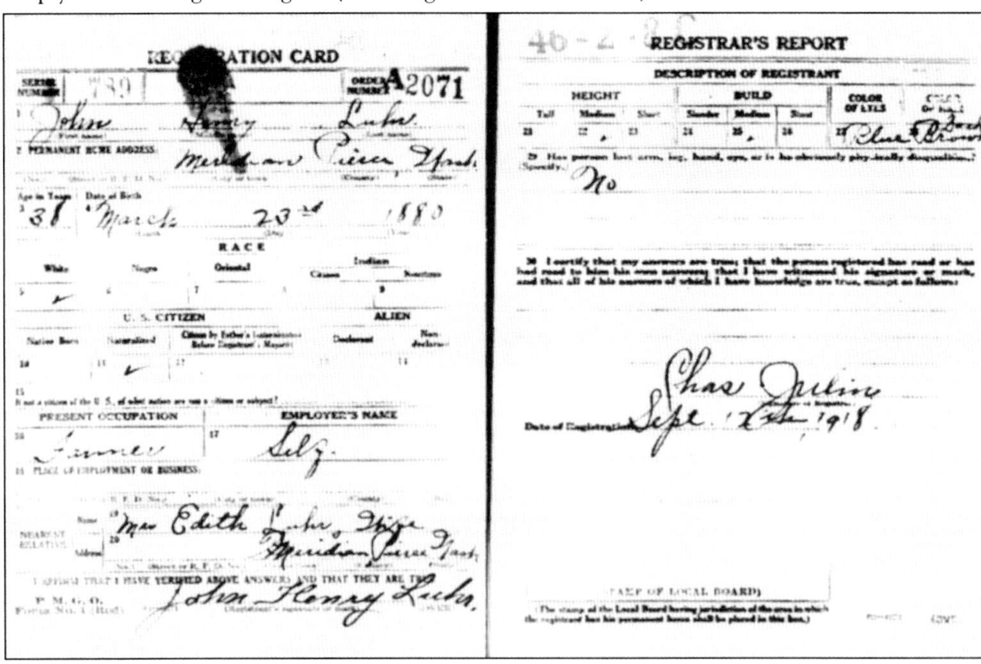

REGISTRATION CARD

SERIAL NUMBER 789 ORDER NUMBER A2071

John Henry Luhr

PERMANENT HOME ADDRESS: Meridian Pierce Wash.

Age in Years 38 Date of Birth March 23rd 1880

RACE

White ✓

U. S. CITIZEN

Naturalized ✓

PRESENT OCCUPATION Farmer

EMPLOYER'S NAME Self

NEAREST RELATIVE Name Mrs Edith Luhr, Wife Address Meridian Pierce Wash.

I AFFIRM THAT I HAVE VERIFIED ABOVE ANSWERS AND THAT THEY ARE TRUE

John Henry Luhr

P. M. G. O. Form No. 1 (Red)

REGISTRAR'S REPORT

DESCRIPTION OF REGISTRANT

HEIGHT Medium ✓ BUILD Medium ✓ COLOR OF EYES Blue COLOR OF HAIR Brown

Has person lost arm, leg, hand, eye, or is he obviously physically disqualified? No

I certify that my answers are true; that the person registered has read or has had read to him his own answers; that I have witnessed his signature or mark, and that all of his answers of which I have knowledge are true, except as follows:

Chas Julin

Date of Registration Sept. 12th 1918.

(STAMP OF LOCAL BOARD)

Although McNeil started as the end of the pioneers' Oregon Trail, by 1918, it was fully part of modern society, and residents had to register to vote along with filling out other documents common in bureaucratic societies. This voter registration card is for John Henry Luhr, 38 years old, who lived at Meridian with his wife, Edith, and was self-employed as a farmer. Charles Julin was the registrar and Gertrude's postmaster. (Washington State Archives.)

Elmer Ward registered for the draft, claiming conscientious objector and sole support status for his family. Twenty-four at the time, he had been born on McNeil in 1893 at the homestead his father bought on the southeast side of the island on a bluff near the current ferry slip. Ward also listed his occupation as farmer, as agriculture was definitely the predominant way of life for settlers on McNeil. (Washington State Archives.)

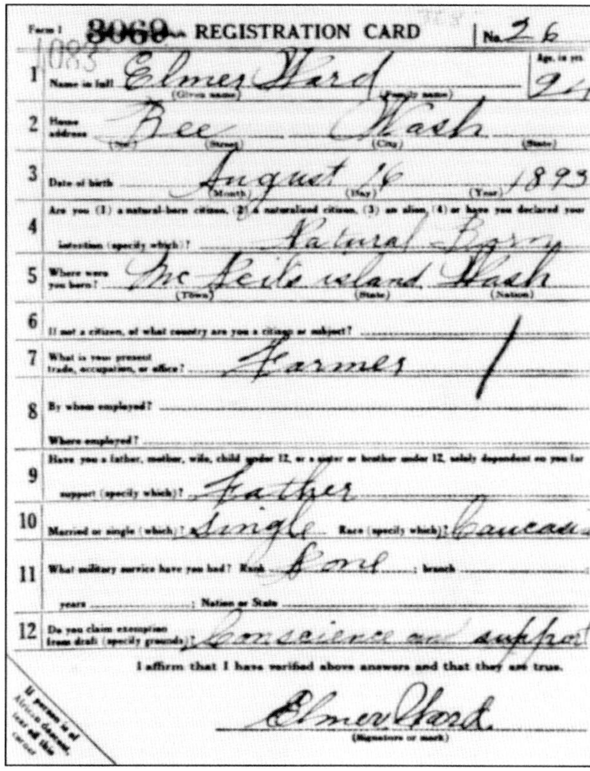

Form 1 8060 REGISTRATION CARD No. 26

1083

1 Name in full: Elmer Ward (Given name) (Family name) — Age, in yrs. 24

2 Home address: (No.) (Street) Bee (City) Wash (State)

3 Date of birth: August (Month) 16 (Day) 1893 (Year)

4 Are you (1) a natural-born citizen, (2) a naturalized citizen, (3) an alien, (4) or have you declared your intention (specify which)? Natural Born

5 Where were you born? McNeil's island (Town) Wash (State) (Nation)

6 If not a citizen, of what country are you a citizen or subject?

7 What is your present trade, occupation, or office? Farmer

8 By whom employed? Where employed?

9 Have you a father, mother, wife, child under 12, or a sister or brother under 12, solely dependent on you for support (specify which)? Father

10 Married or single (which)? Single Race (specify which)? Caucasian

11 What military service have you had? Rank None ; branch years ; Nation or State

12 Do you claim exemption from draft (specify grounds)? Conscience and support

I affirm that I have verified above answers and that they are true.

Elmer Ward (Signature or mark)

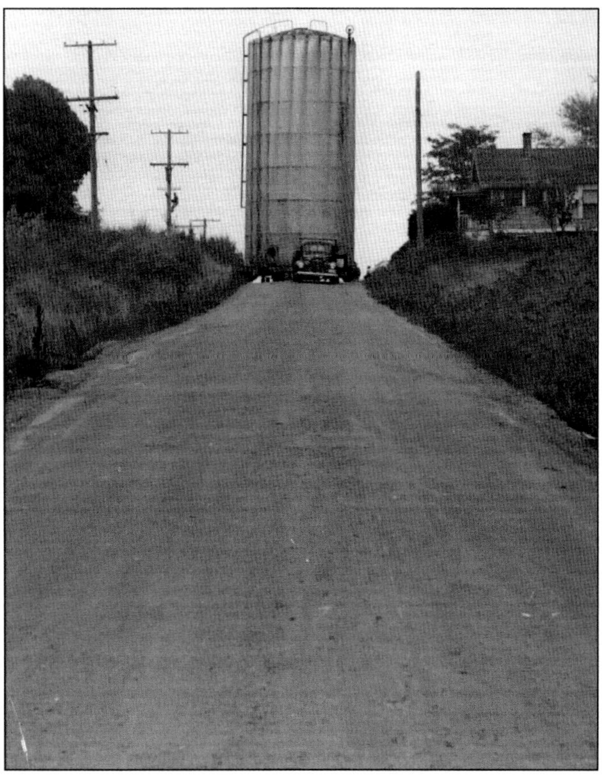

This amazing photograph demonstrates the hard work required to supply a prison island with necessities. A 1900s settler house sits beside a dirt road as a small 1920s farm truck carries a giant silo to the prison honor farm where it will hold grain to feed the inmates. Things had to be done to make McNeil run, and the capable staff always figured out a way. McNeil had spirit. (Washington State Archives.)

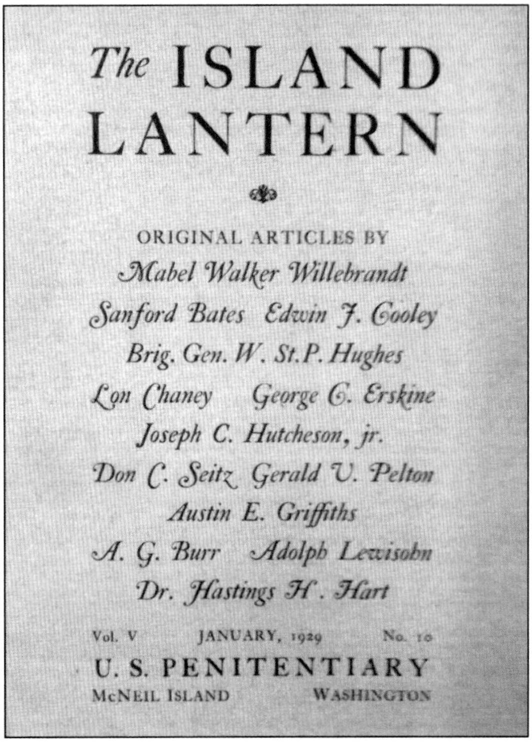

In 1928, *The Island Lantern* earned the Best Prison Magazine Award for the United States by the American War Mothers, attracting national attention. Besides the usual penology experts like Hastings H. Hart, movie star Lon Chaney also contributed an article, as rehabilitation was a cause célèbre. Its theme, "Smile, Strive, Be Game," prevailed until the final edition in 1980. Proceeds from sales were divided among deserving prisoner families. (National Archives and Records Administration.)

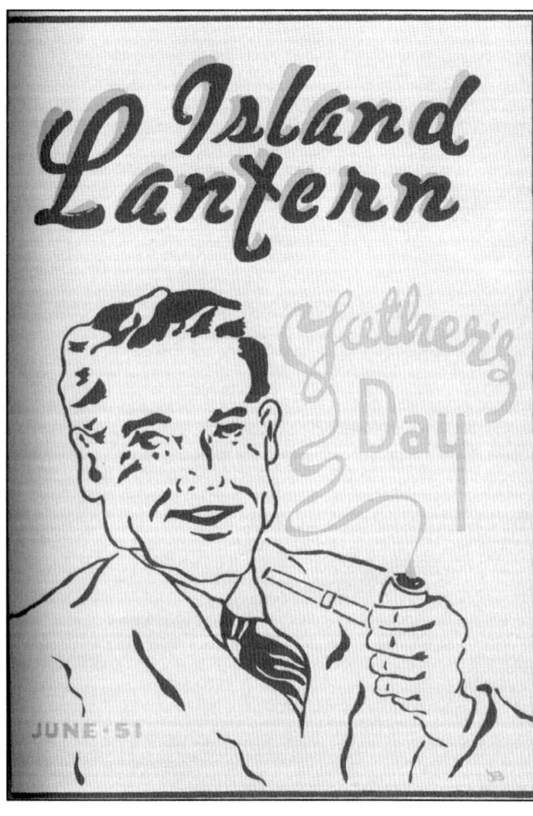

This *Island Lantern* from June 1951 celebrates Father's Day by using a cover drawing with a classic dad look. A prison is like a small town. Inmates have the same hopes, dreams, and fears (plus some additional ones) as the rest of society, so of course, the *Lantern* was filled with heartwarming articles about fatherhood, as well as enviable original inmate artwork. (National Archives and Records Administration.)

Warden Fench Archer feeds chicks at the new honor farm in 1927. He had a true concern for the inmates and was among them as much as possible, keeping abreast of the feelings of the men and the rhythms of the prison and farm. The improvements set in motion at McNeil helped it become the premier federal penitentiary. (Washington State Archives.)

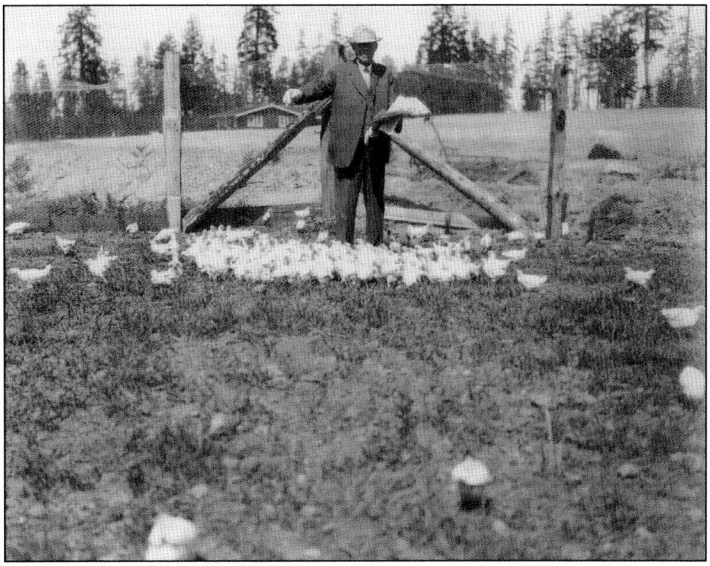

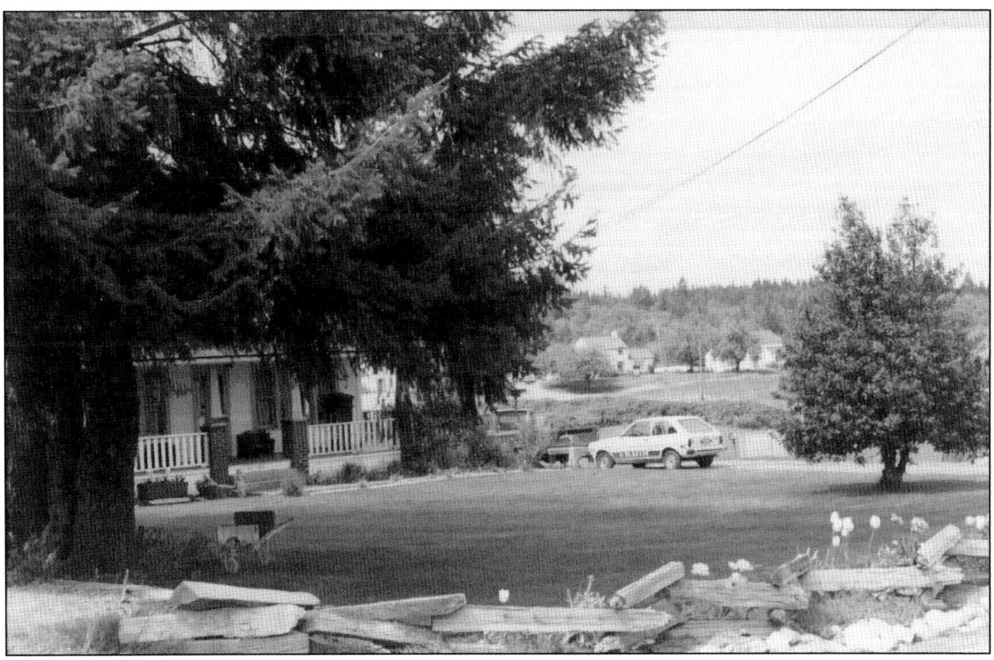

Constructed in 1920, Residence 321 was M. Christofferson's home before the prison purchased it in 1936. In the background, two houses on Holly Hill, built by federal prisoners in the 1940s, can be seen on what was Emma Tangen's property. Interestingly, state people called Holly Hill "Lieutenant's Row," but that was what Center Hill actually was, under the feds. Ultimately, this was home to very closely knit people. (Washington State Archives.)

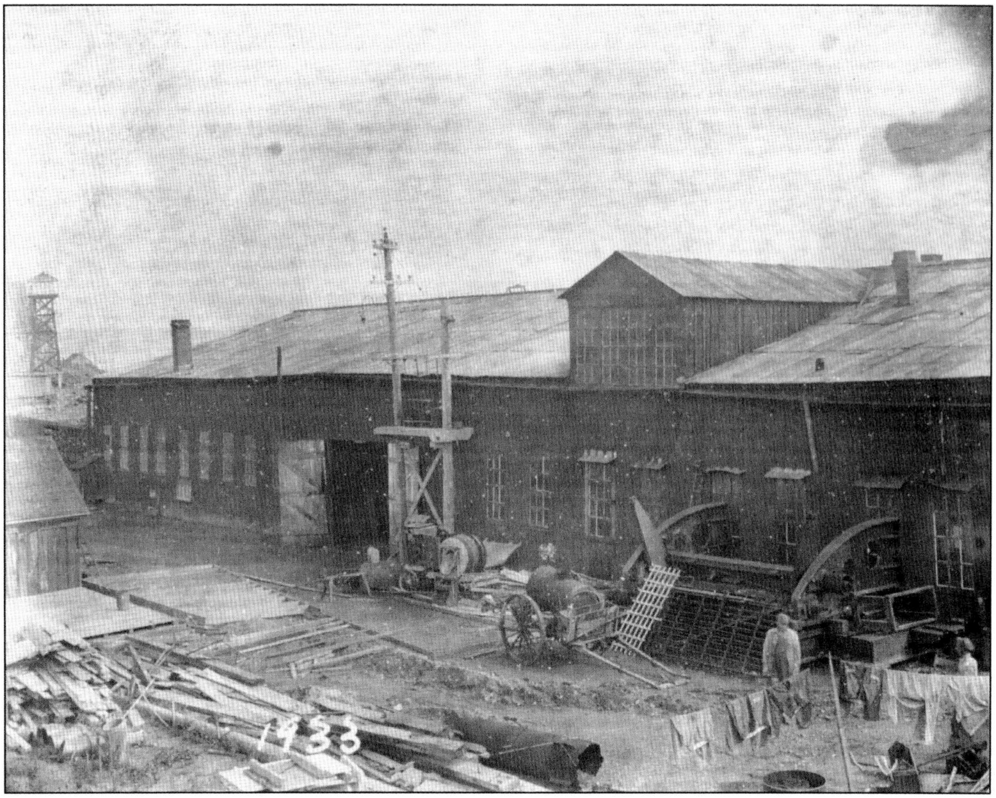

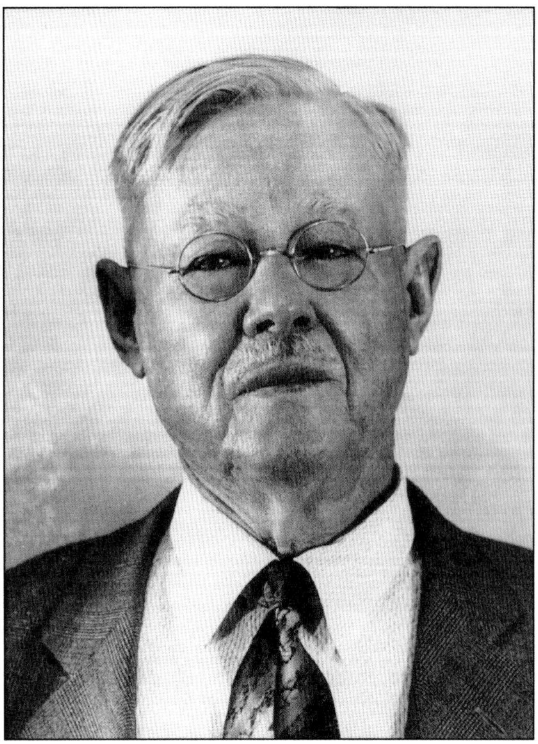

Basic necessities surrounded the 1933 auto and machine shops. Clothes dry on a makeshift clothesline before two inmates beside a cart holding a cement mixer. Shop Row was built over an easement the state leased to the feds, which was finally filled in 1911. These buildings replaced earlier versions from 1912. The three-acre area was the final purchase during BOP ownership of the island. (Washington State Department of Corrections.)

In 1922, Fench W. Archer became the last politically appointed warden. During his 12 years, 600 men lived on less than 100 acres; despite this, Archer's connections and outlook transformed McNeil. Archer believed that any man could run afoul of the law, so therefore, every man should be given opportunities to improve his condition. This philosophy continued on McNeil until its closure in 2011. (Washington State Department of Corrections.)

Four

Federal Bureau of Prisons

The Federal Bureau of Prisons took ownership of McNeil Island in 1937, although a final 3.3-acre parcel leased from Washington State was not acquired until 1940.

Standardization became the norm, with the newly created BOP director initiating streamlined operation procedures at all institutions. This was mostly true, but McNeil benefited from distance and her island location, and retained some autonomy. With her giant library and progressive rehabilitation programs, McNeil became the model for all other federal facilities.

The BOP promoted based on merit rather than patronage, and in 1934, Warden E.W. Swope became the first thus appointed at McNeil. Career BOP personnel stationed throughout the prison system typically spent two years at a facility before moving, but often returned to a favored location at a higher rank. These standardized operations created a smoother national process and better experiences for both incarcerated and staff. Communication between penitentiaries and within the prison system was of primary concern and was distilled via the BOP newsletter, the *Bulletin*, which contained best practice articles as well as information and policies from national headquarters. This concept was individualized at each penitentiary, and McNeil's newsletter had a few specific interests. *The Island Lantern* was an inmate publication, although with administration approval, and followed the proscribed line. The staff version was *Soundings*, of which there are special souvenir editions from the early 1960s. McNeil also ran the *Newsbuoy*; the *Monitor*, an informational publication named after the first US ironclad warship; and the island telephone book, which kept everyone connected via party line, although it was usually full of scratch-outs and write-ins as people moved houses and others transferred, trying to make it to "Silk Stocking" territory on the two hills.

The Island Store and gas station at Still Harbor also circulated communication, as after 1936, staff took turns operating it, and kids worked there part-time, as they would do at the mainland dock launch and McNeil's community center bowling alley, where they set pins and risked injury while dishing the local dirt beside white-collar criminal caretakers.

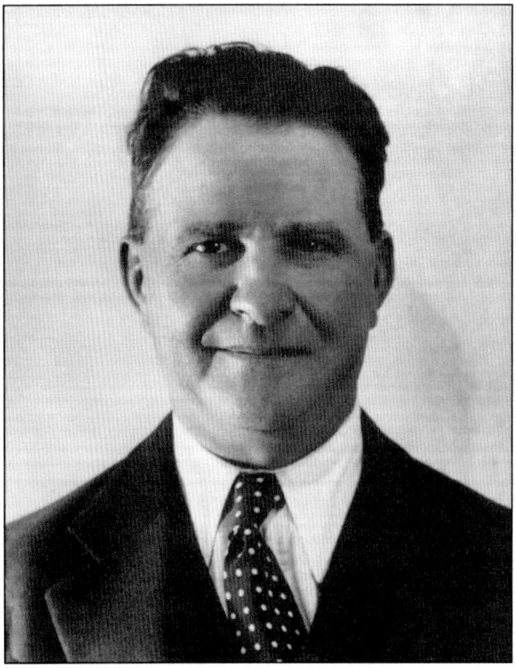

When E.W. Swope became the first BOP warden chosen on merit and experience, McNeil's prisoner count was at 810, down from a high of 1,350. Swope made the most of his time at McNeil, acquiring the entire island, adding two wings to the hospital, and constructing the utility building, a multifunctional facility, and staff housing designed by Heath, Gove, & Bell, all despite the Depression. (Washington State Archives.)

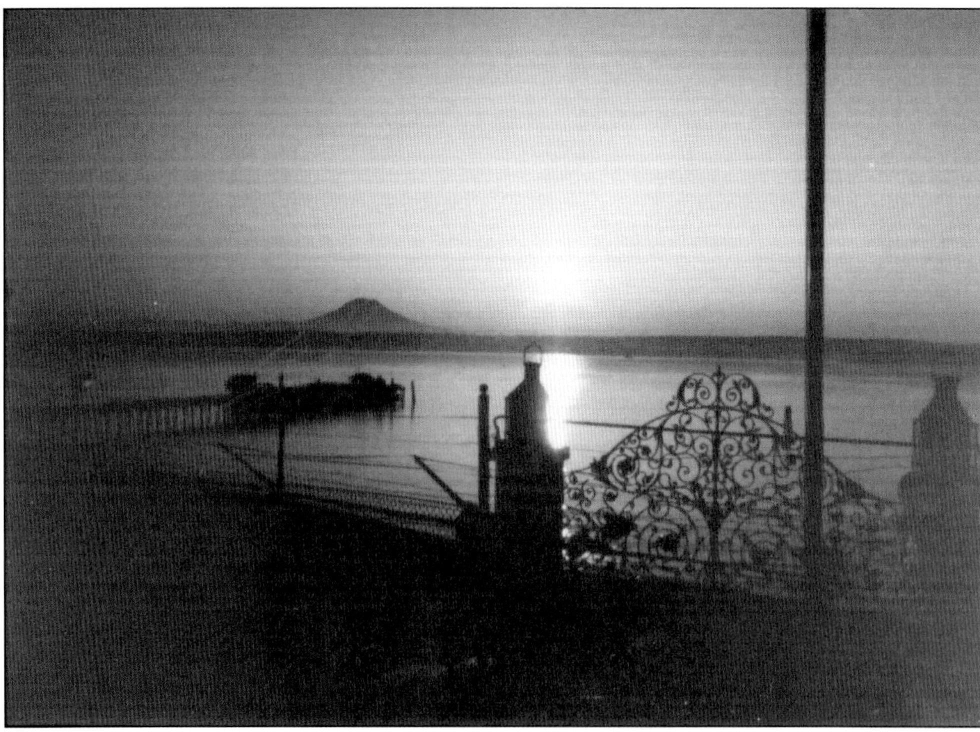

This beautiful view from the front steps of the administration building is McNeil's heart. Rapturous Mt. Rainier, washed by the sound, bathed in the sunrise, and framed by the ornate gate and brass lanterns of McNeil, with the main dock stoically awaiting the day, captures the essence of what made McNeil so special. Its location, surrounded by natural beauty, put peace in everyone's soul and made positive interactions a reality. (Washington State Department of Corrections.)

Two House was designed by architects Proctor & Farrell in 1907. John Proctor lived on McNeil. He also designed Olympia's first capitol building and is the namesake for Tacoma's Proctor Street. He later sold the BOP his land, where the community center now stands. Two House was once the preferred facility at McNeil, with magnificent views of Rainier. Later, its age and painted-over windows made it "the hole." (Washington State Department of Corrections.)

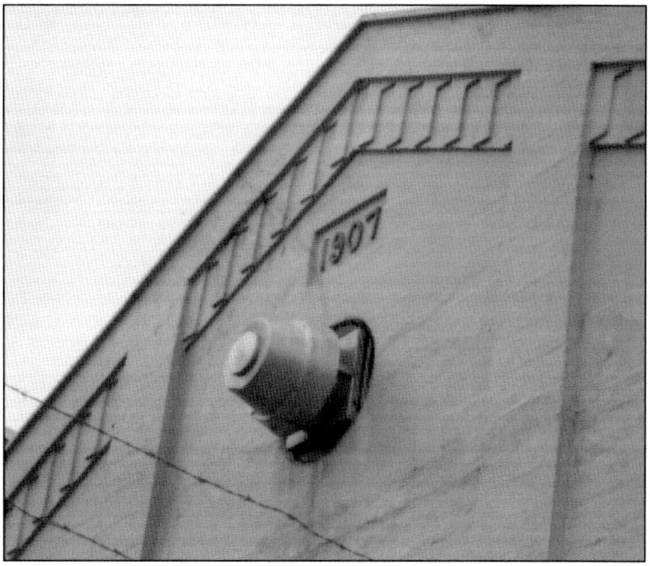

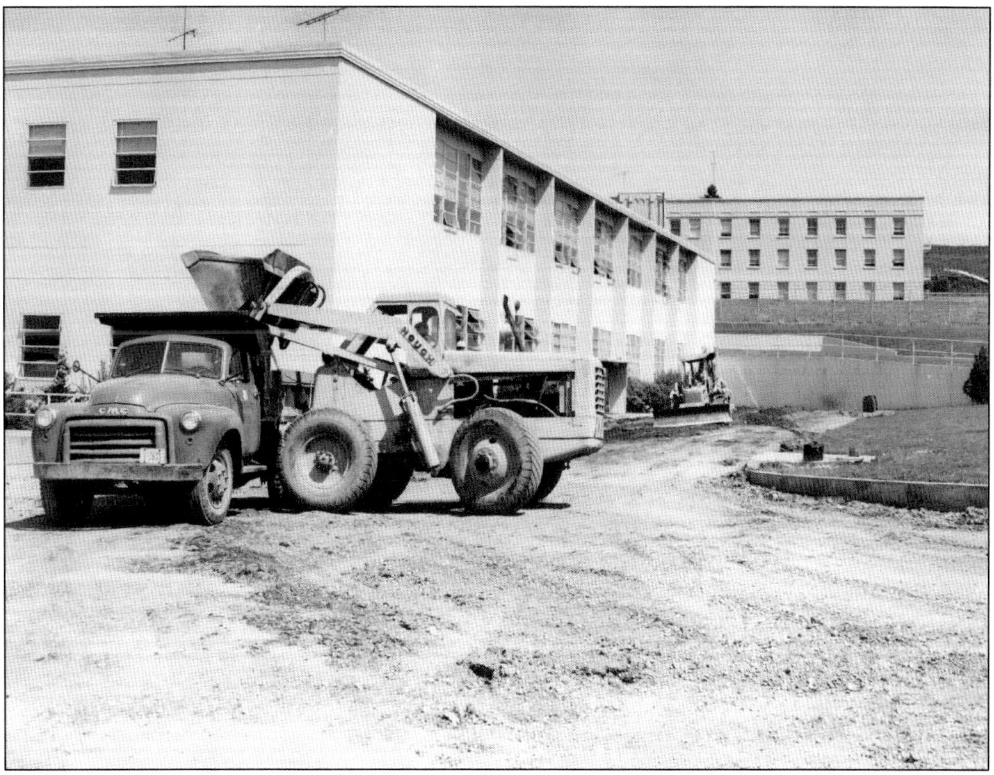

Construction was the name of the game at McNeil. At any time, two major and several minor projects could be happening. Federal Prison Industries' need for more space and better facilities was only part of the program. Bulldozers and flatbeds were always seen about the island, whether repairing water lines, grading roadbeds, or digging foundations. The outside foreman and his crew really knew their stuff and got it done. (Courtesy of Loren Else.)

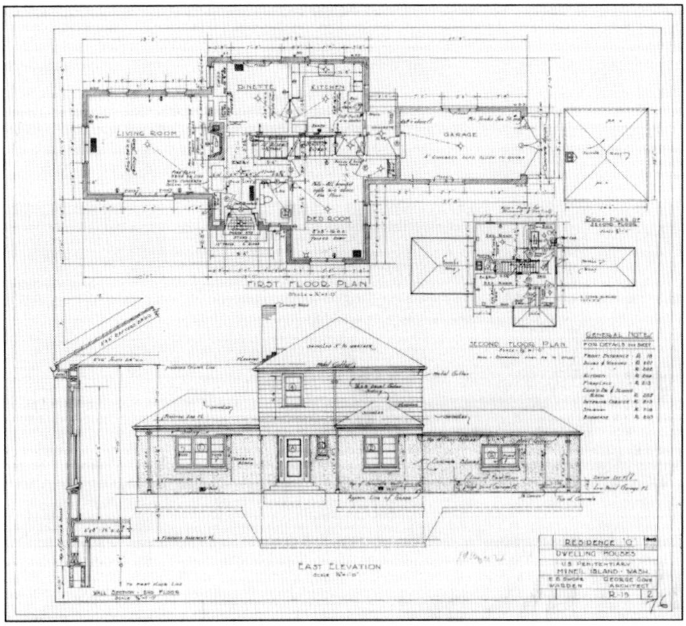

The "G" floorplan of the staff housing development created for McNeil by Heath, Gove, & Bell in 1935 is seen here. The "G" was typical of homes on Center and Holly Hill. All had hardwood floors, built-in cabinets, window seats, covered entrances, and attached garages. Styles varied and ranged through "H." Staff homes began in 1935 and continued through 1941. Frequently, a former settler outbuilding was included in a plot. (Washington Department of Corrections.)

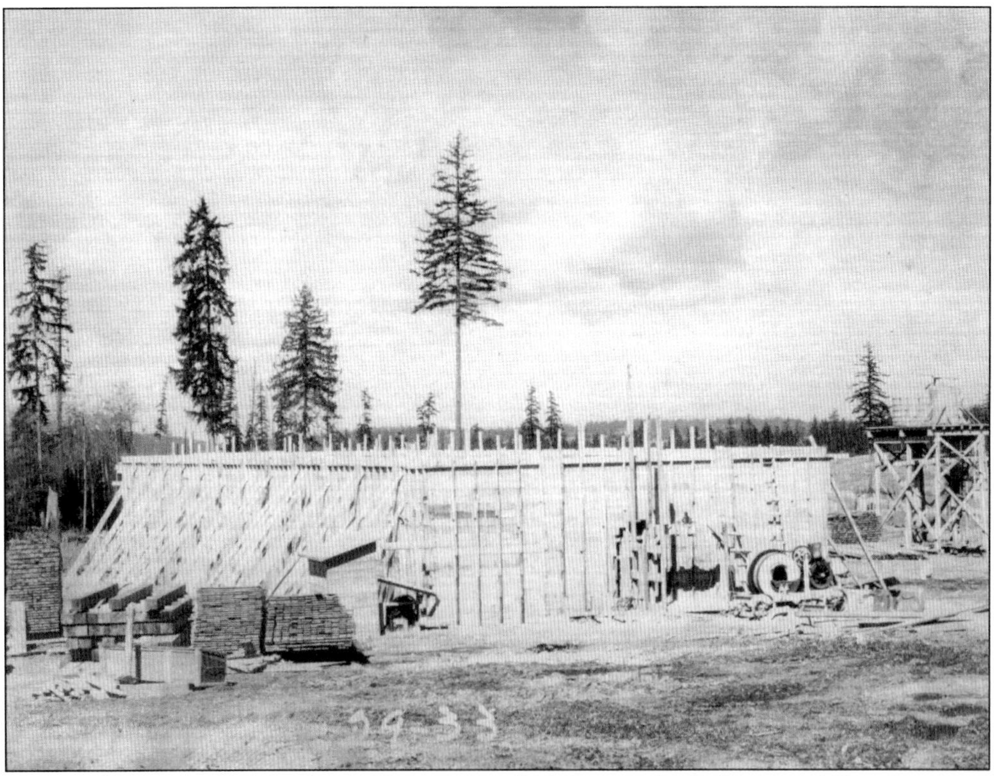

A camp dormitory is seen under construction in 1933. Inmates built their own lodgings, so they did their best. Enabling a man to utilize his capabilities and function as a human being, not a caged animal, brought out the best in the incarcerated, who appreciated the relative freedom of working outside the bars, under their own impetus (and inmate foreman), simply reporting their progress to their staff supervisor at the day's end. (Washington State Archives.)

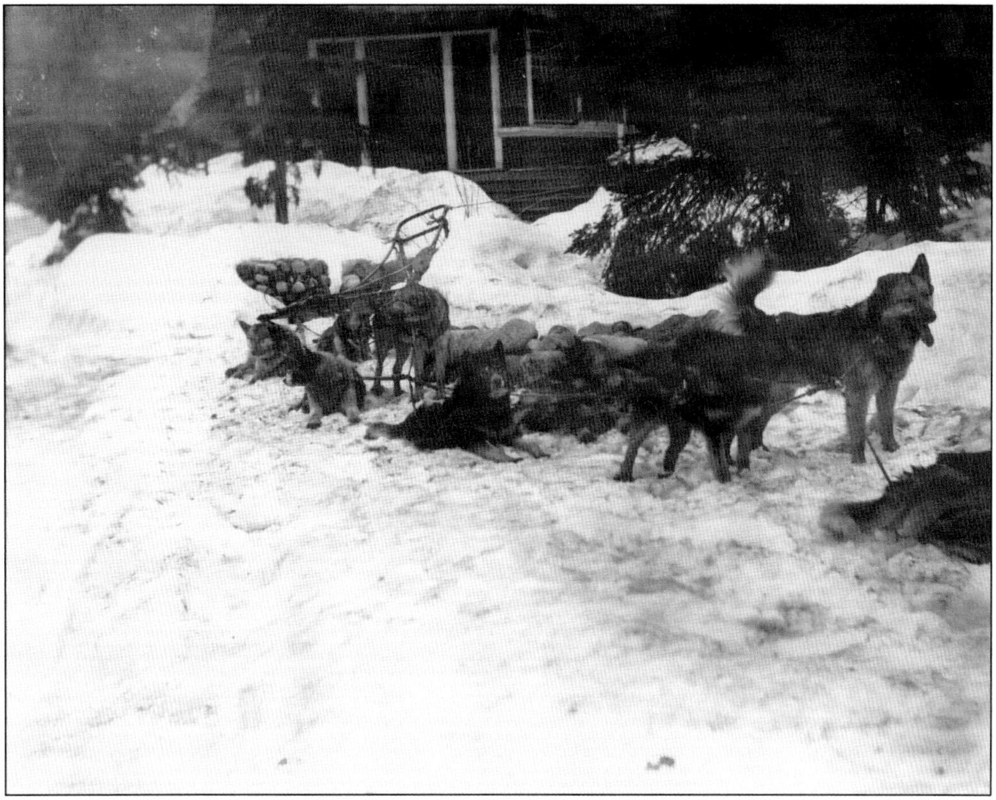

McNeil had dog teams and handlers throughout the years. Mostly used for tracking escapees and assigned to one handler, they also had teams that were capable of transport in adverse winter conditions. Every contingency was considered and prepared for on the isolated island. Self-sufficiency and effectiveness were always bywords at McNeil. The loyal canine officers were ready to give their lives to apprehend criminals and save others. (Washington State Archives.)

McNeil's machine shop is seen here when new in 1933. It replaced a 1912 version that was built on a slough filled in between 1904 and 1911. The shop's industrial machines were are all original and fully functional. The overhead lift and tool room cubbies are to die for. The best part is that it looks exactly the same today and is still in use. (Washington State Archives.)

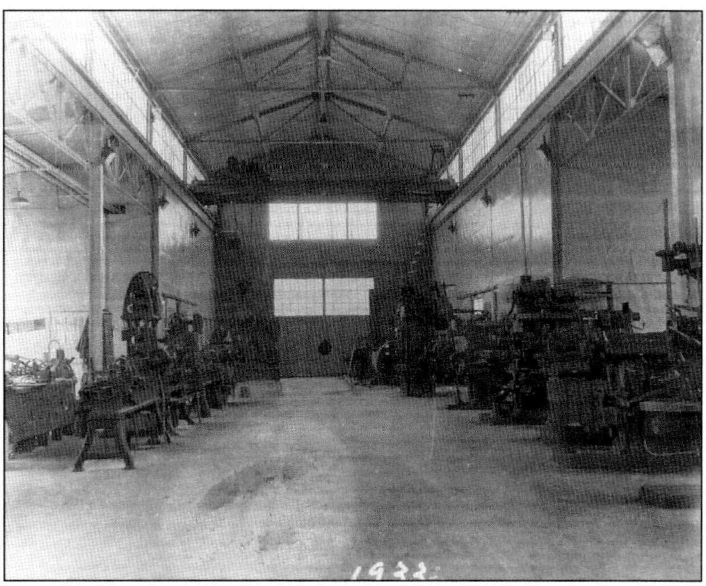

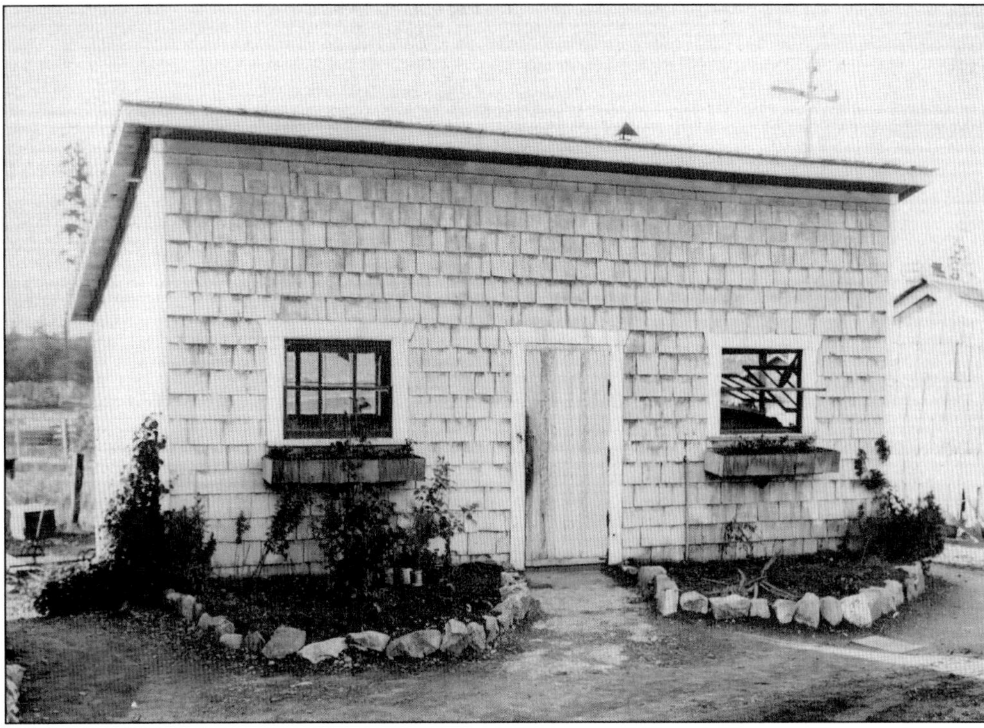

The plantings on this camp office are typical of the beautification seen throughout McNeil during the BOP years. Inmates volunteered, were paid, and sought jobs in groundskeeping because it got them outside in the beautiful Pacific Northwest; earned them a small amount of money for the canteen, commissary, and phone calls; and just made them feel better to work with something where they could see the results of their labor. (Washington State Archives.)

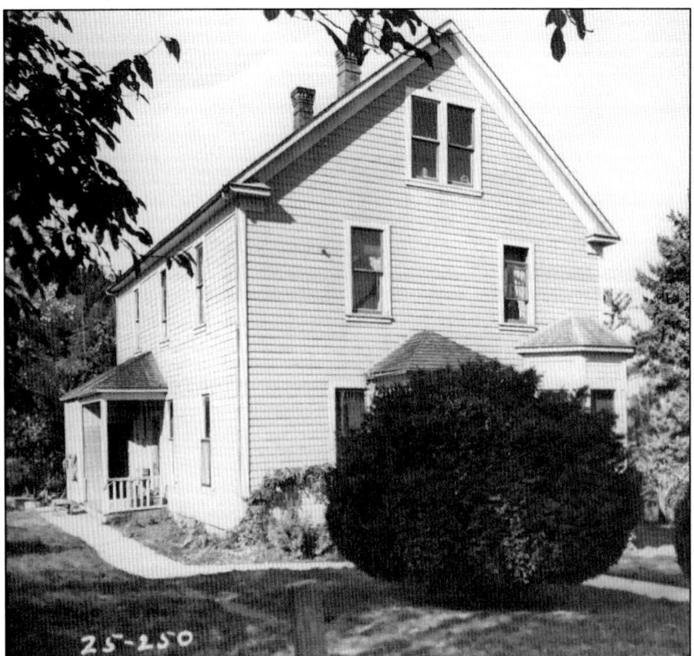

Residence 250, formerly the Julin Holm at Still Harbor, housed the largest staff families and was a kid hangout. The main entrance changed since its 1890 start, but the warmth stayed. Residence 250 was much loved by the Parkers, Swingens, and many others over the decades. Horses were kept at the barn for years, and rumors say it was a brothel for sawmill workers and BOP bachelors and dignitaries. (Washington State Archives.)

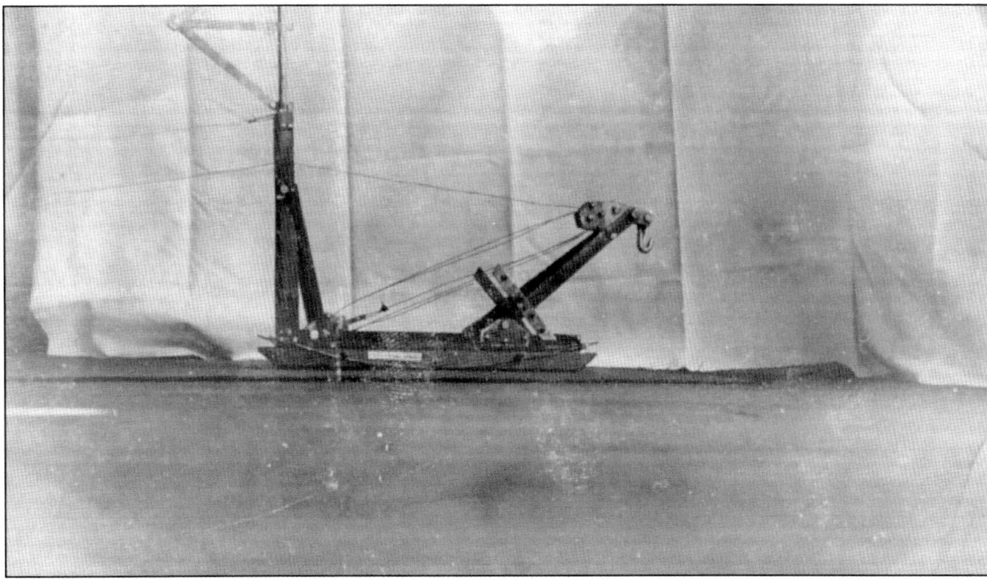

Charles Larson created this cable machine for use in hauling ships and such out of the sound. A winch and cable were always needed for heavy lifting jobs, and having one mounted to a barge allowed for salvage operations to proceed smoothly and profitably for Larson and any others involved. This was another case where the prison took a concept from McNeil's settlers and ran with it. (Jean Cammon Findlay.)

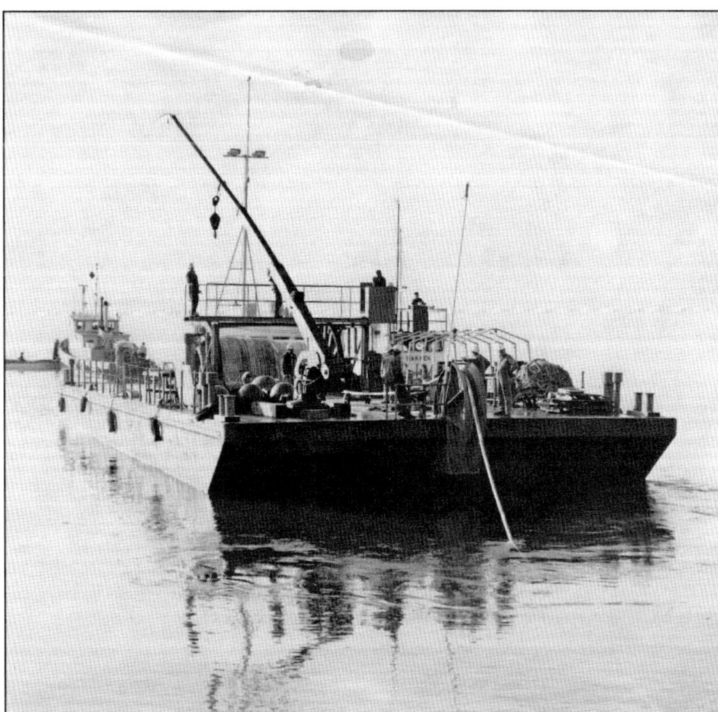

One of the McNeil tugboats pulls a barge laying cable. During World War II, McNeil helped the US Navy by creating and laying submarine cable in the sound. It was designed to echo if contacted or to snare subs if they ran afoul of it. After the war, the extra submarine cable was used as bulkhead wrap on the beachheads of McNeil to prevent erosion. (Washington State Archives.)

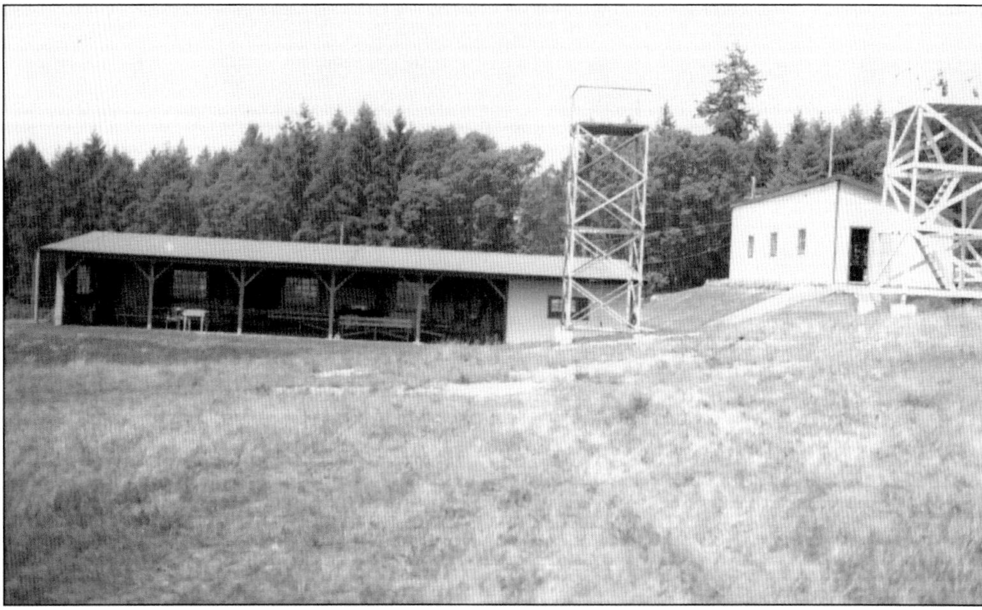

The 1930s-era rifle range and its bunkers and obstacles are still in use today, as they were so well constructed and in such an isolated location that exercises can proceed unhindered by prying eyes or stray bullets. Built into the side of a cliff, there is a natural stop for strays, and it works as a sound barrier as well. Hostage negotiation training was conducted here too. (Washington State Archives.)

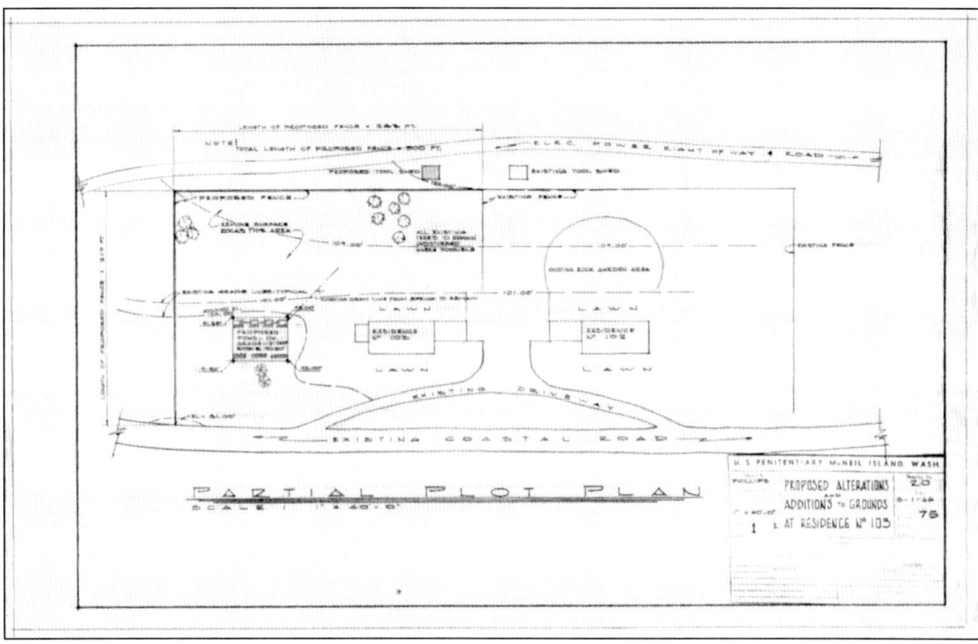

This is a plan for the doctor's and associate warden's houses. Approved in 1935 for $15,000 and $10,000, respectively, in 1966, it was decided to add a water feature beside Dr. Kyle's home to complement the rock garden behind the associate warden's house. Giving staff decompression space was a key in McNeil's success—happy staff, happy pen—although satisfied inmates made the institution run. (Washington Department of Corrections.)

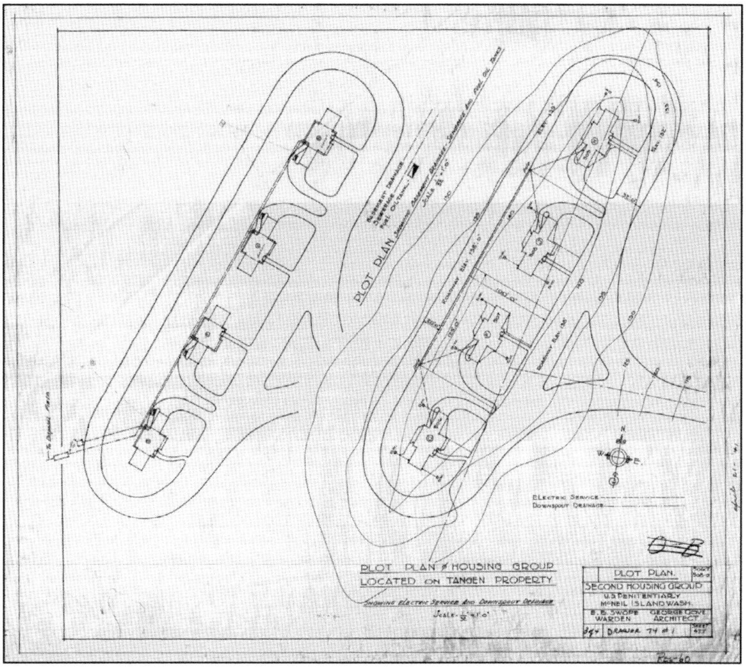

This is architect George Gove's 1941 plan for the plumbing utility lines of the staff houses on the former Tangen Property at Holly Hill. Attention to detail was important, as McNeil always had a water supply issue, and Gove knew this as he built minimum and maximum allowances for flow into his plans. (Washington Department of Corrections.)

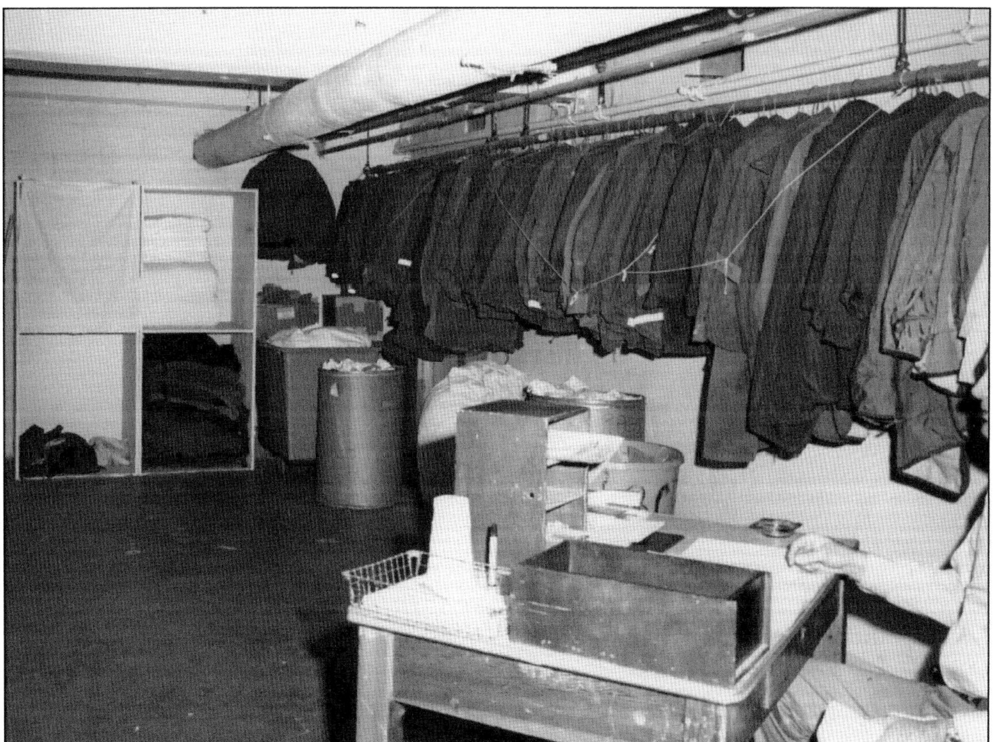

Prisoner and staff coats hang in the coat room of the laundry office. The laundry manager or staff supervisor sat at the desk at right, keeping track of inventory. Essentially, everything in the prison had to be accounted for, because anything could be used as a weapon or as escape materials. Certainly, extra clothing would be helpful in an escape. (Washington State Archives.)

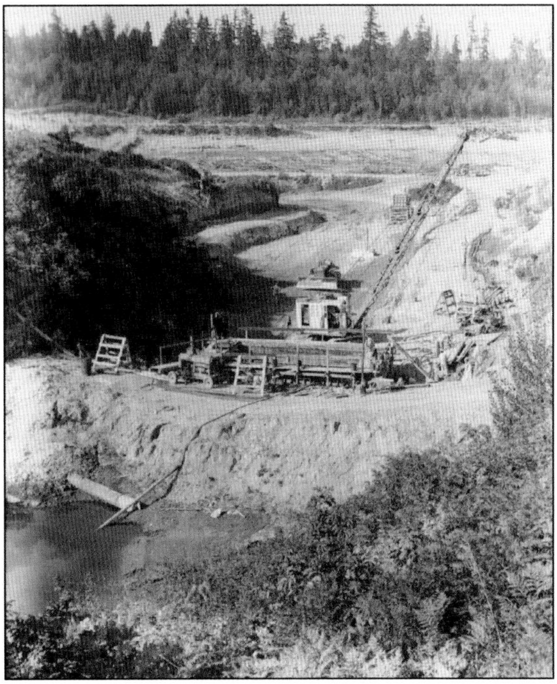

This is the 1944 beginning of Butterworth Dam, named after an engineer helpful to the prison. Butterworth lake emptied in dry season, so damming up the feeder streams would create a year-round water supply. It would also make a great lake for staff families to enjoy fishing and boating. One inmate, after imbibing too much pruno or locoweed, swam it, thinking he had escaped to the mainland—not so much. (Washington State Archives.)

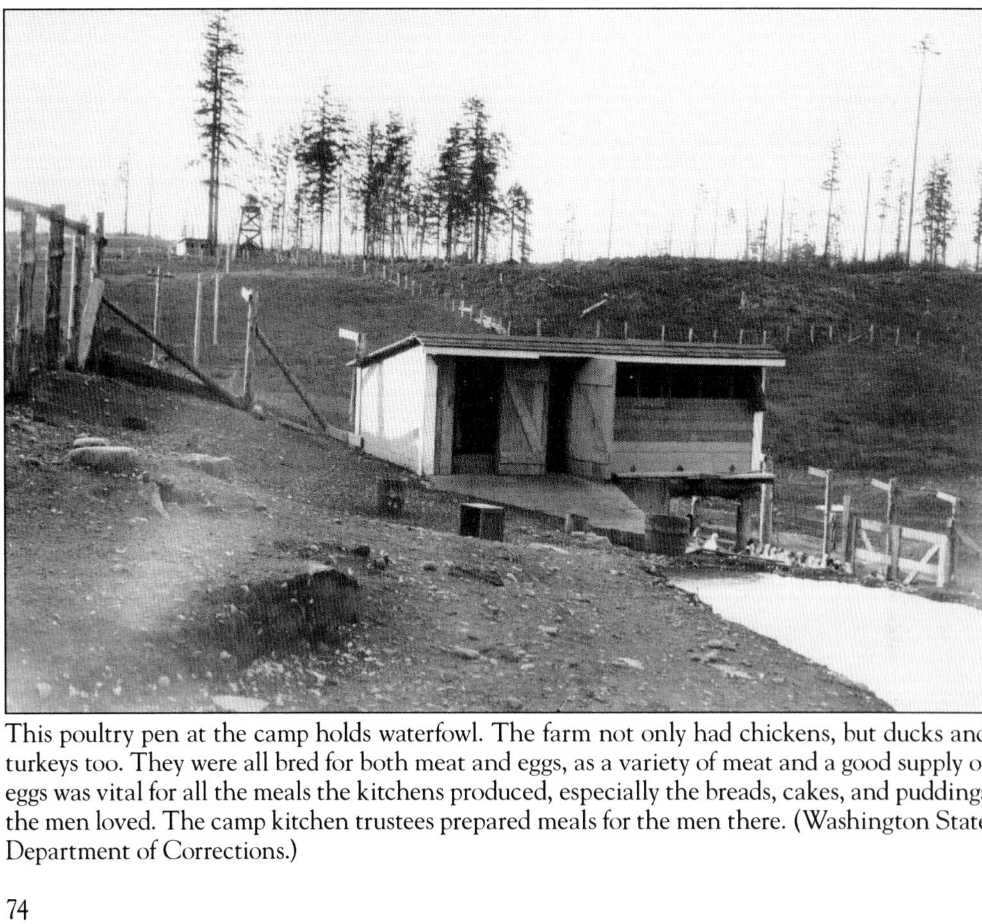

This poultry pen at the camp holds waterfowl. The farm not only had chickens, but ducks and turkeys too. They were all bred for both meat and eggs, as a variety of meat and a good supply of eggs was vital for all the meals the kitchens produced, especially the breads, cakes, and puddings the men loved. The camp kitchen trustees prepared meals for the men there. (Washington State Department of Corrections.)

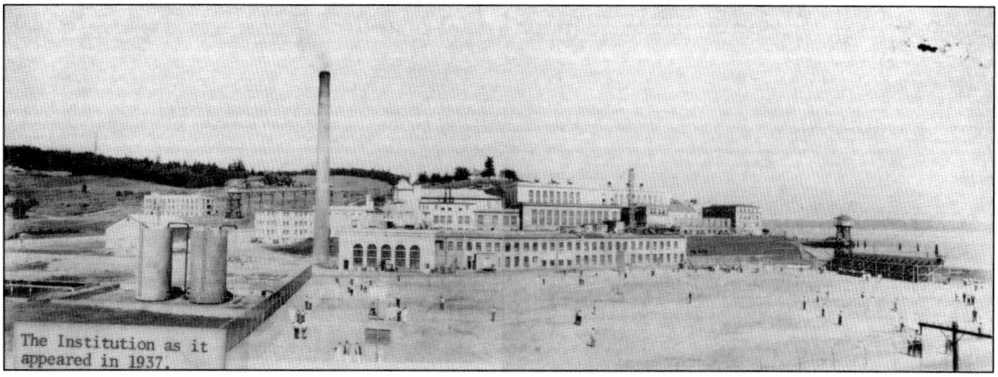

This 1937 panoramic view of the institution shows how much it had grown since its austere beginnings. The big yard, with its great waterfront view, is in the foreground, with scaffolding at center where the utility building and auditorium are being worked on. At far left is the materials building for the warden's house, which was converted into a 750,000-gallon water reservoir. (Washington State Department of Corrections.)

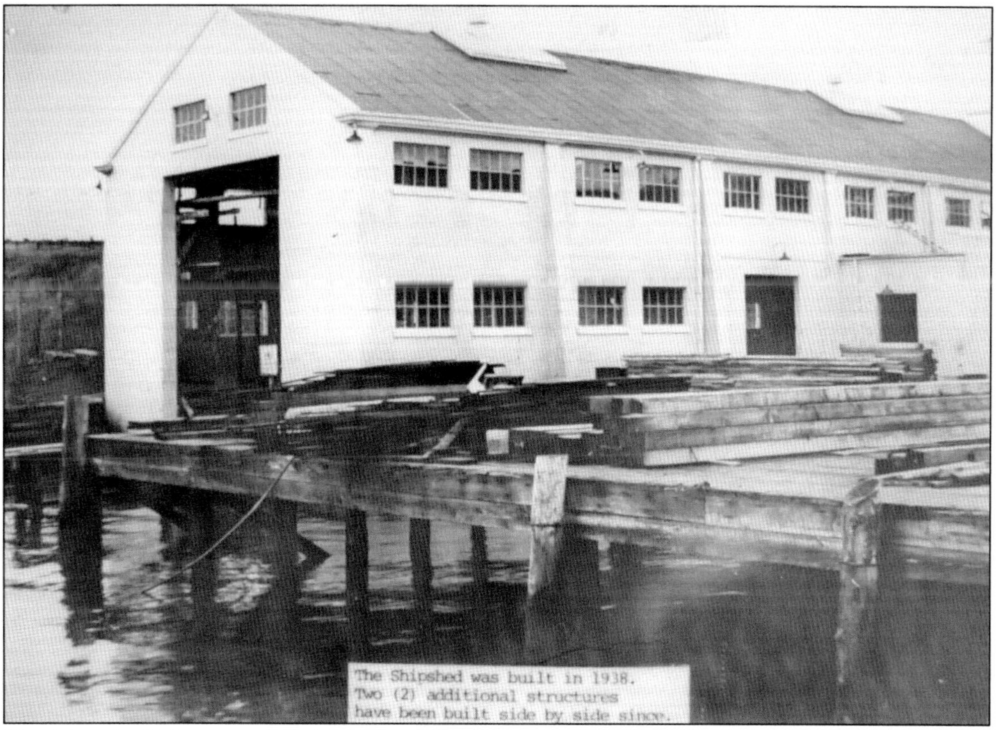

The "shipshed" that stands at the former institution now was built in 1938. It followed a temporary structure built in 1912, which itself had followed an earlier makeshift boat shed farther up the eastern shore of McNeil. The site of the current shipshed is next to the slough that was slowly filled in beginning in 1904. The site is also where Ezra Meeker's cabin was located in 1853. (Washington State Archives.)

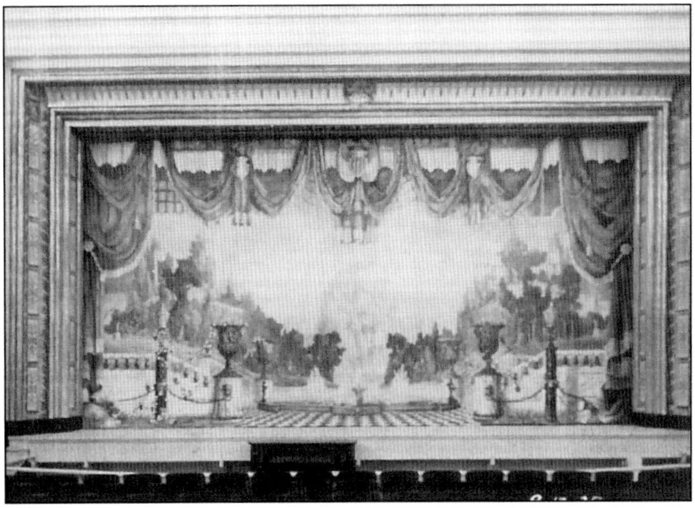

This fabulous *trompe l'oeil* painting of theater curtains hung in the original 500-seat movie theater built in 1928 under Warden Archer. Inmate artist Clifford Vernon Vincent blessed the institution with his talent in other areas as well. Having art such as this gave the men inside a sense of normalcy that was very beneficial to morale. (National Archives and Records Administration.)

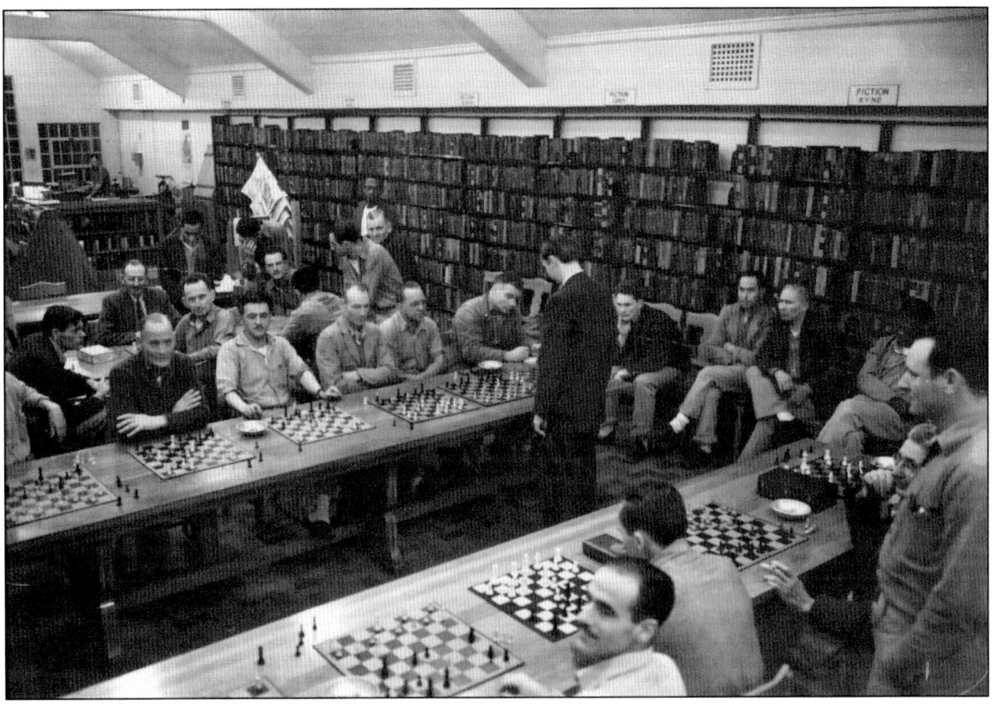

This is the famous McNeil library, which all Federal Bureau of Prison libraries were modeled after. Early on, the library acquired an extensive catalog of 10,000 books through Warden Archer's solicitations and community donations, which were considered an investment in future society. Over time, the collection grew to average 15,000 books, and meetings and games were held in the library's pleasant interior. (Washington State Archives.)

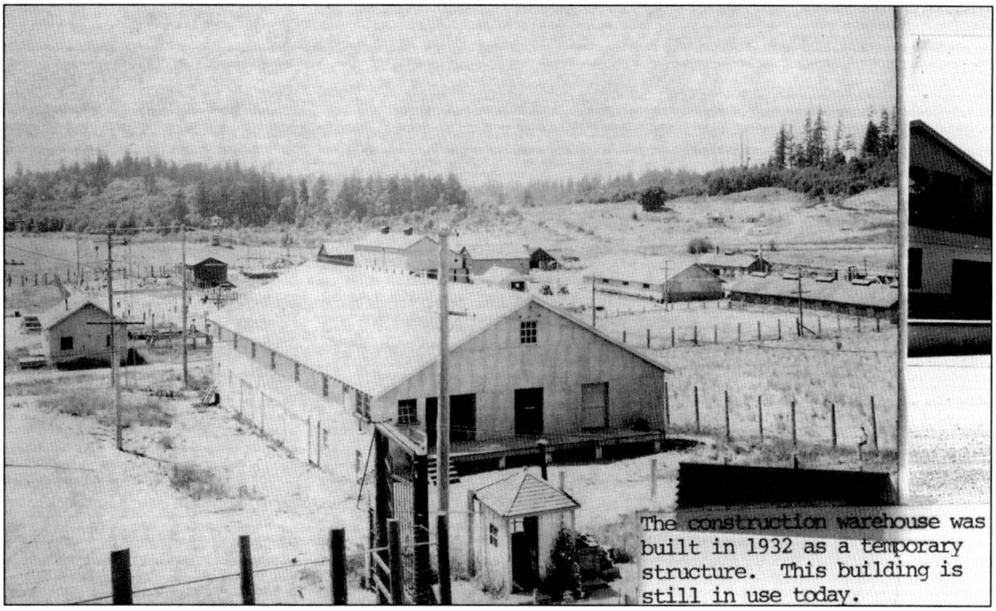

The 1932 construction warehouse was created to hold materials for building the Warden's house, the utility building, and staff housing. McNeil was very rural, and settlers still lived by the prison then. John Holm's house and the four trees over his son's grave are in the background. The wooden buildings by the warehouse were replaced, but the solid warehouse remained in use. (Washington State Archives.)

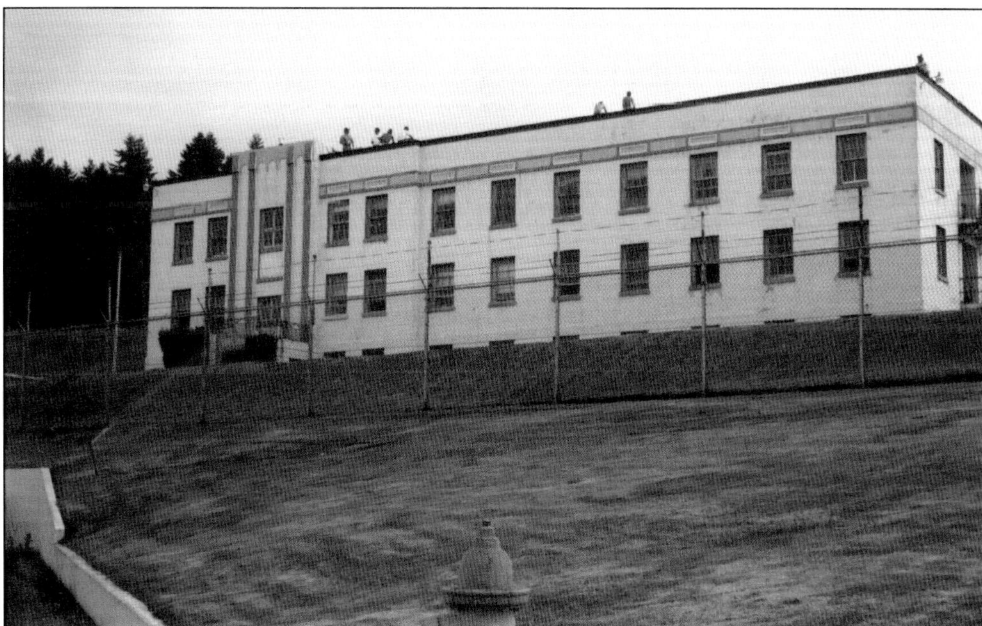

Inmates work on the roof of Summit house, which was originally the bachelor officer's quarters and sat on a hill outside the fence. Minimum custody prisoners lived here in preparation for societal re-entry. In the late 1960s, former public enemy No. 1 Al Karpis was a trustee there, supervising maintenance and the younger inmates, who were awed enough by him to benefit from his wisdom, as was noted by staff. (Washington State Archives.)

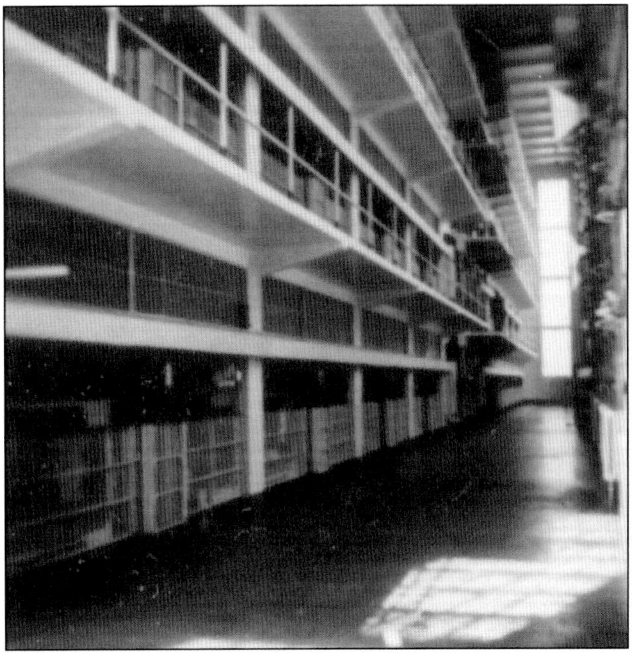

Here are the notorious five tiers of Three/Four House, with its main corridor, "Broadway," below. Built by Heath, Gove, & Bell, first as Three House, with Four House attached later, the cells were made to hold five men each in 1921, but population growth caused another row of bunks to go in, making a 10-man cell. It was a busy place to work. (Washington State Archives.)

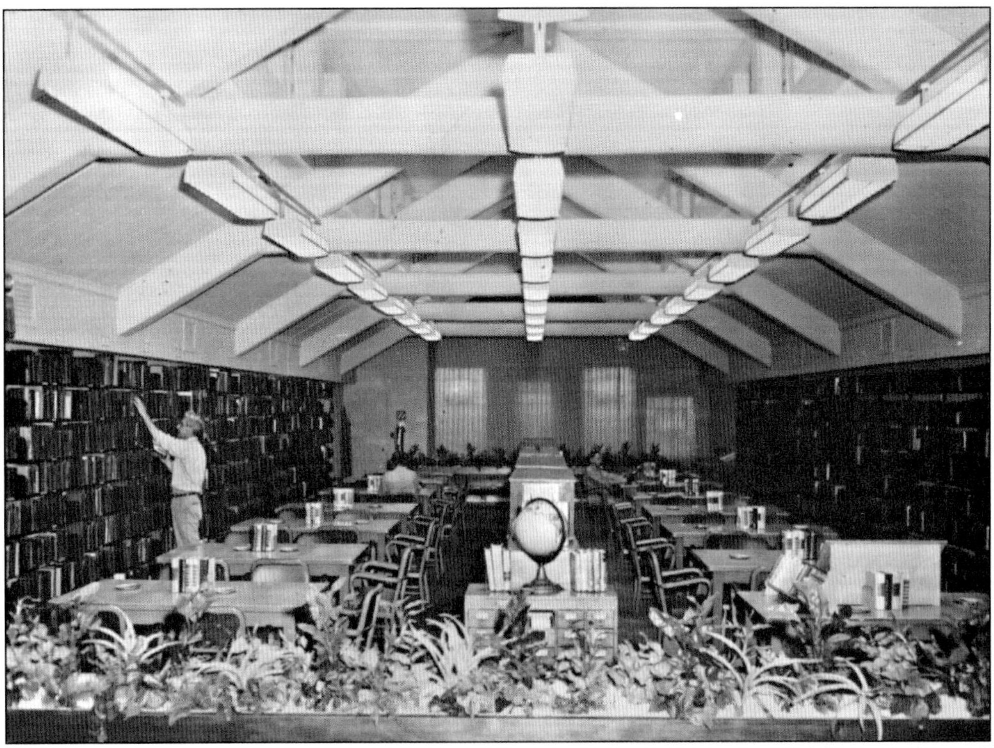

Here is a better view of the volumes in McNeil's aesthetically pleasing inmate library. (The staff also had a library in the community center.) Note the skillful arrangement of live plants that graces the front. The men truly enjoyed using their gifts to improve their surroundings. Feeling a sense of purpose and achievement is helpful to everyone, and the library and its tomes certainly engendered this. (Washington State Archives.)

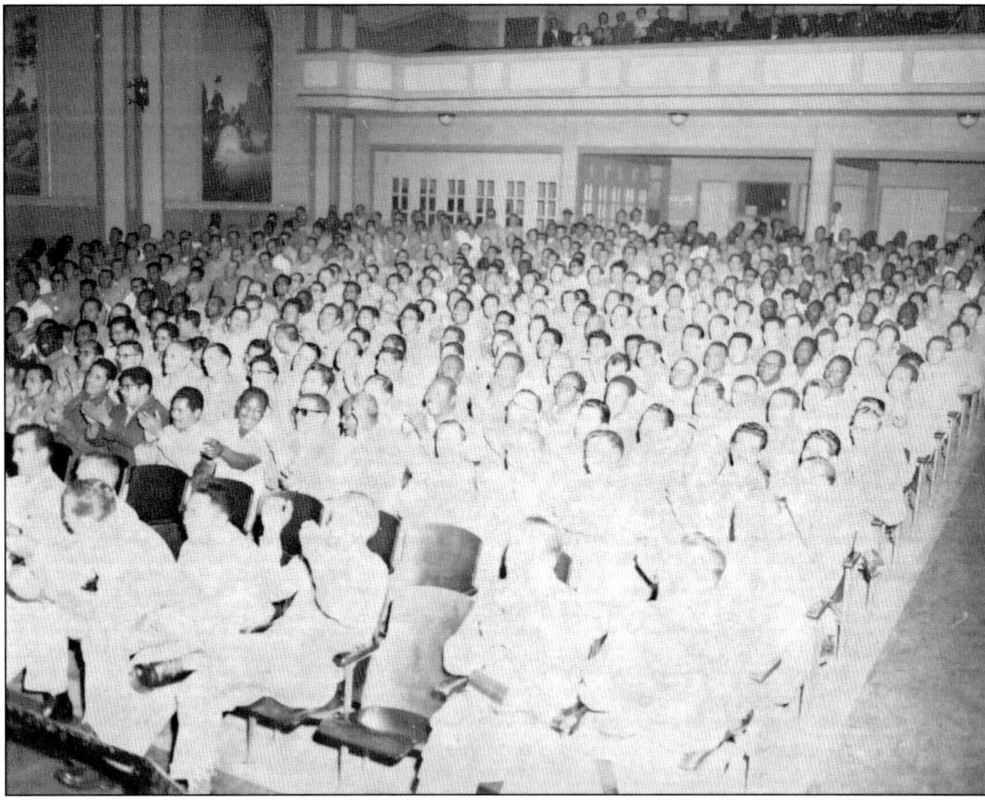

This prison movie theater/auditorium shows how fully integrated McNeil was in the 1960s. The auditorium was donated by Marie Claude in the 1930s. Pleasant surroundings have a beneficial effect on outlook, and the lovely murals improved everyone's mood. Staff and their family members can be seen on the balcony also enjoying the show. Having entertainers perform for the inmates was a common occurrence, and the staff watched the shows as well. (National Archives and Records Administration.)

This little "guard shack" started as a settler shed. It is similar to the more open shacks that were used for bus stops on McNeil. The big difference is, the guard shack had electricity. Power came to McNeil in 1911, which was pretty early on, as a lot of places in America did not have electricity then, including Anderson Island, which did not get it until 1961. (Washington State Archives.)

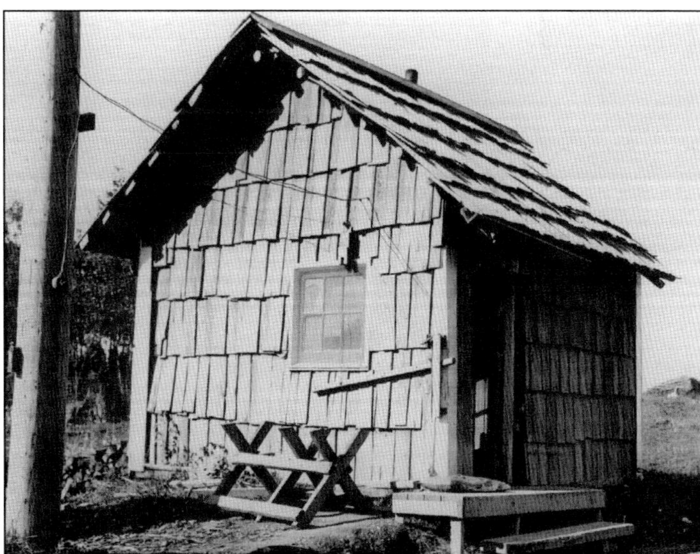

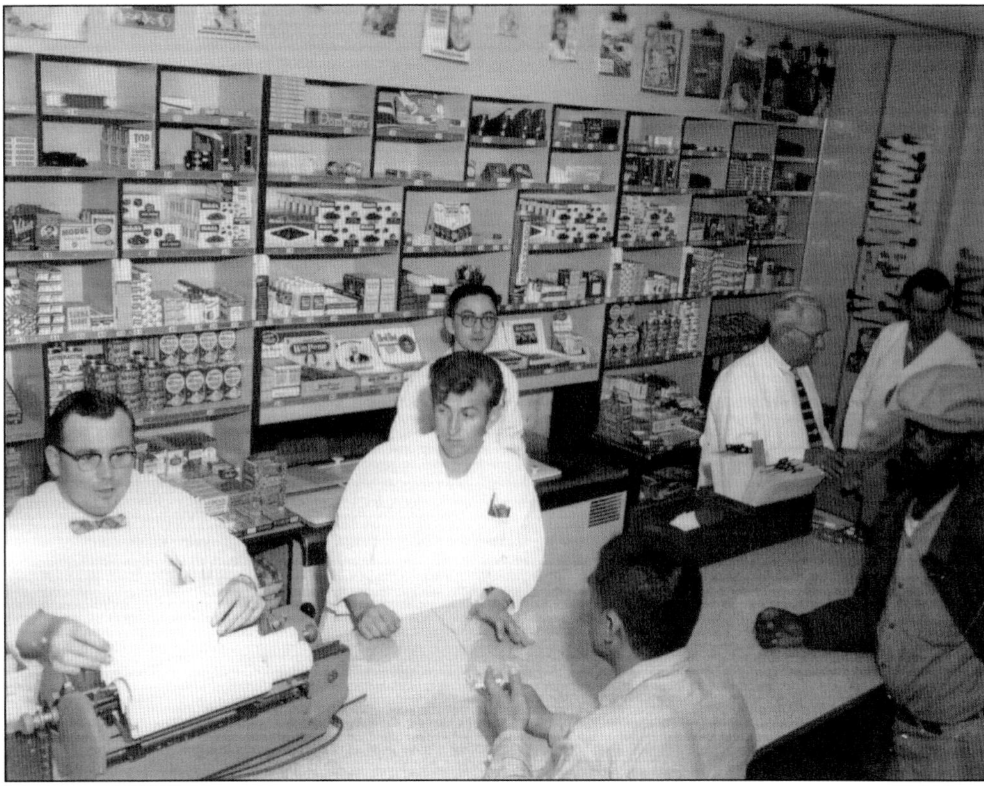

This is the inmate commissary, where prisoners bought snacks, toiletries, and sundries with the money they earned from their jobs or were given. Certain items were greatly valued, and inmates would amass quantities that they could resell or trade for things they desired. There was always a "fixer" in the pen who could get things other inmates wanted. Where there is a will—and lots of time—there is a way. (Washington State Archives.)

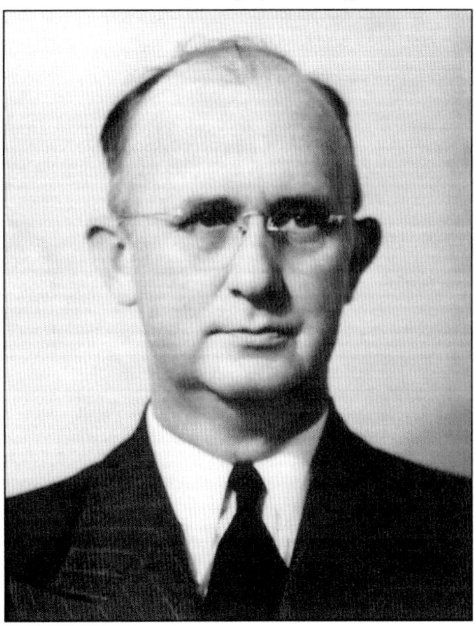

Paul J. Squier became warden in 1940. It was his second McNeil tour, as he began his career as a guard there in 1924. He and his associate warden continued to standardize operations as begun by Swope. Bringing McNeil up to speed did not endear him to everyone. Squiers was not progressive, but he was systematic and predictable despite a reliance on stool pigeons for intel; they play all sides. (Washington State Archives.)

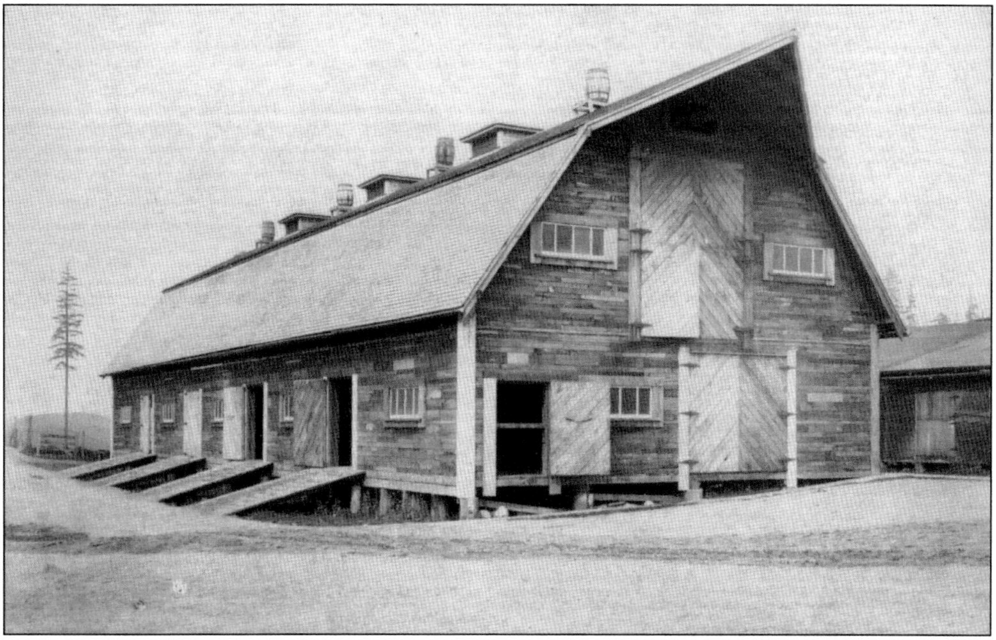

Here is a great shot of the livestock barn begun in 1929 and finished in 1933. The Douglas fir trees for the barns were felled on McNeil and cut and planed into lumber there as well. Inmate laborers built the very modern barn, with its mud ramps, according to plans drawn by Heath, Gove, & Bell, the innovative, preeminent Northwest architecture firm of the era. (Washington State Archives.)

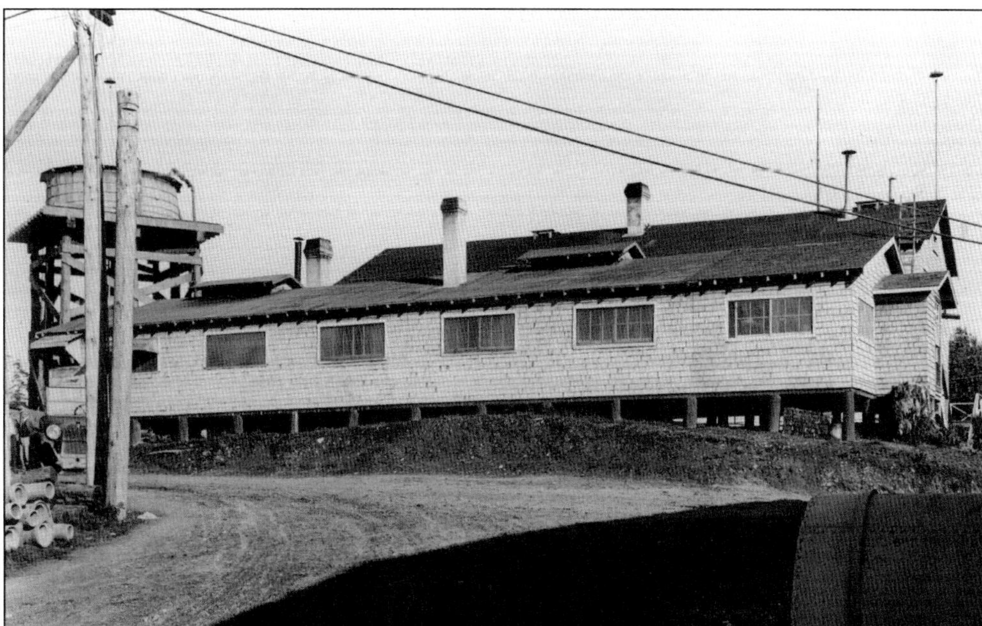

The camp dormitories and water tower are seen here when new in 1933. The camp started in 1927 when land was appropriated for the honor farm, and the first dorm was completed in 1930, according to plans drawn by George Gove. Having the overflow area for trustees and minimum security prisoners really helped relieve overcrowding in the main joint. (Washington State Archives.)

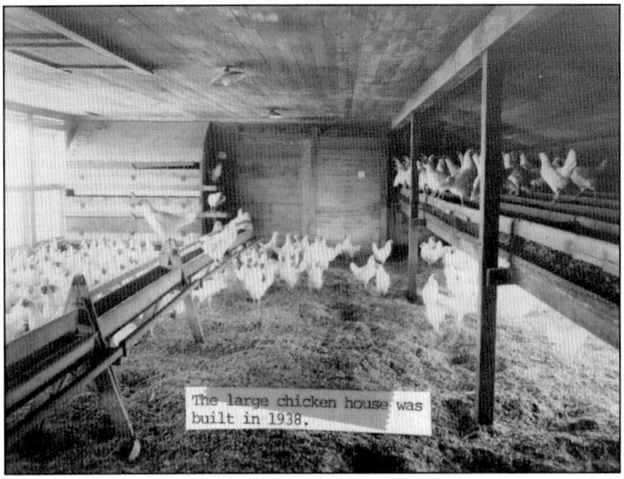

The large chicken house was built in 1938 as conditions continually improved at McNeil and operations expanded. The care for the chickens fell to inmate trustees and laborers at the camp. Trustee inmates acted as foremen directing jobs under indirect supervision from prison staff. The truly beneficial thing about the farm, apart from the extra provisions, was that it allowed inmates to function as capable men, furthering their self-esteem and skills. (Washington State Archives.)

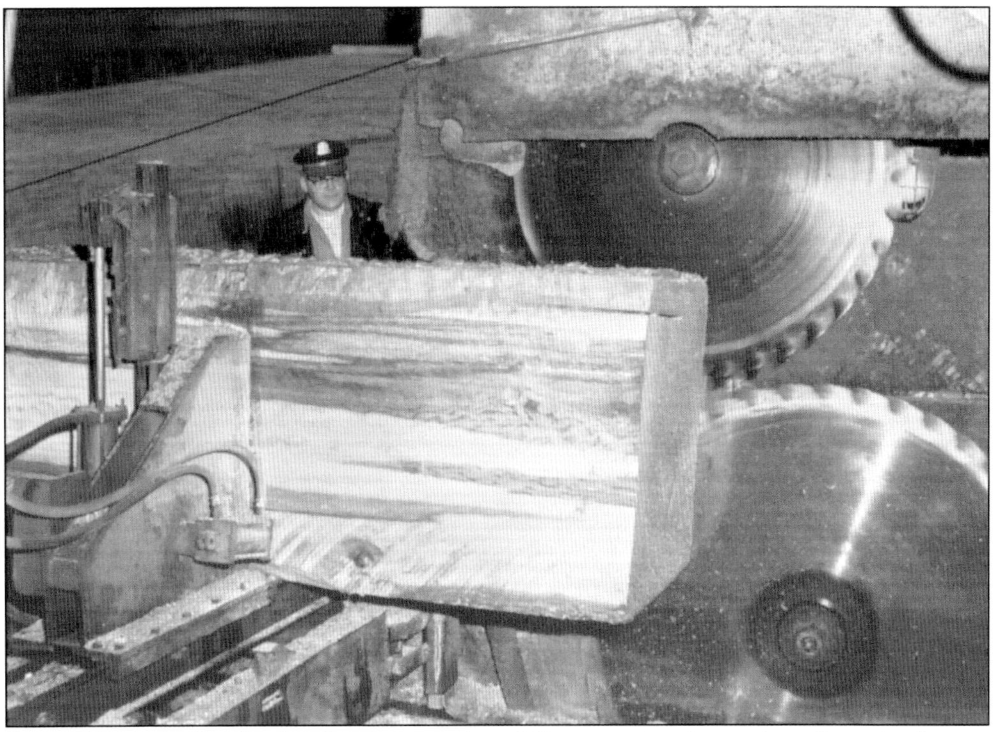

Sawmill manager Charles Scanlon is pictured in 1965 supervising the cutting of massive fir trees into lumber, by the equally massive circular wood saws housed in the sawmill. The sawmill was partially burned down in an inmate-set fire during the turbulent post-Attica late 1970s. However, the old saws and tools were still around for use in cutting bubble wrap or whatever else was needed by the state until closure. (Scanlon family.)

An inmate listens to music through headphones in his cell in the 1930s. Giving the men a chance to relax and fill their time peacefully was always on the administration's agenda. Although silence prevailed in the early days, Fench Archer had an inmate orchestra play at lunch and dinner every day. Keeping inmates happily occupied kept the pen riot-free. (McNeil Island Historical Society.)

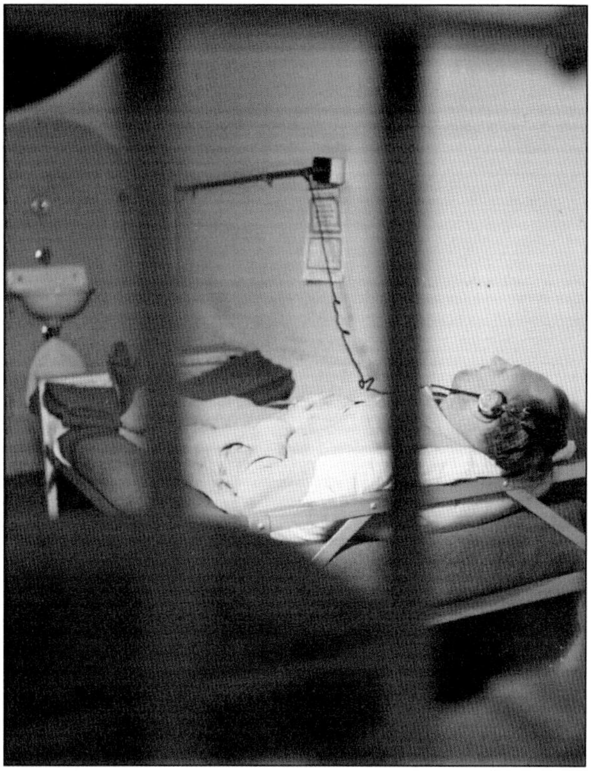

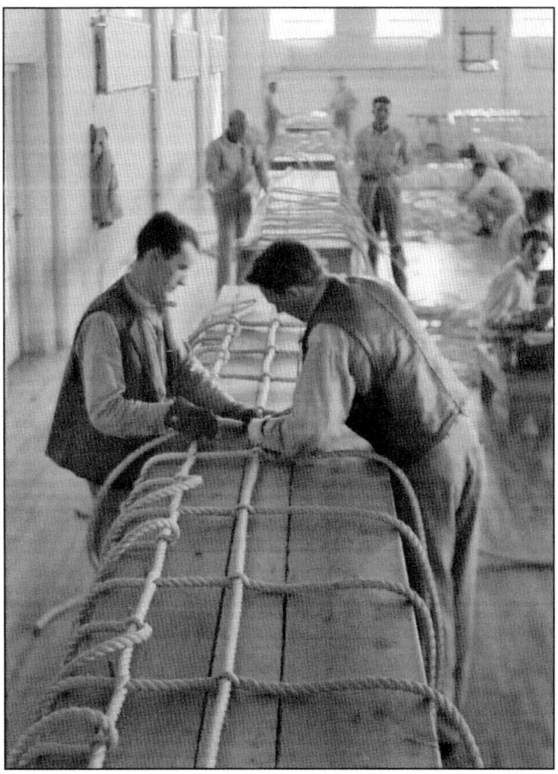

Inmates work on cargo netting for the US Navy during World War II. Cargo nets were an important industry, as they could not only load ship cargo, but also hold it in place or be used as barriers if need be. The inmates volunteered to work for the war effort, but they were paid 12¢ an hour for their labor. (Museum of History and Industry, Seattle.)

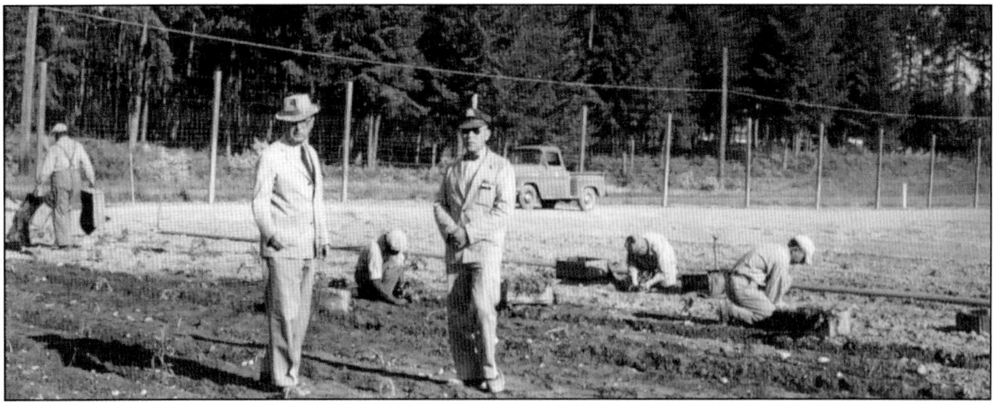

Farm manager Joe Havelka (left) and camp supervisor Jerry Zemon look over plantings at the farm in the early 1960s. Farm manager was a very important job because the food administrator relied on solid production to feed the inmates. The soil on McNeil was not especially good, so it had to be augmented, and of course, it was in use for decades, so crops were rotated to rest the fields. (Washington State Archives.)

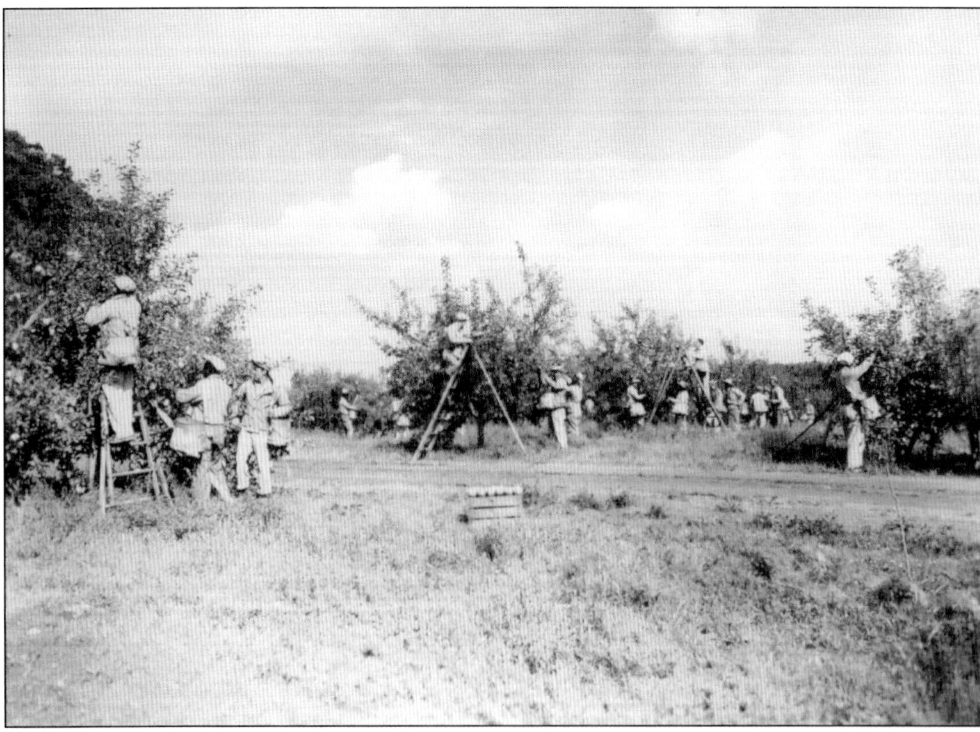

Inmates are harvesting the fall apple crop in 1942. The orchards were created in the late 1930s and were used extensively to supply canned goods to the military during World War II. The orchard ceased production in 1979, although families still went to pick apples and pears. The trees still bear fruit despite years of neglect and no care at all since the 2011 closure. (Washington State Archives.)

Five

Island Waves

Life on McNeil rolled with the tide, constantly moving forward as prison staff kept prisoners safe and mostly doing good time while caring for their own families. As inmates repaired typewriters, worked in industries (both federal and state), or studied for high school or college diplomas, the Island Residents Association pooled funds from raffles, cookbook and bake sales, and the like to continually improve quality of life. Children participated in island Boy and Girl Scouts, bowling leagues, karate and piano lessons, played organ, or were altar servers at chapel, and rode their bikes all over McNeil—even going down Center Hill handless. Children and teens explored McNeil's beauty for hours on end and learned to drive cars and heavy equipment at ages well below 15. There was a limitless sense of freedom, as they felt they were not beholden to state law since they were on federal property. Interaction with trustees was always positive, and fear was never a factor.

Families clammed, dug geoducks, found clay babies, and watched seals and orca cavort. Walks along Sandy beach and picnics there or near the "Big Rock" by the ferry slip happened frequently. Holiday celebrations included sack races, an egg toss, greased pig chase, and greased flagpole climbing, highlighted by viewing fireworks from the bluff overlooking Commencement Bay. The Ladies Auxiliary arranged luncheons through prison telephone operators like Harriett Taylor (who thwarted an escape), did crafts and flower arranging, and made meals for the needy while they supported each other with the unique understanding of prison island life.

Roaming the island selecting Christmas trees, watching an inmate variety show, or checking out the farm produce and orchard progress was always fun. Seeing the auto barn and heavy equipment or being safety trained by the firemen made life full. The self-sufficiency instilled on McNeil went beyond that at other islands because of added security issues. Luhr Creek saw several escape attempts, and everyone knew to be alert. A real sense of family prevailed on McNeil, and island brats did summer camps together yearly at Miracle Ranch. Truly, it was the people who made McNeil special.

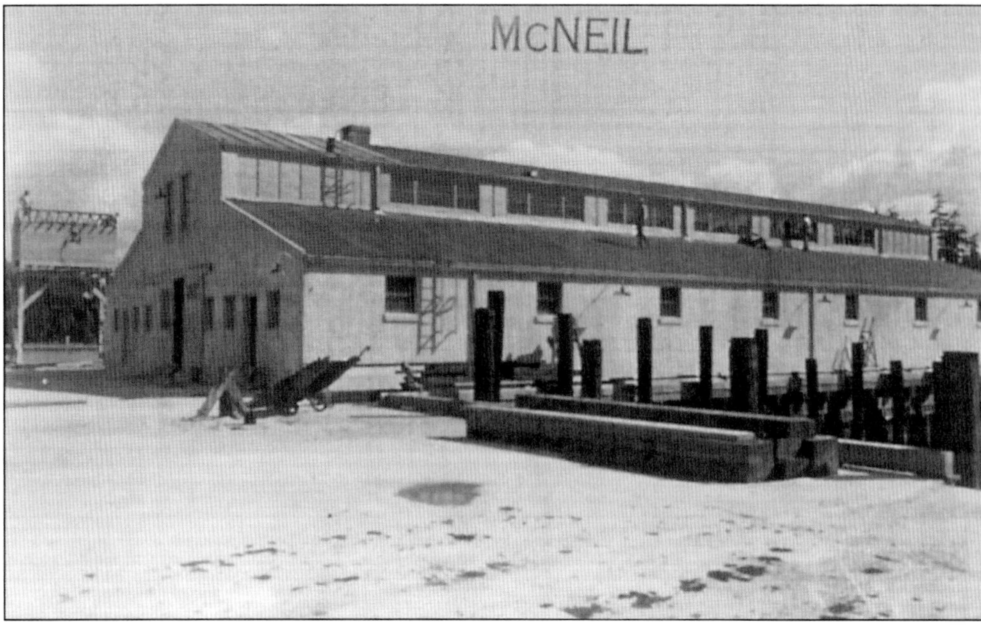

This was a really cool warehouse dock designed by George Gove of Heath, Gove, & Bell. The dock sat on springs, which allowed it to flex with waves and tidal flow, as well as any boat collisions that might occur while loading and unloading freight, leaving the cargo inside undamaged. It was a truly innovative design. Inmates put the finishing touches on its roofing in 1941. (Washington State Archives.)

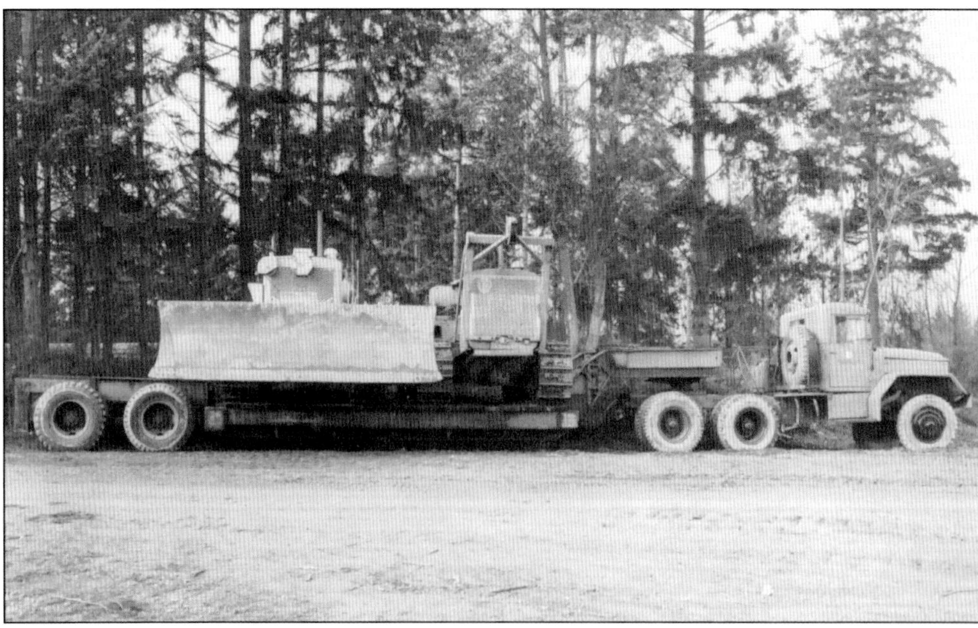

The bulldozer and tractor on a flatbed truck in the 1960s are just some of the vehicles the outdoor foreman and crew used to keep McNeil shipshape. Kids on McNeil also learned to drive them at young ages, thanks to federal status and nothing else to do. The gravel pits were busy with excavators, cranes, and other heavy equipment that were needed to maintain the institution. (Washington State Archives.)

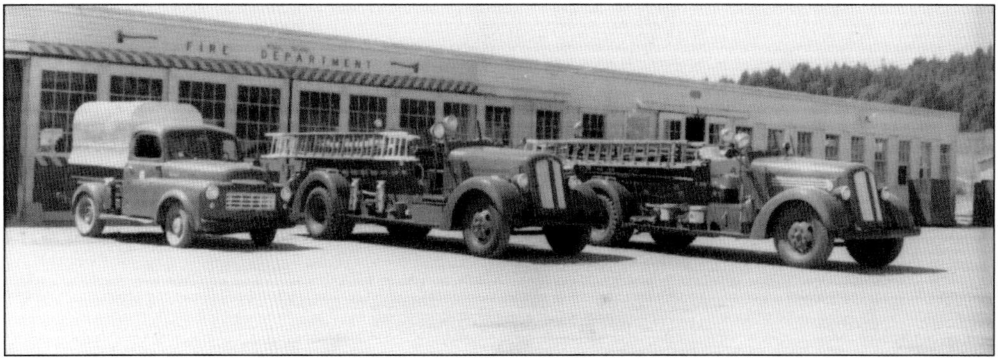

This is McNeil's fire department fleet in the late 1950s. McNeil's trucks were always a bit antiquated owing to the island location, but that never stopped them from getting the job done. Fires were a real danger at prisons, so even the children were given training on what to do in the event of a fire. The staff trained regularly, and many had prior firefighting experience from military service. (Loren Else.)

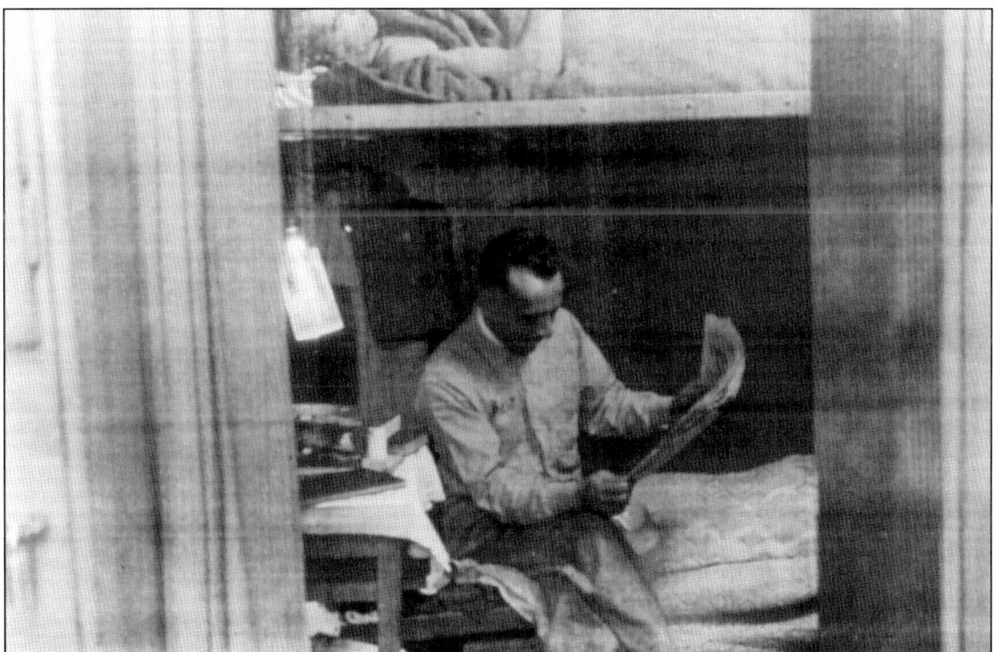

This image of inmates relaxing and reading the newspaper in their 1940s-era cell is rather poignant. One can only imagine what it feels like to be locked up every day and have no freedom. It is a consequence of their own actions, but still, it makes one reflect on how easily such a simple joy can be lost. (McNeil Island Historical Society.)

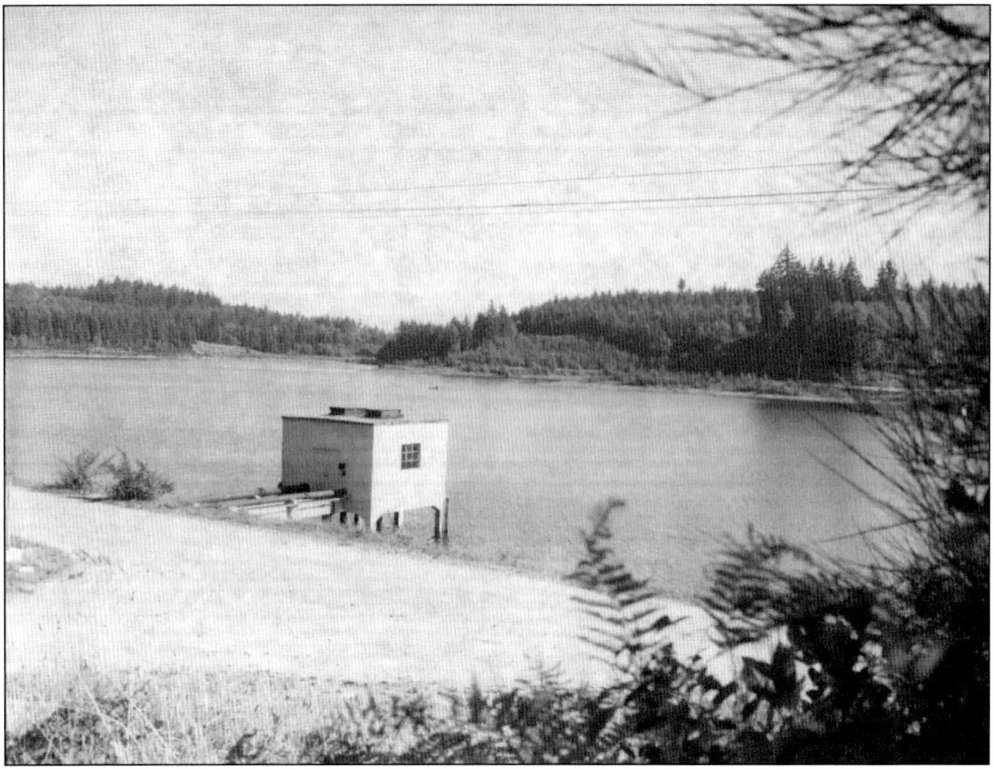

The blockhouse at Butterworth Lake is seen here at center, while a canoe drifts in the background on the lake. This beautiful bucolic scene hides the fact that the lake is actually the main source of water for McNeil Island. A water filtration plant sits below the lake and dam at the mouth of Eden Creek. All water on the island flows through there. (Washington State Archives.)

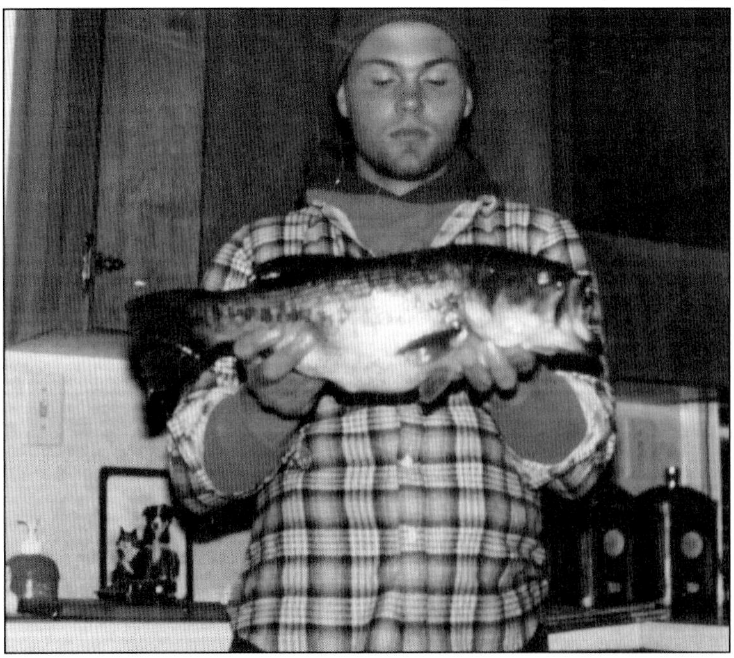

This local displays a bass he caught in Butterworth Lake in the 1980s. There was an annual fishing derby that began with the feds and continued until closure. The rewards were the tall tales one could retell and repeatedly embellish—and also, the much sought-after trophy. (Washington State Archives.)

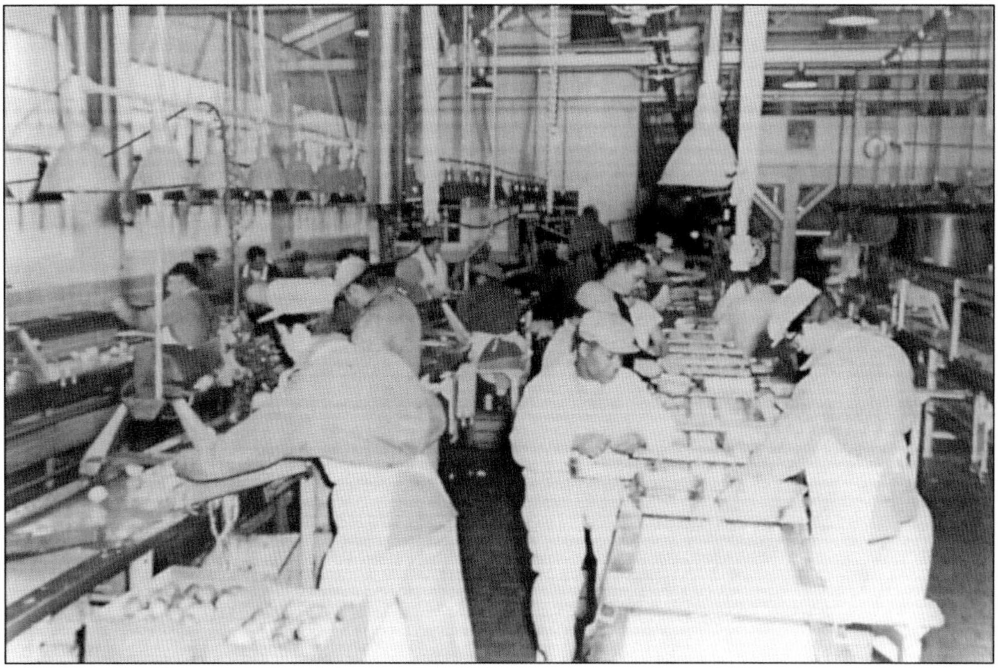

Prisoners work in the cannery in 1942. During World War II, the cannery was big business. Crops from the farm, along with apples and pears from the orchard, were harvested and brought to the cannery for processing and shipping to the military and civilian buyers. The cannery prospered after the war, but complaints from private business about unfair labor cost advantages caused the cessation of outside sales. (Washington State Archives.)

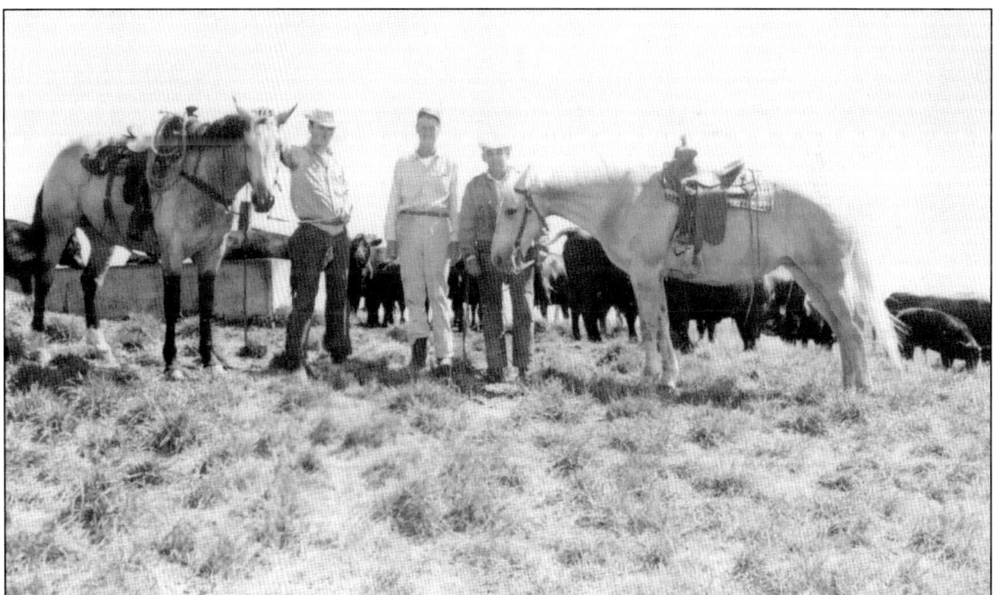

An inmate cowboy with his horse (left) stands beside Al Karpis, a former member of the Ma Barker gang, center. The staff cowboy supervisor is at right. The Angus beef cattle that roamed the pastures are behind them. Island children felt fortunate to have "pet" cows that came daily to their back fences. Author Ann Burkly's pet Hereford was named Spot. (Washington State Archives.)

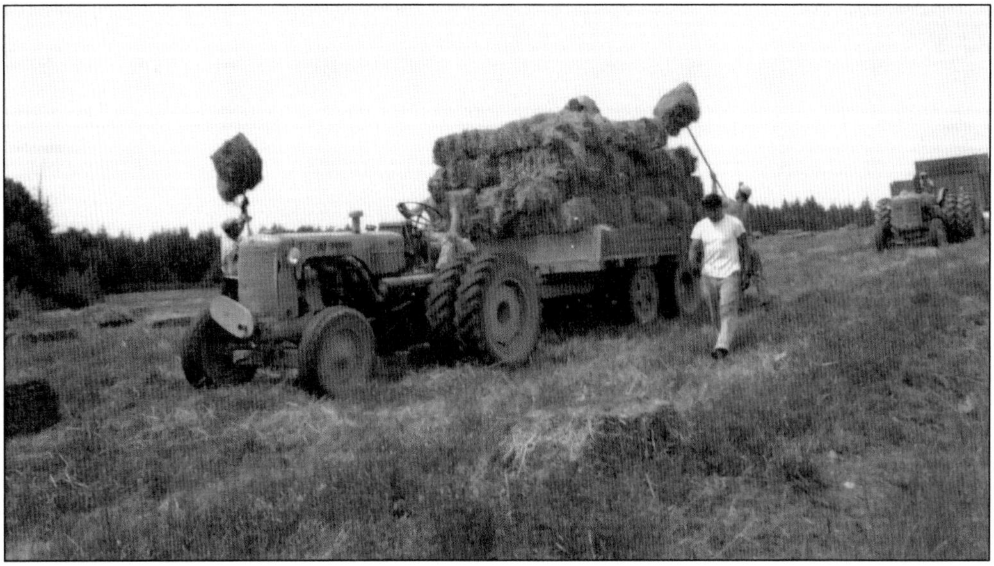

Two inmates drive tractors pulling trailers, while inmates with pitchforks load bales of hay onto the back of the trailer. Harvesting and baling hay was an annual job on McNeil, and although hard work physically, the inmates looked forward to being outside in the sunny weather, on their beautiful prison island framed by the Cascade and Olympic mountain ranges. (Washington State Archives.)

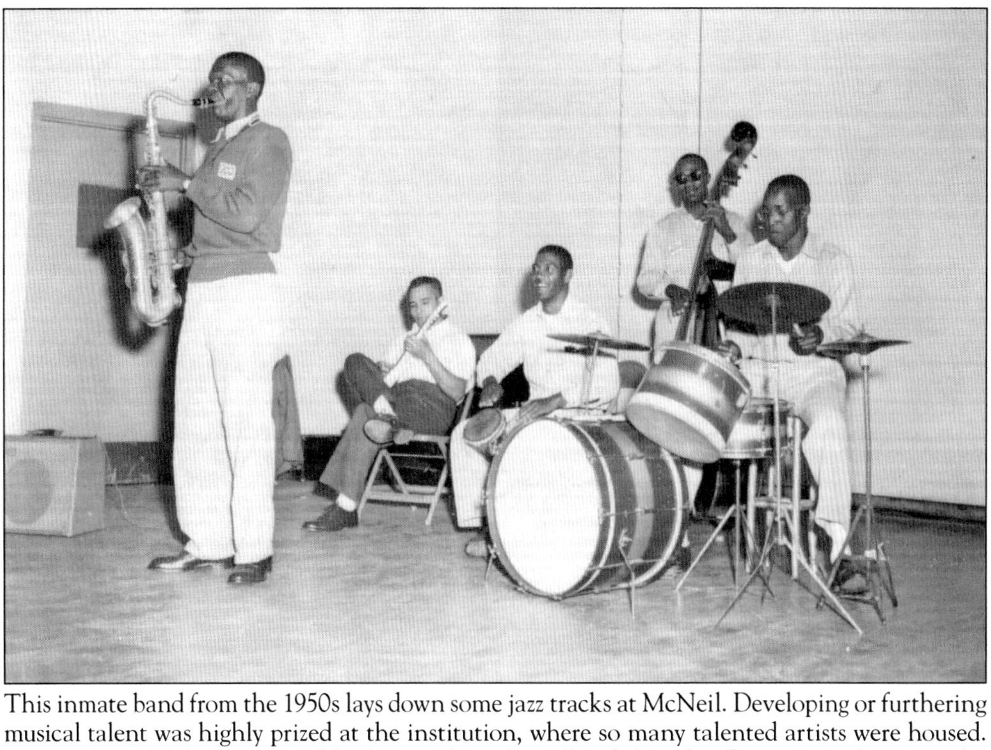

This inmate band from the 1950s lays down some jazz tracks at McNeil. Developing or furthering musical talent was highly prized at the institution, where so many talented artists were housed. Variety shows took place monthly, frequently with staff and their families in attendance, so the musicians always wanted to do their best and, of course, show up the other performers. (Washington State Archives.)

The marine department was a huge component of McNeil's functionality. From its earliest beginnings, water access was a constant struggle, as boats had to be built and maintained. The rails beside the pier made it easier to haul out the larger old wooden vessels. They would then be worked on either ashore or in the marine shed. Inmate crews still help, although they are now brought in daily. (Washington State Archives.)

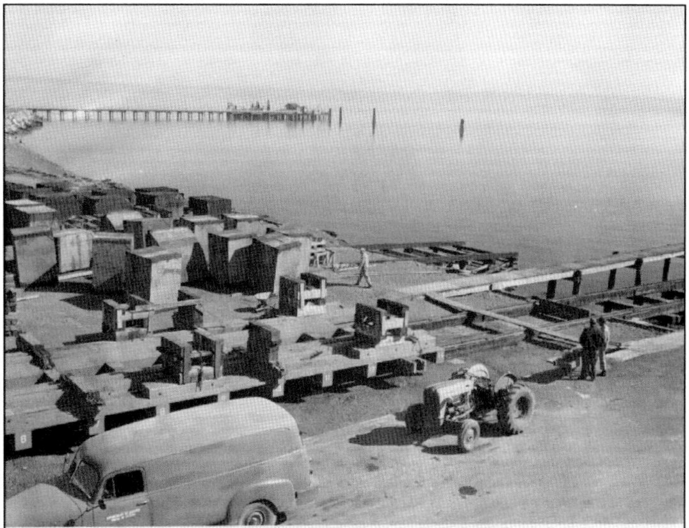

PARTIAL VIEW OF MARINE WAY & PONTOONS

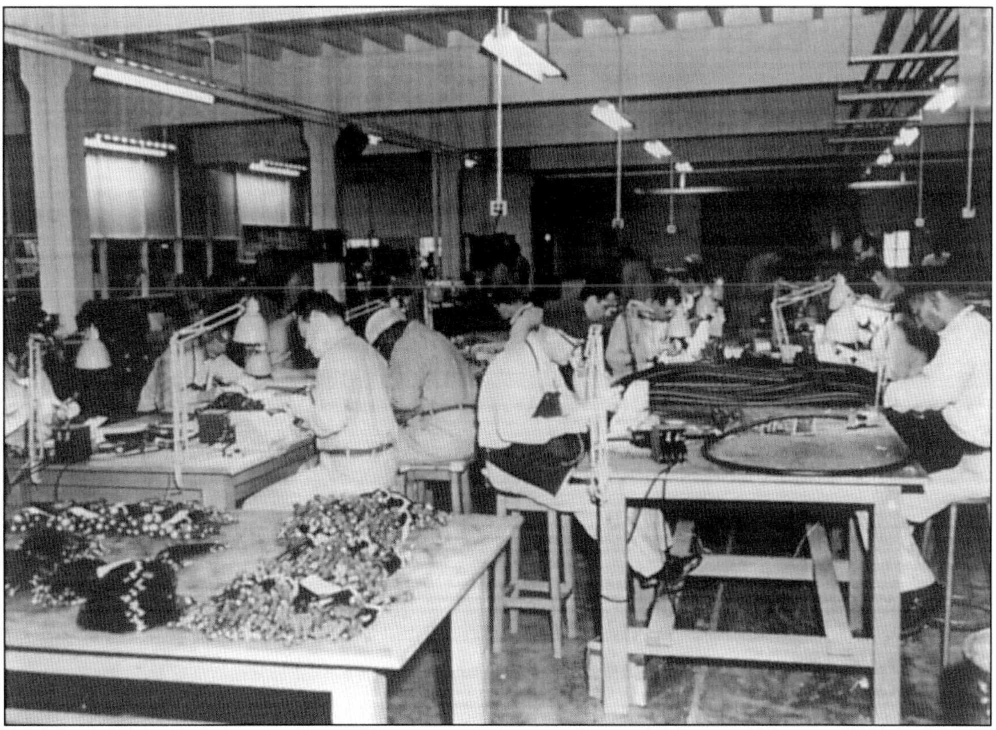

Inmates processed roughly 85 tons of salvaged cable monthly for the Navy. Most of the scrap cable came from ships damaged at Pearl Harbor. The inmates stripped it of its insulation and returned the cables in usable condition. One staff supervisor was awarded an $800 bonus because his suggestion for more efficiently processing the cable resulted in a $22,000-a-year savings. (Washington State Archives.)

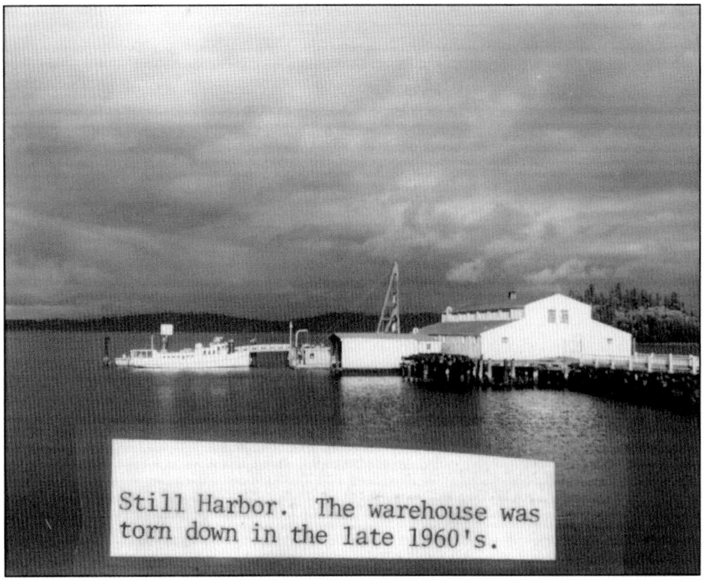

Still Harbor is on McNeil's leeward side and was used in foul weather. The *Captain Conner* is moored at the dock, probably being held in reserve as it was the smallest launch. The *Steilacoom* was usually used in rough seas, as she handled the best. Sadly, the progressively engineered spring base dock was torn down, but Still Harbor is where the DOC boats still moor today. (Washington State Archives.)

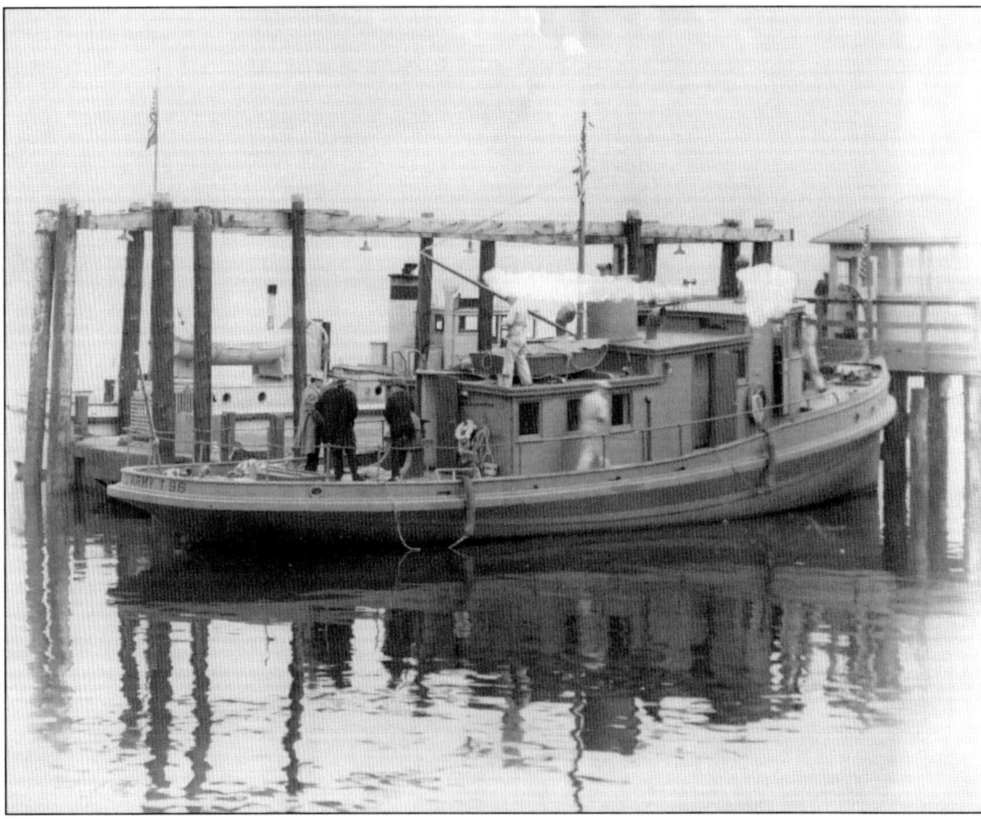

T-96 was built for the Army in World War II. The tug launched in 1942, followed by another in 1943, and finally, the *Captain Conner* in 1945. Since the war was over, *Captain Conner* went directly into the penitentiary fleet, where she served until the state took over in 1981. This was a truly patriotic effort on behalf of the inmates who volunteered to build the boats under staff direction. (Washington State Archives.)

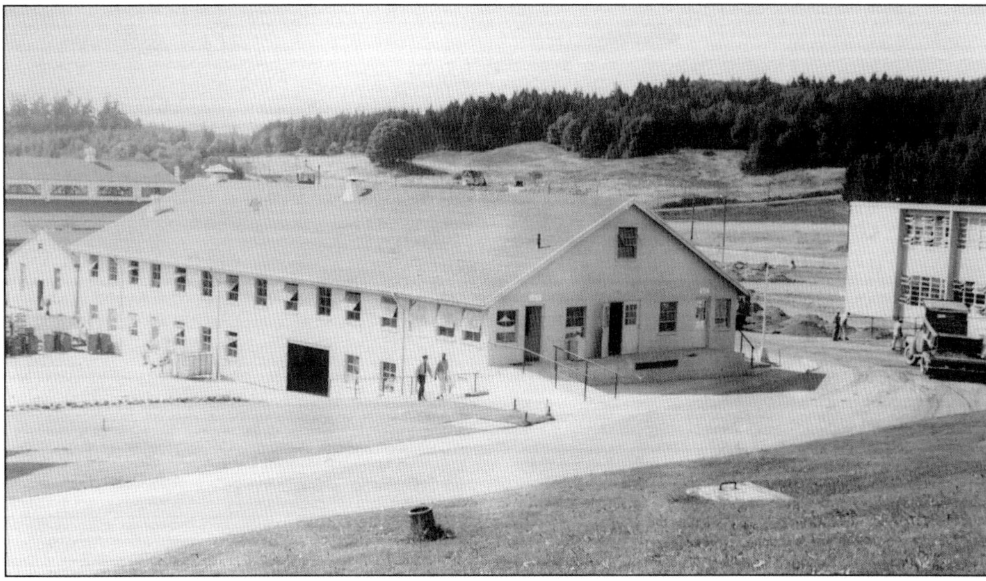

Part of the story of McNeil is useful repurposing, and the construction warehouse is proof of this. After the burst of construction waned and World War II arrived with its need for supplies, the warehouse became part of prison industries, whose modern buildings are seen to the right in this photograph from the 1950s. The 1932 building remained part of prison industries, even under the state, until closure in 2011. (Washington State Archives.)

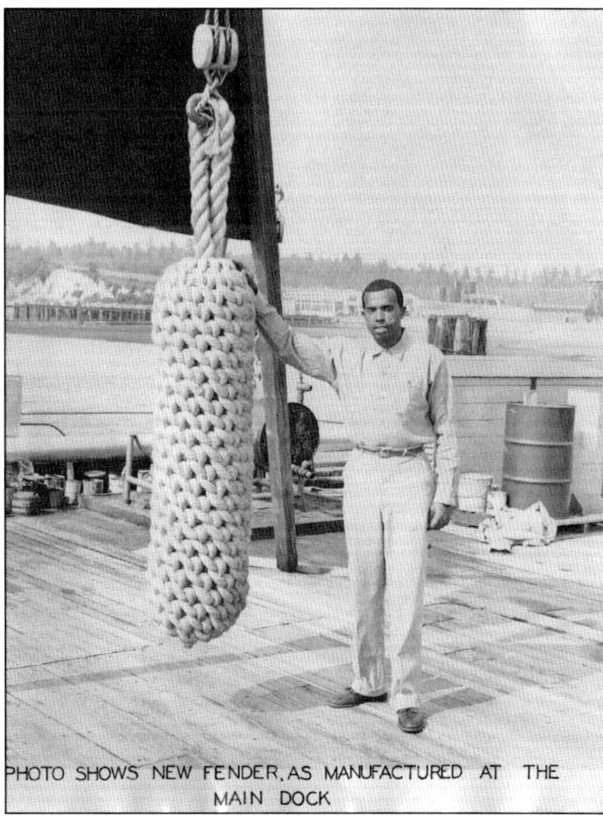

An inmate poses with a new rope fender he helped make at the main dock in the 1950s. The marine department had a lot of jobs that needed to be done and were open to inmates deemed deserving of a job. Making fenders was one of them. The inmates had facilities for working with rope from when nets were made for the Navy. (Washington State Archives.)

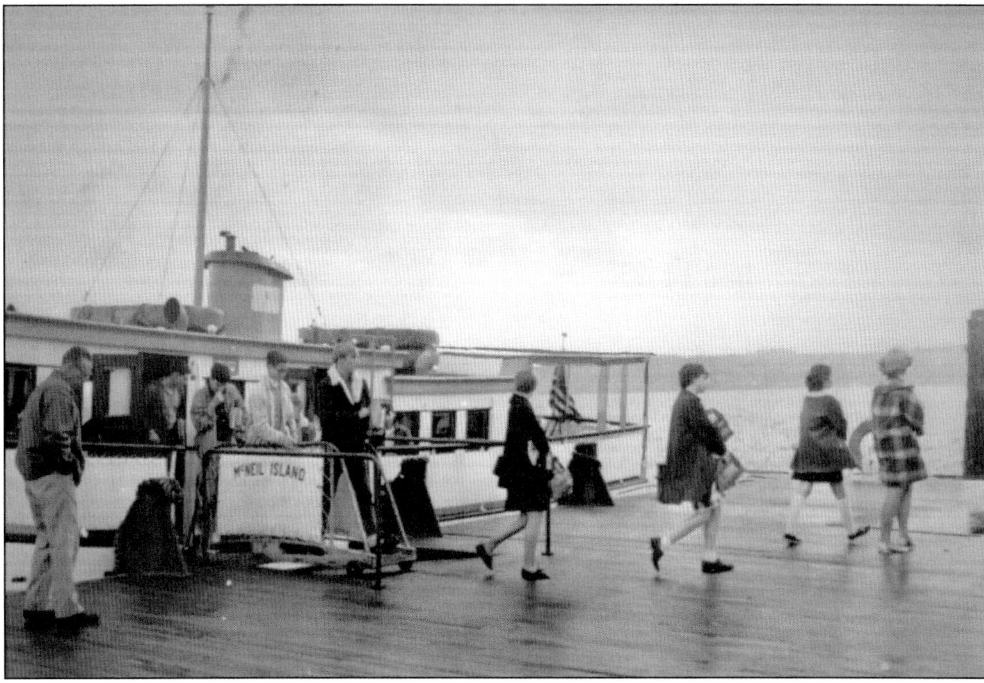

In this December 1961 photograph, McNeil teens head to school in town. Riding the boat was fun and a great experience. McNeil youth rode the launches daily once they matriculated out of the two-room McNeil Island Elementary, which went up to sixth grade. In the 1976–1977 term, fifth grade became the cap, and even more kids road the boat daily; this continued through 2010. (McNeil Island Historical Society.)

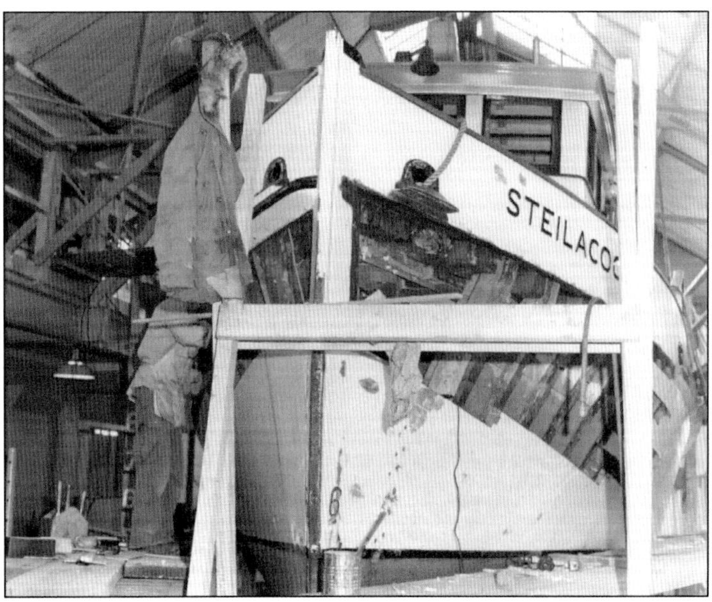

An inmate does restoration on the *Steilacoom*, built in 1943. She served in World War II, and Capt. John "Jack" Zukowski sailed her from the East Coast to McNeil in 1961 via the Panama Canal. The *Steilacoom* had the best heater and was beloved. She stayed at McNeil, remaining in service until 2005. There are a lot of great memories of the below-deck card room. (Washington State Archives.)

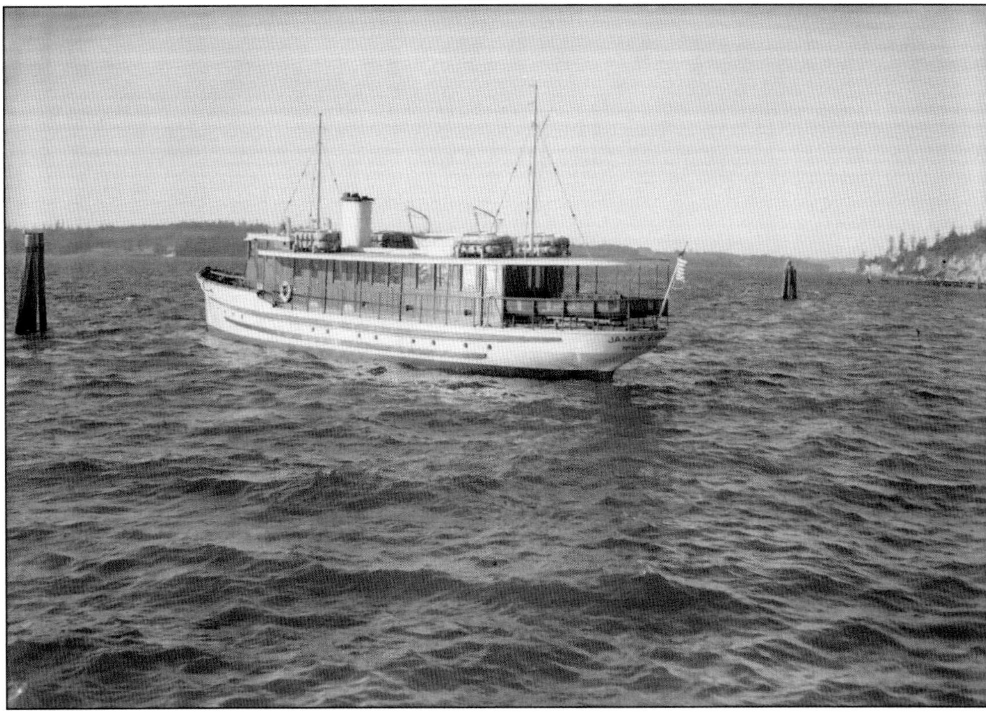

The *James V. Bennett*, named after a director of the Federal Bureau of Prisons, started life in 1931 as the *Holiday*, an 87-foot yacht. Designed for the William Morris ad agency, she ferried celebrities. In War World II, she carried troops; afterward, she was refitted and served McNeil until 1980. Renamed *Discovery* by her current owners, she cruises between Alaska and Puget Sound. (Washington State Archives.)

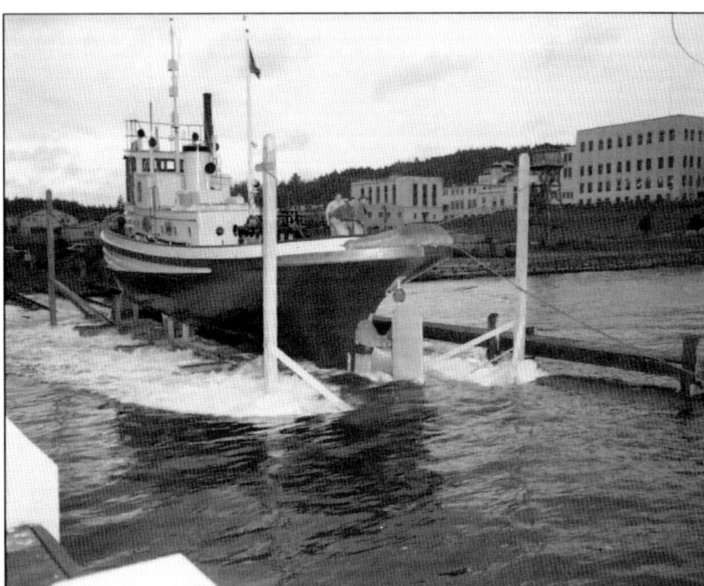

The beautiful *Butte* is being launched off the marine rails in front of the prison. Built in 1954 for the Army, she wound up at Alcatraz and came to McNeil after Alcatraz closed in 1963. She pushed barges carrying freight to McNeil and around the sound. A wonderful inmate-painted portrait of her hung in the marine office for years, even after the 2011 closure. She sails in Mexico now. (Washington State Archives.)

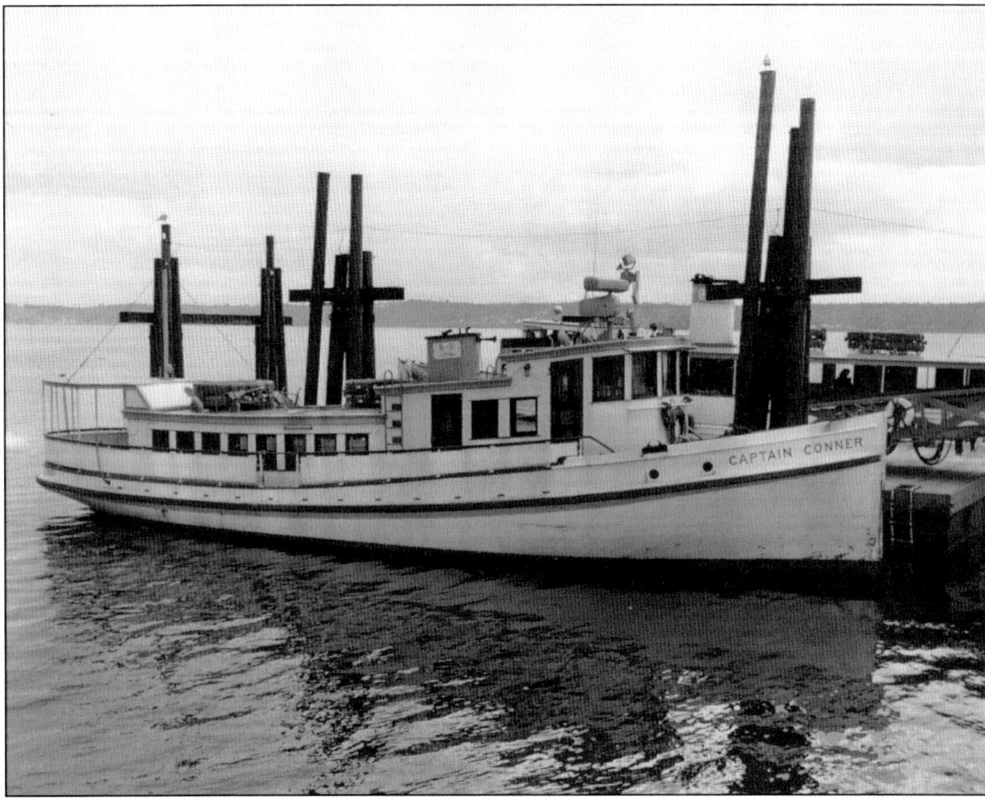

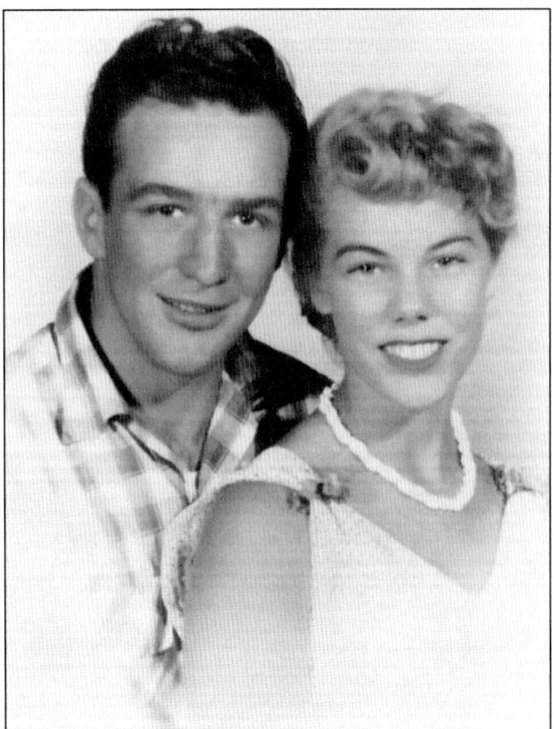

The inmate-built *Captain Conner* launched at McNeil in 1945, where she stayed until 1980. She was the site of an attempted escape and gave thrilling rides in rough weather. A tough little tug launch, designed by naval architect L.E. Coolidge, she is still afloat, touring the Columbia River between Ilwaco and Astoria, Oregon. (Washington State Archives.)

Seen here are Jack and Sue Zukowski. Jack was a young relief operator when he was attacked by his two inmate crew with a pipe at 3:00 a.m. on December 1960. Jack fought them off, radioed for help, and chased one with the *Captain Conner* after he dove overboard. They were sent to Alcatraz. Jack was stitched up and given a citation and monetary reward from the BOP. (Andrew Zukowski.)

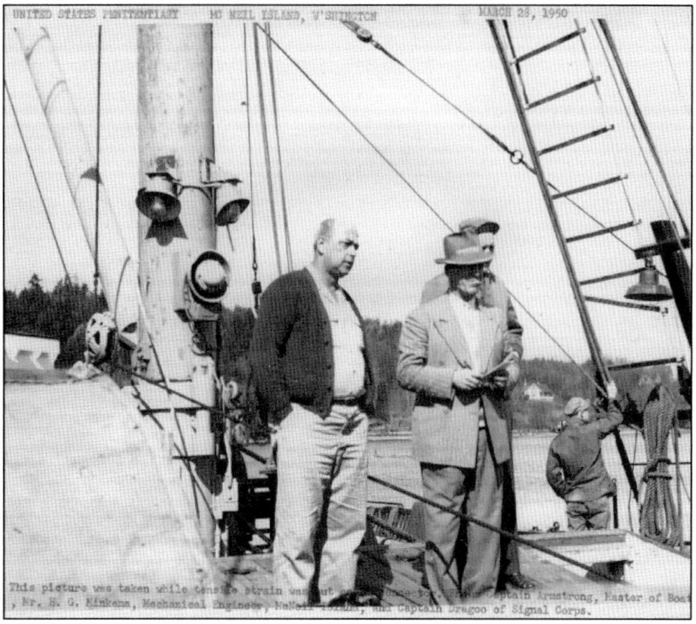

From left to right, Captain Armstrong, master of boats for McNeil Island; Henry Minkema, McNeil's mechanical engineer; and Captain Dragoo of the Signal Corps test out the tensile strength of a connector on a cable ship in the 1950s. This was a typical event on any day for McNeil's marine department. (Washington State Archives.)

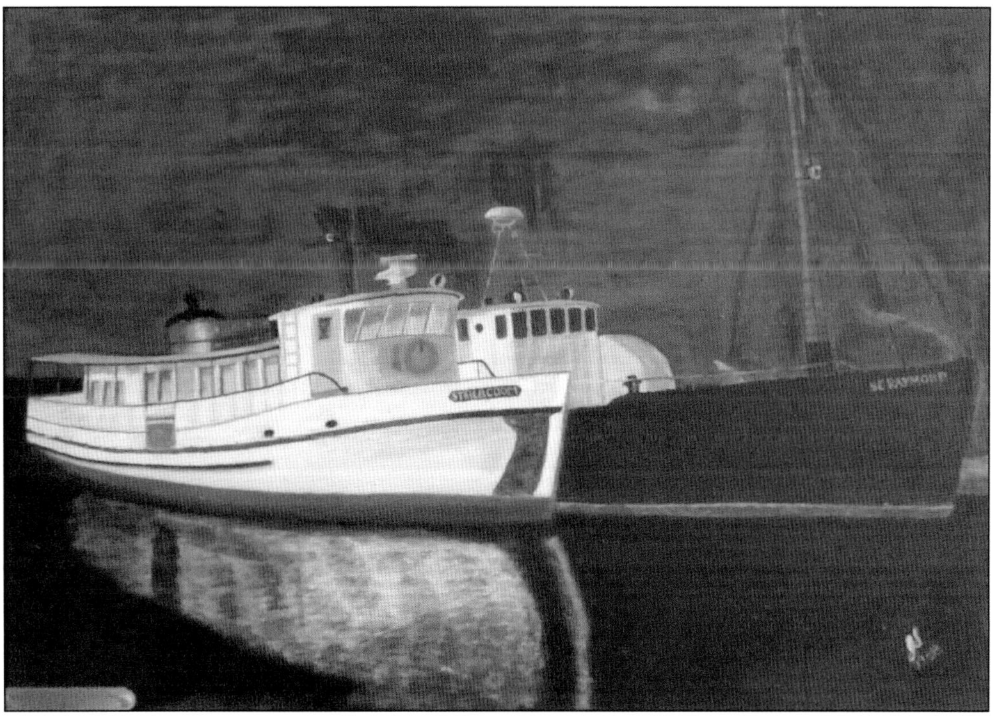

This is a painting of the launch *Steilacoom* moored beside the *S.E. Raymond*, done in 1988 by McNeil Island boat captain Jack Splawn. McNeil's launches were popular painting subjects, and this is very representative of the work done by inmates and given to well-regarded staff at their retirement or departure from McNeil. The painting was a gift to fellow marine department member Chris Hawke from the captain. (Courtesy Charmaine Hawke.)

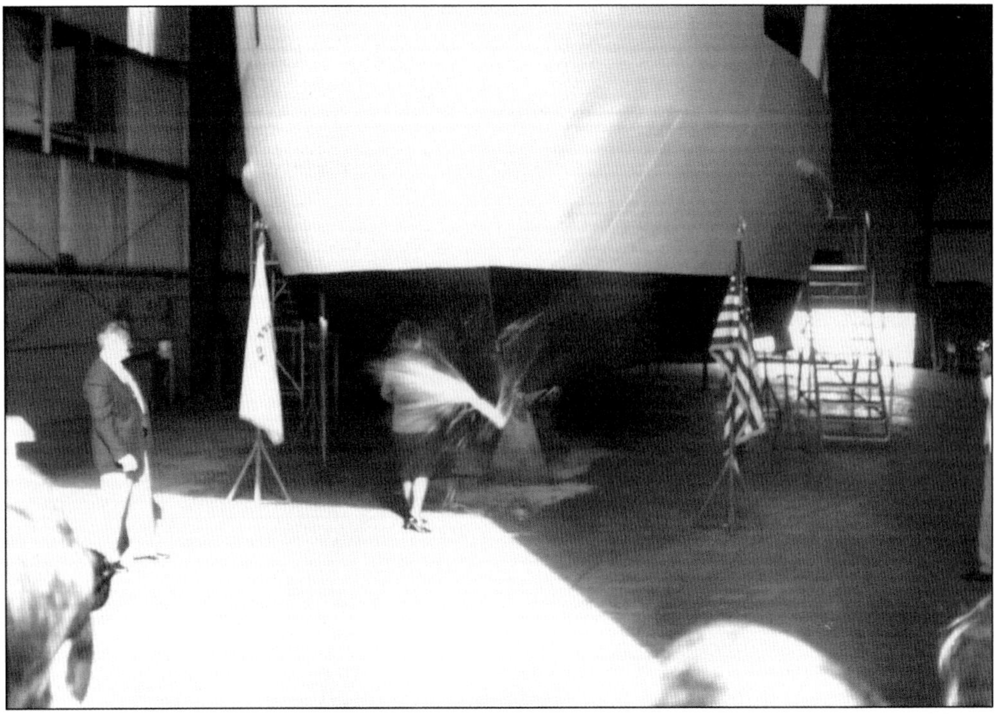

Sharon Callahan christens the *William Callahan* in 1991, when the ferry became the newest addition to the MICC fleet. She was named after William "Bill" Callahan, the first superintendent of McNeil Island for the Washington Department of Corrections. Callahan was a very well-regarded superintendent who liked to answer to "warden," since McNeil was an ancient pen. The *Callahan* is still in service for McNeil. (Washington State Archives.)

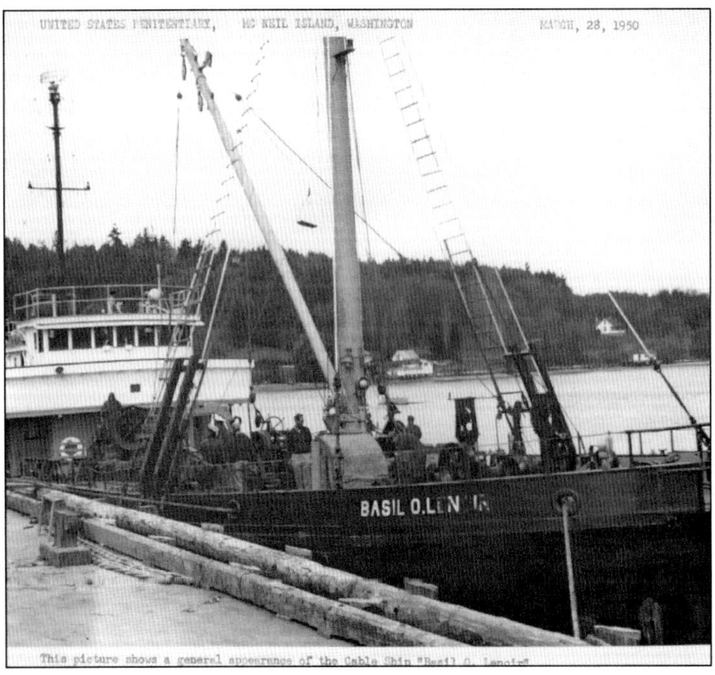

The cable ship *Basil O. Lenoir* is tied up at the dock between cable runs. It was used to lay submarine cable around McNeil Island to protect its shores from erosion. Periodically, maintenance must be done, and cable ships such as this were used to complete repairs and lay down more cable if needed. These boats required a lot of maintenance because metal fatigue was a concern. (Washington State Archives.)

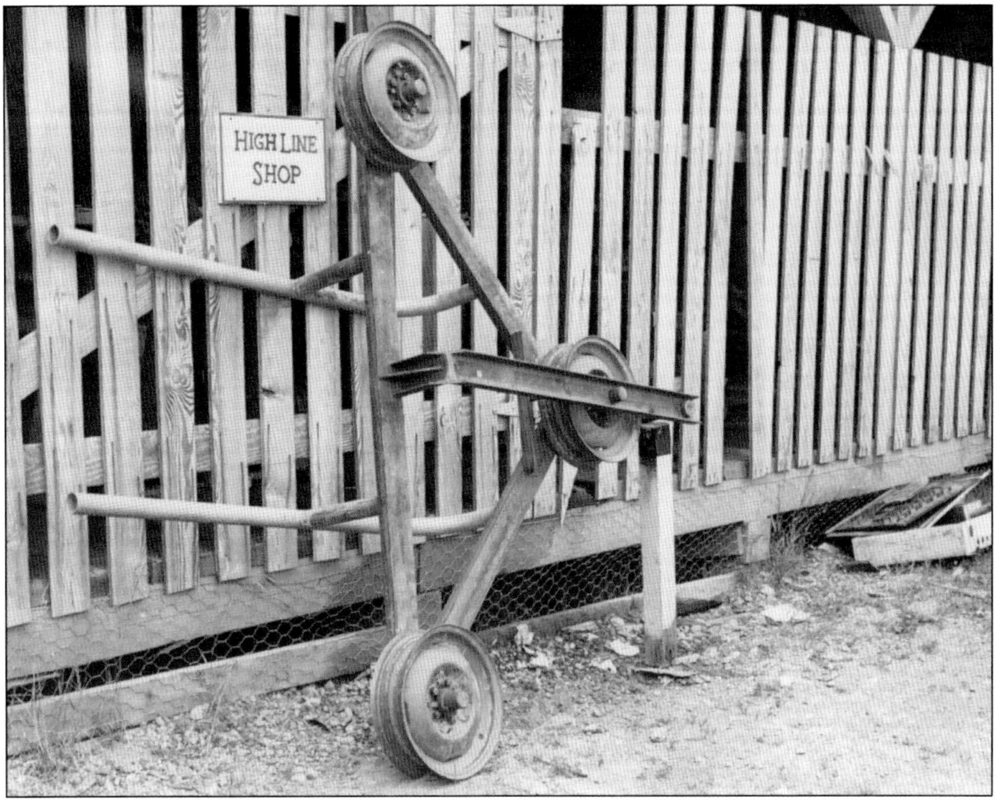

This is a piece of cable-laying equipment designed by McNeil Island mechanical engineer Henry Minkema. He was hired by the Federal Bureau of Prisons specifically because of his mechanical engineering degree, and although considered an officer, he was not involved with inmate custody. Minkema did a lot of good work at McNeil and constantly tried to improve conditions for the marine department especially. (Washington State Archives.)

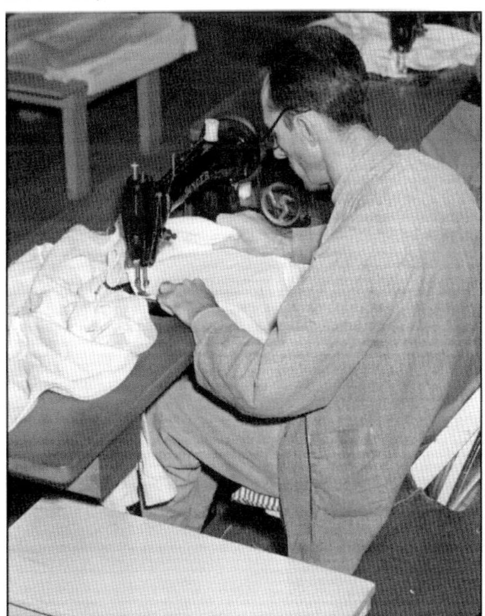

An inmate is working in the tailor shop in the 1940s. Sewing was just one of the handy skills an inmate could learn or utilize at McNeil. Inmate tailors made prison uniforms, tailored staff uniforms, made tablecloths and linens, designed costumes, sewed stage backdrop accessories for skits, and could do basically anything else asked of them. The work also earned them money toward phone calls or commissary goods. (McNeil Island Historical Society.)

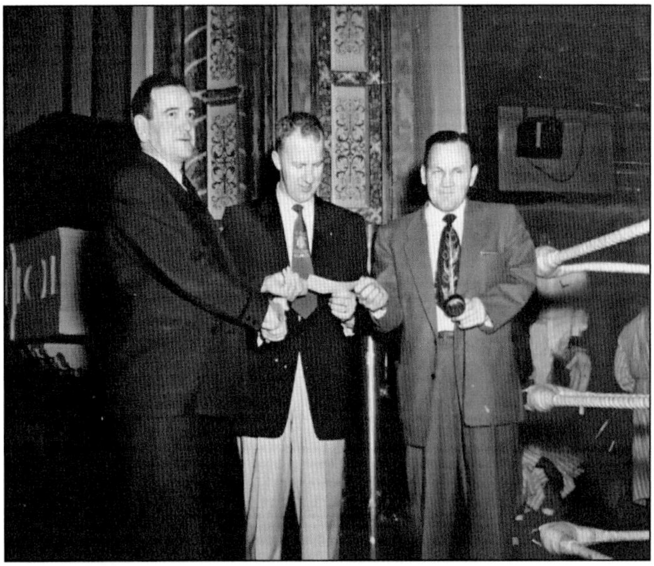

From left to right, officer and athletic director William "Cy" Rubado, an unidentified staff member, and Warden Fred Wilkinson announce winners and hand out certificates at a banquet held for inmate athletes. Wilkerson, known as "Friendly Fred," took office in 1951 and encouraged inmates in industries. He believed that inmates "went to prison as punishment, not for punishment." His philosophy paid off; there were no inmate murders during this three-year tenure. (Rubado family.)

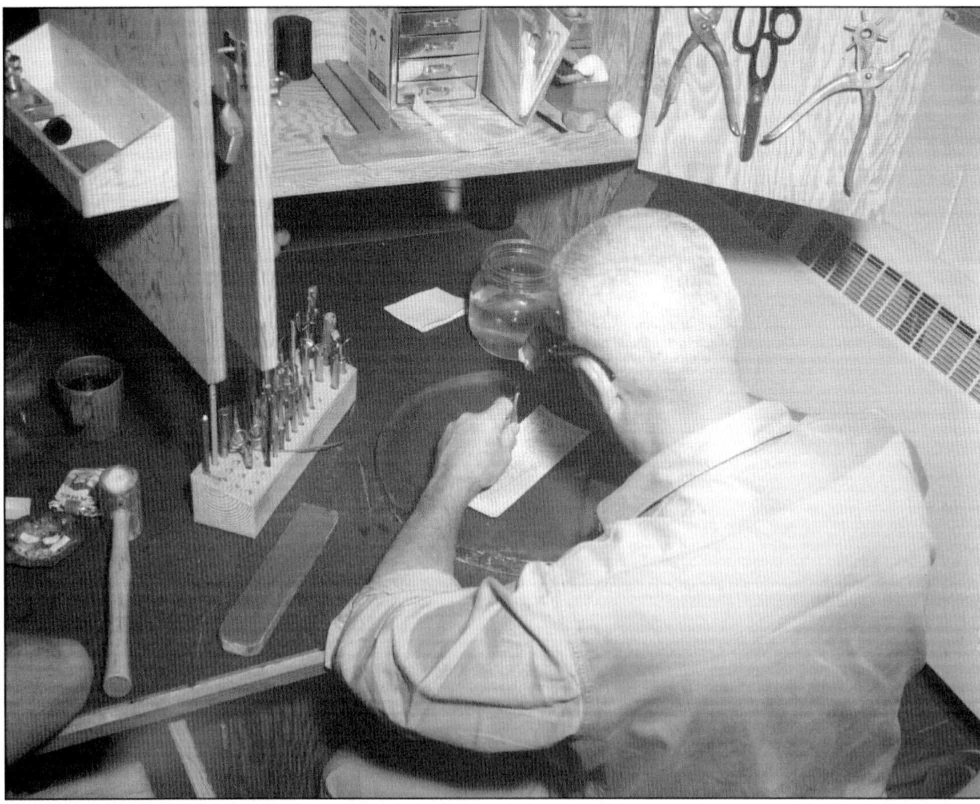

A federal prisoner works in the hobby shop, creating a wood carving or engraving. Housed in the English-style basement under the administration building, the hobby shop was open seven days a week into the evening so inmates could explore hobbies there at their leisure. Every imaginable hobby was there, including painting, ceramics, woodwork, and leather and copper works, to name a few. The tools required for these skills had specific spots outlined on a pegboard and were closely inventoried. (National Archives and Records Administration.)

The warden's greenhouse is being worked on by inmates in the 1940s. The greenhouse was part of the original design drawn by George Gove of Heath, Gove, & Bell, who loved flowers as much as Dora Archer did. It had a little room at the back so the yard boys could take a break with a cup of coffee. The greenhouse supplied McNeil with flowers year-round and was much appreciated. (National Archives and Records Administration.)

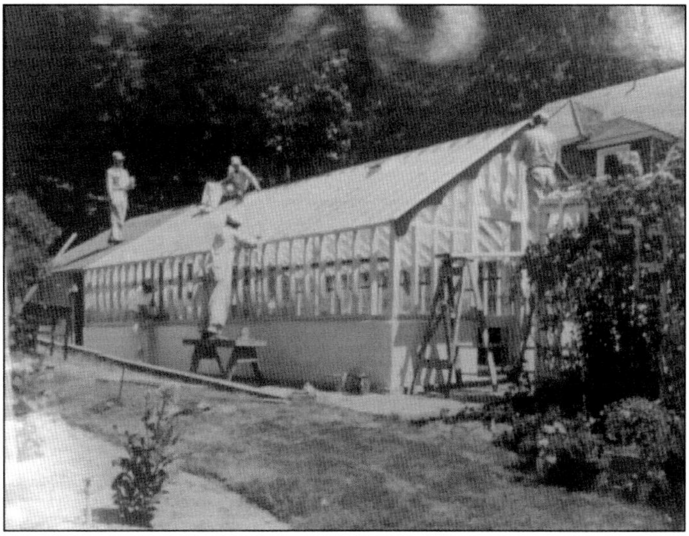

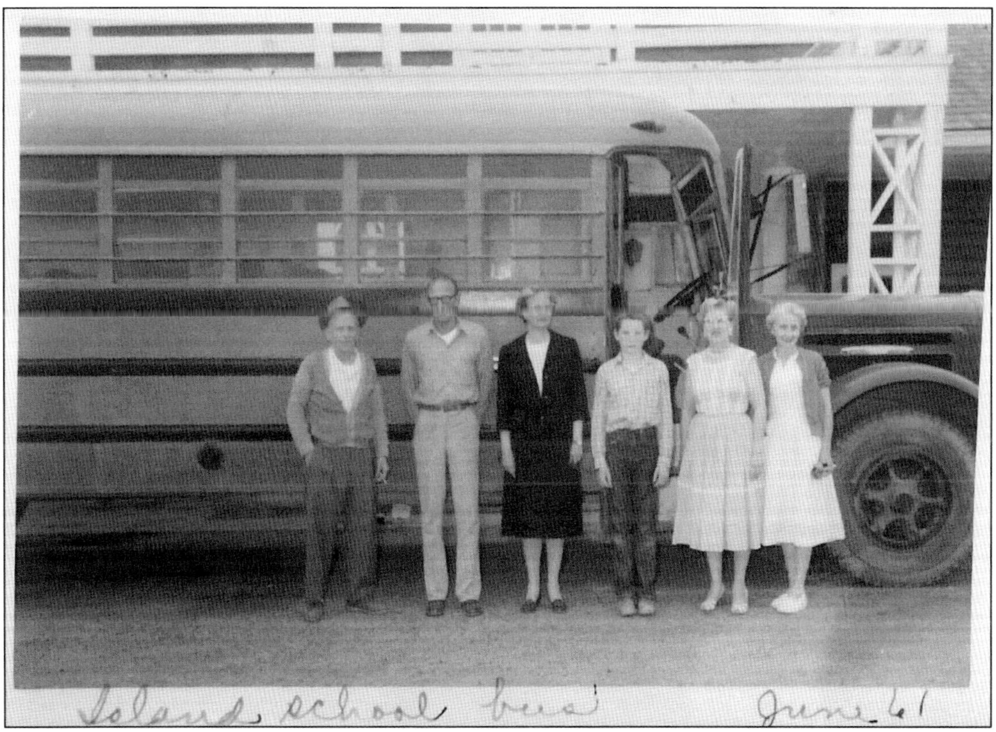

Student David Wisehart (third from right) is pictured with a staff supervisor (far left), an inmate bus driver (second from left) and his teachers in front of the McNeil Island Elementary School bus. Riding the bus was exciting as trusted inmates, including "Creepy" Al Karpis, the former gangster, drove, and the engine frequently failed near the top of Center Hill. The bus would careen wildly backward down the hill, with children screaming all the way. They all wondered if the inmates were practicing reverse getaway driving. (David Wisehart.)

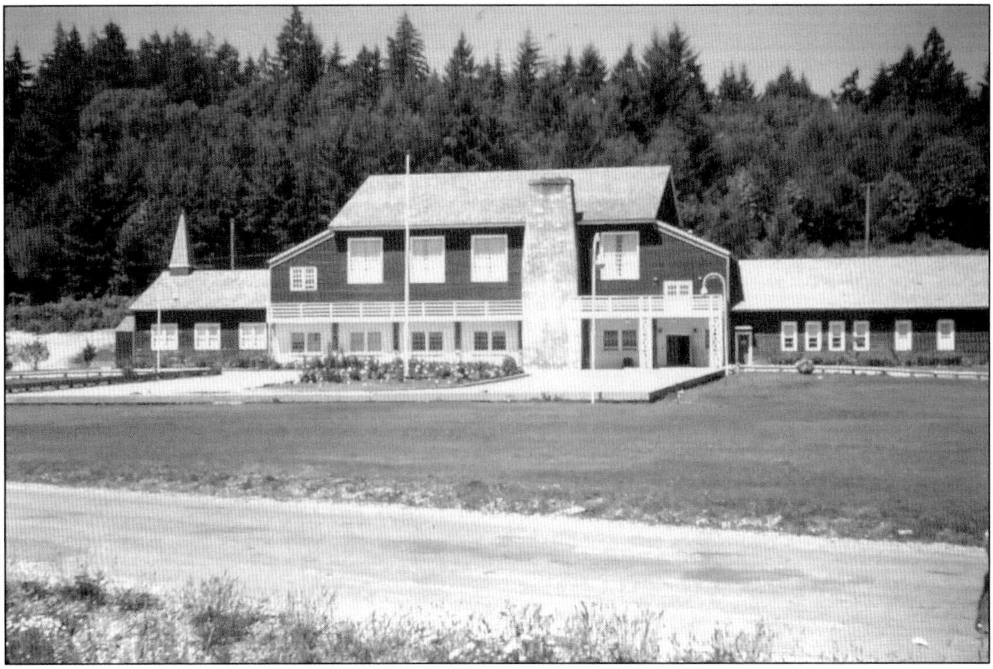

On Friday nights, the community center showed 25¢ movies. It had bowling lanes, a gym that also held school plays, a kitchen, a game room, a chapel, and a two-room schoolhouse with a library. A playground held a tether ball, swings, tennis courts, and a baseball diamond. It had a pool, kiddie pool, and pool house. There was also an outdoor pavilion for celebrations, where they greased the flagpole and pigs. (Washington State Archives.)

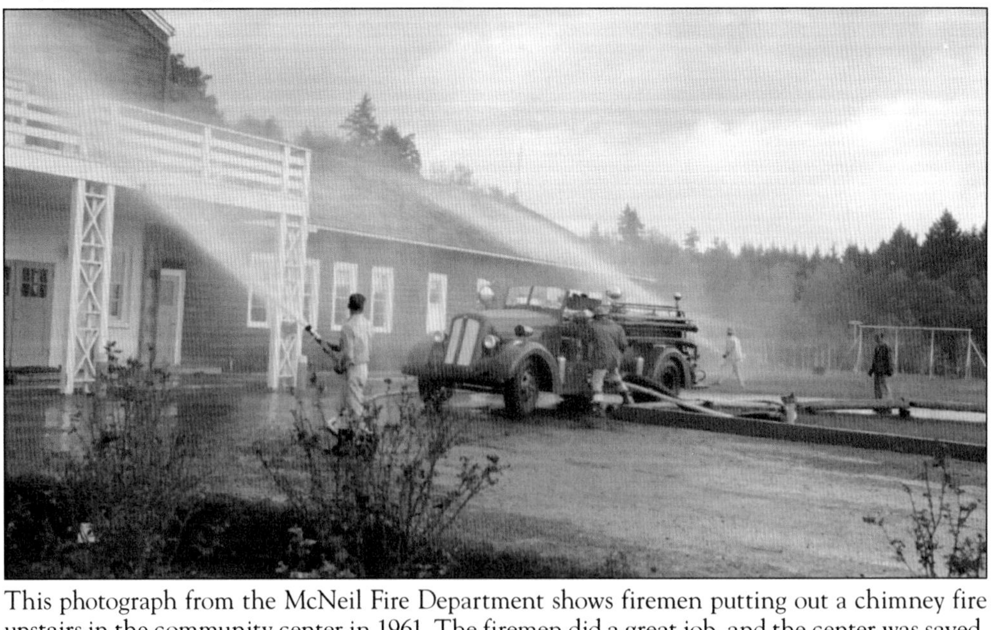

This photograph from the McNeil Fire Department shows firemen putting out a chimney fire upstairs in the community center in 1961. The firemen did a great job, and the center was saved, with only minimal smoke and water damage. Smoke entered the attic that ran upstairs above the school. The community center and school opened in 1952, so faulty systems were not to blame. (Loren Else.)

The Floyd's Cove pump station and pond are seen while under development in the 1950s, with Longbranch in the background across Pitt's passage. Engineer Henry Minkema (left) and probably the outside foreman walk along while discussing progress. Floyd's Cove was always very well maintained and had beautiful flower beds and fencing around it through 1980. The vehicle in the photograph looks like those driven on McNeil in the late 1970s. Some things never change. (Washington State Archives.)

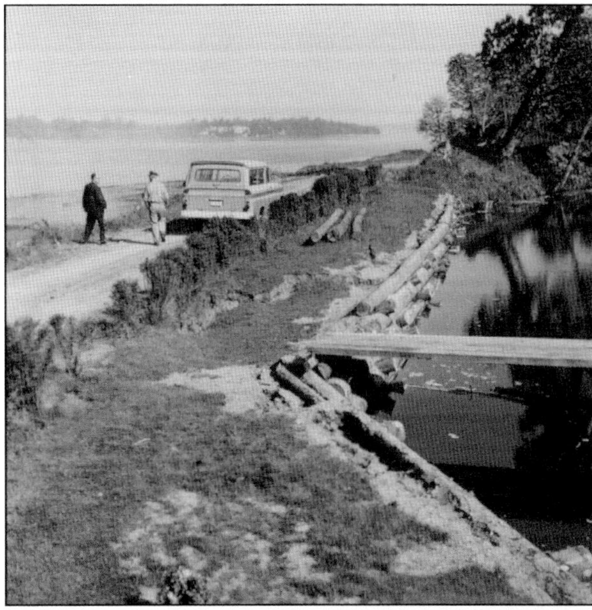

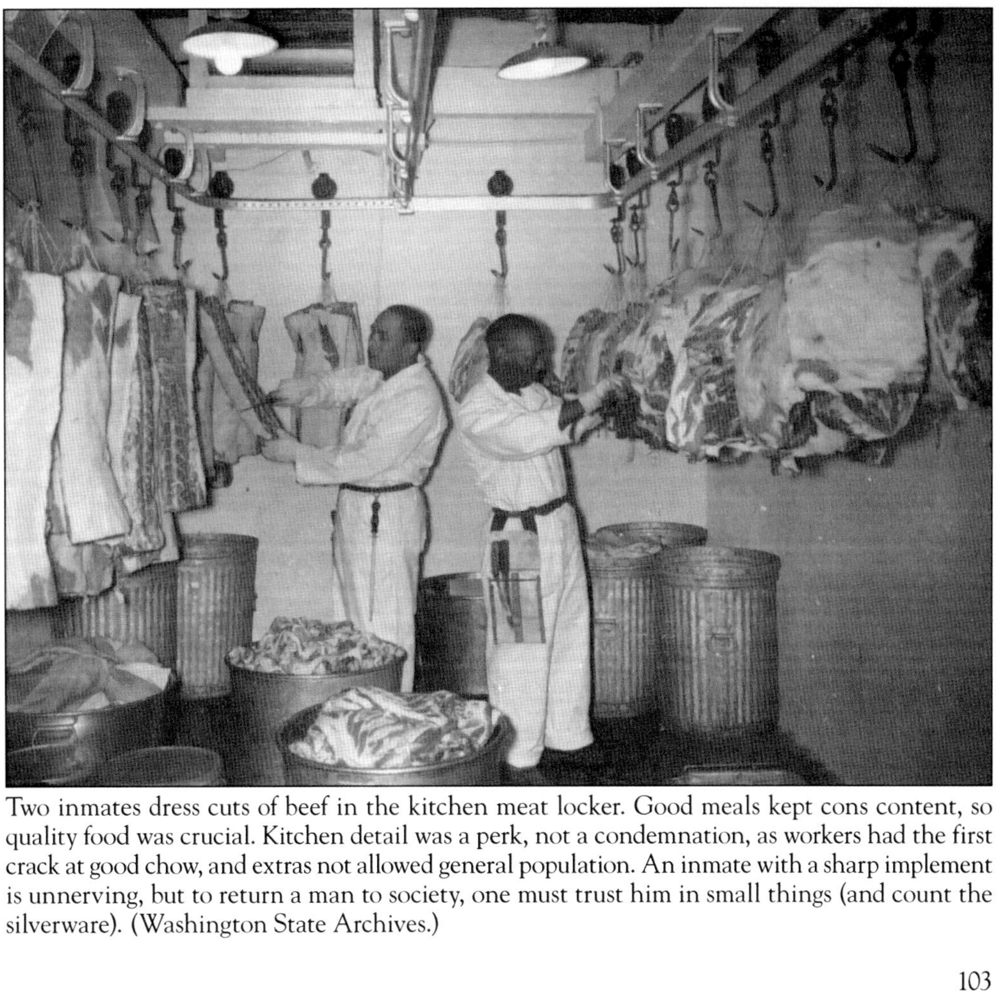

Two inmates dress cuts of beef in the kitchen meat locker. Good meals kept cons content, so quality food was crucial. Kitchen detail was a perk, not a condemnation, as workers had the first crack at good chow, and extras not allowed general population. An inmate with a sharp implement is unnerving, but to return a man to society, one must trust him in small things (and count the silverware). (Washington State Archives.)

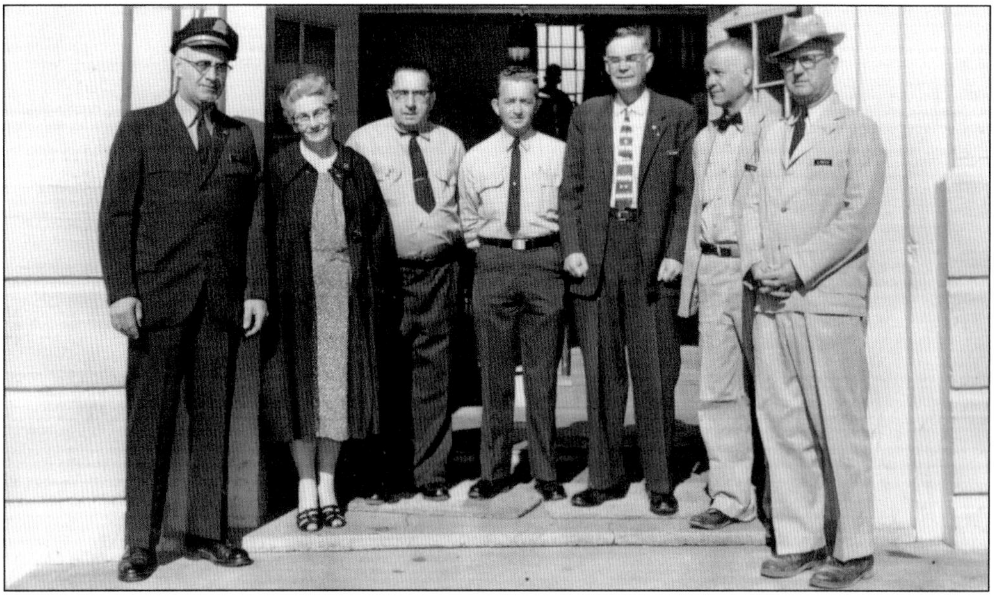

Staff members are pictured on the administration building steps about 1960. From left to right are Lieutenant Prosser, who burned down old settler cabins that teenagers were using at the rear of Holly Hill; an unidentified woman who appears to be the wife of the tall man in the dark suit; officer Jack Henderson; the Four Trees author; unidentified staff, unidentified; the assistant farm or dairy manager; and Joe Havelka, the farm manager. (Washington State Archives.)

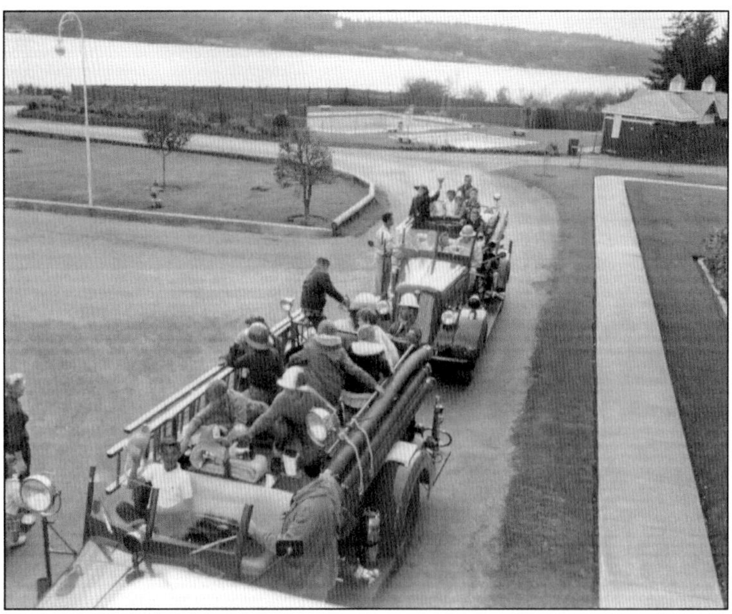

McNeil Island Elementary children are pictured on the island fire trucks in front of the school at the community center in 1956. The fire department did annual fire safety training for the children and practice fire drills. Fires were taken very seriously on McNeil, and everyone learned best practices, thanks to the well-trained fire department. (Loren Else.)

Six

Cons and Current Events

A boy and his inmate school bus driver was McNeil's unique mix. Besides families, plenty of cons called McNeil home too: the Weyerhaeuser kidnappers, a German spy, murderers; all were part of McNeil's story, which continues today with the SCC and Emergency Response Team, but a few cons stand out.

Robert Stroud, the "Birdman of Alcatraz," began life behind bars at McNeil in 1909, sentenced for manslaughter. He left McNeil after he stabbed an orderly who snitched about his drug smuggling. That sent him to the tougher Leavenworth, Kansas, pen. Killing a guard there landed him on "the Rock" in the 1930s.

Roy Gardner, the last of the great train robbers of the 1920s, dubbed the "Smiling Bandit" and the "King of the Escape Artists," was said to be the most hunted man in Pacific Coast history, alongside hijacker D.B. Cooper.

The "King of Seattle Bootleggers," Roy Olmstead, stayed four years on McNeil, while confidence man Fred Peters chauffeured the warden and was given a farewell watch by him, only to depart and charge an indulgent Seattle shopping spree to Warden Archer.

Ralph "Bottles" Capone did time for tax evasion, peeling potatoes in the 1930s. Los Angeles mob boss Mickey Cohen got in a few fights due to his germaphobia in the early 1950s.

There were World War II conscientious objectors, notably Auburn-born Gordon Hirabayashi, who refused the order for Japanese Americans to "evacuate" to internment camps. Hirabayashi considered the orders a violation of his Constitutional rights. He was convicted and appealed to the Supreme Court, which upheld the order, but it was overturned in the 1980s.

Progressive Party nominee Vincent Hallinan ran for president in 1952 from behind McNeil's bars, and former teamster president Dave Beck McNeil left 40 pounds lighter in 1964 after being sentenced for fraudulent organization reporting.

Charles Manson landed on McNeil in 1961 for pimping and forgery. Serving a seven-year sentence, he learned guitar and Scientology here. The con who taught Manson guitar was Ma Barker Gang member Alvin "Creepy Karpis" Karpavicz. While Manson considered Karpis a friend, the feeling was not mutual.

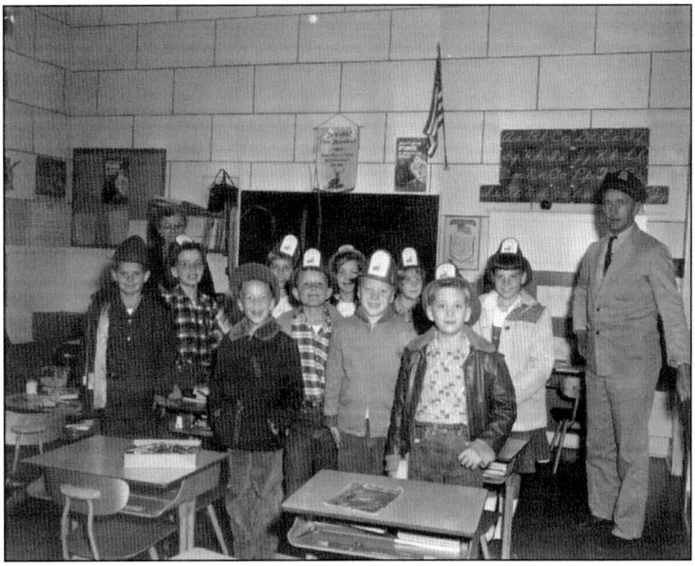

In 1955, the fourth-, fifth-, and sixth-grade class of the two-room schoolhouse of McNeil Island Elementary had an exciting fire safety class. Three grades in one room worked amazingly well, and having older children in class probably increased the aptitude of the younger students. Having the firemen visit was always a big hit with the kids. (Loren Else.)

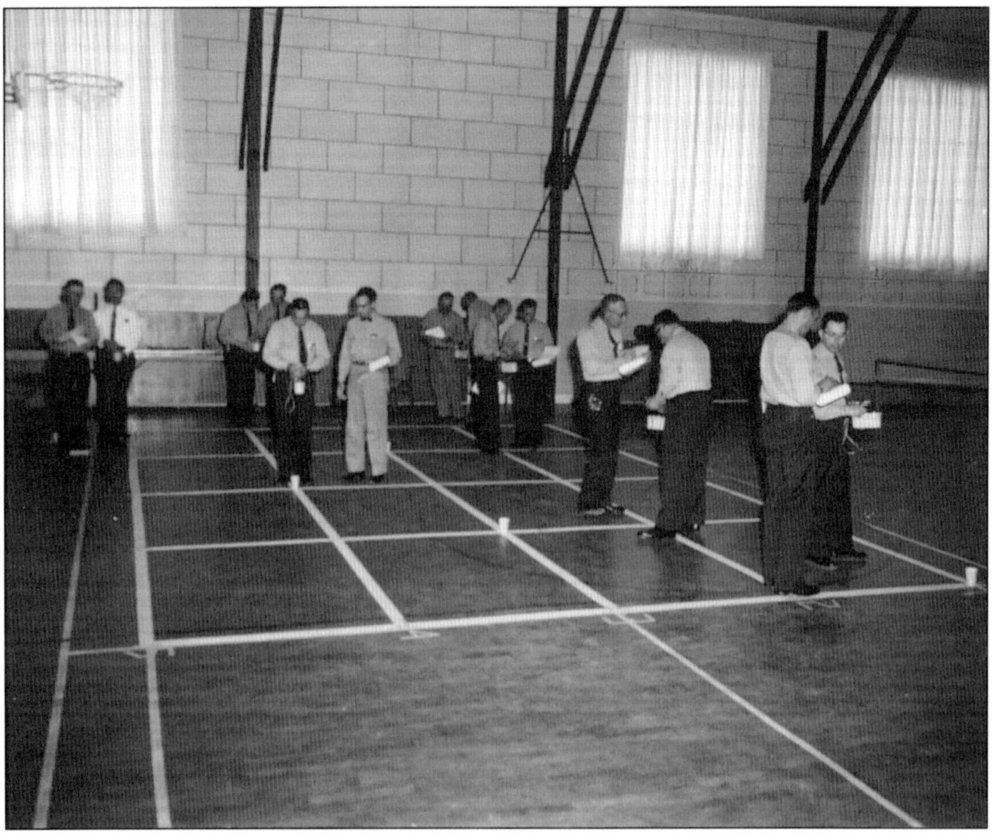

Correctional officers train in the community center in 1953. The Island Resident Association found a loophole where they could get funds for a community center if it was used for training, so the multiuse training center was born. Staff did train in it, but mostly, it was used for school and community events. Awesome Halloween parties and Christmas programs were held there, but Friday movie night was the best. (Loren Else.)

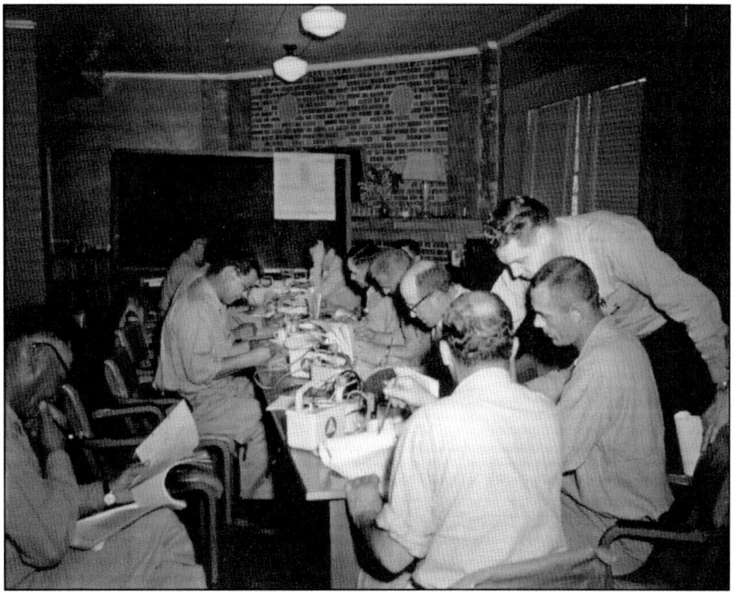

Staff train in the lower-level training room of the community center in the mid-1950s. This room was called the recreation room, or rec room for short. It was where most of the casual socializing happened in the community center because it had a big fireplace and was next to the pool tables, kitchen, and bathrooms. It was a great location, even for training. (Loren Else.)

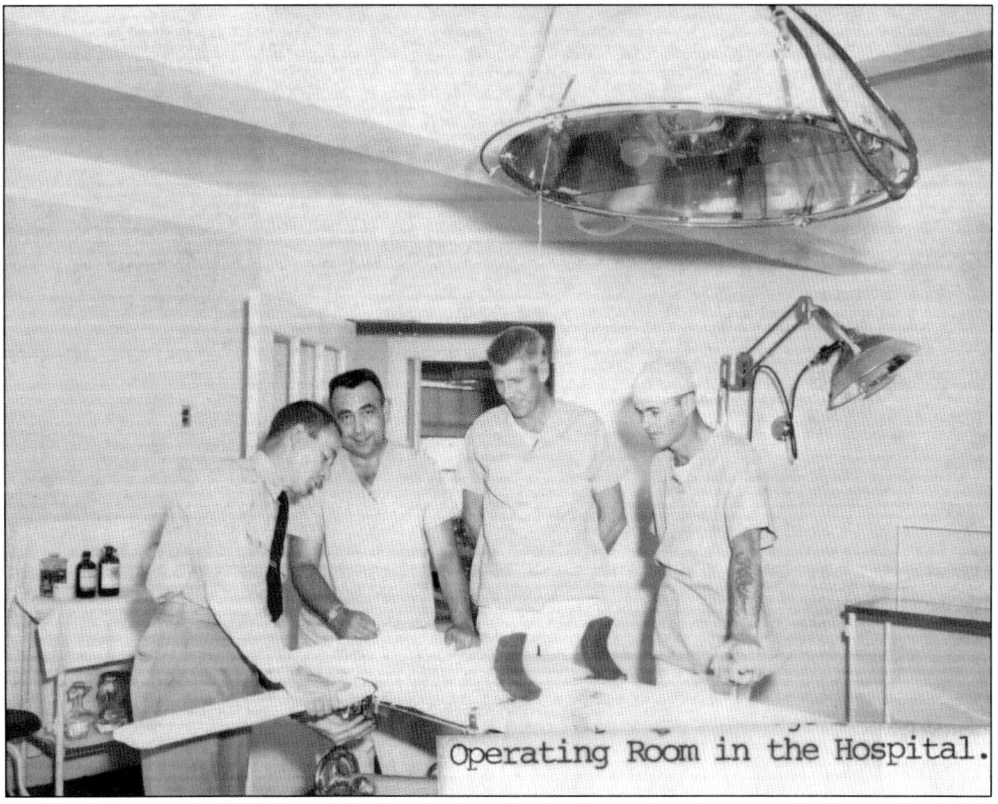

Built in 1926, McNeil's hospital had a chief medical officer, two physicians, a dentist, and two nurses. The hospital was fully accredited in 1955, a distinction that is seldom achieved by prison facilities. Unfortunately, medical testing occurred at McNeil. Forbidden since 1976, in the 1950s, it was common practice to grant good time to test subjects. Sadly, two cons died of hepatitis, but others gained early release thanks to testing. (Washington State Archives.)

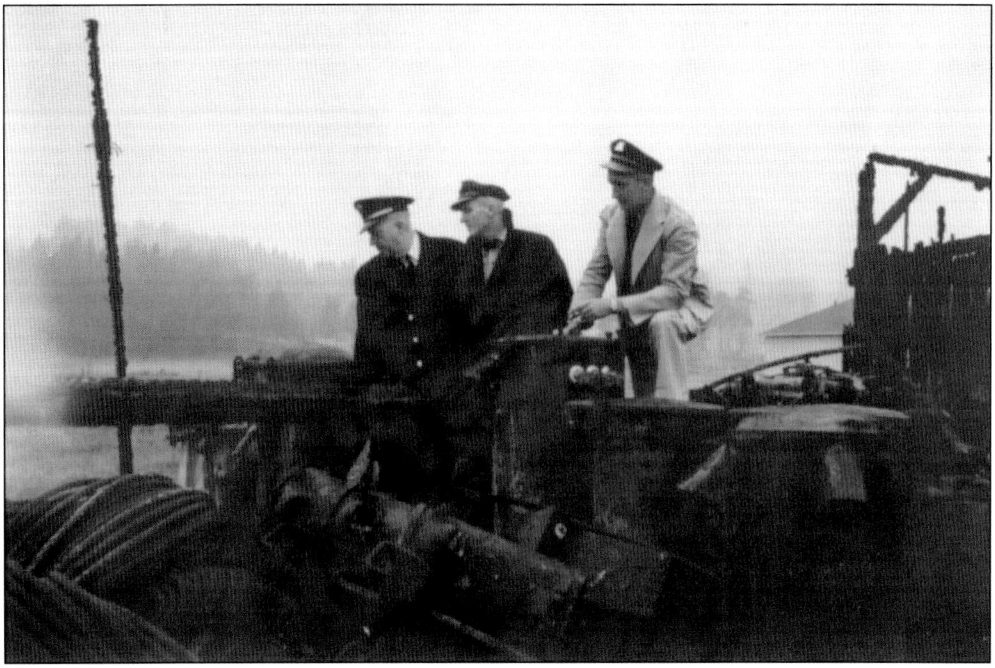

From left to right, the fire marshal, Warden Donald Byington, and McNeil's fire chief survey damage after the huge inmate-set 1961 farm fire. A substantial industrial portion of the farm was destroyed. The fire can be attributed to unrest caused by Byington's lax leadership. Previously a capable administrator, he was sidetracked by an affair with his secretary, creating a power vacuum. The BOP transferred him to Arizona, and he resigned. (Loren Else.)

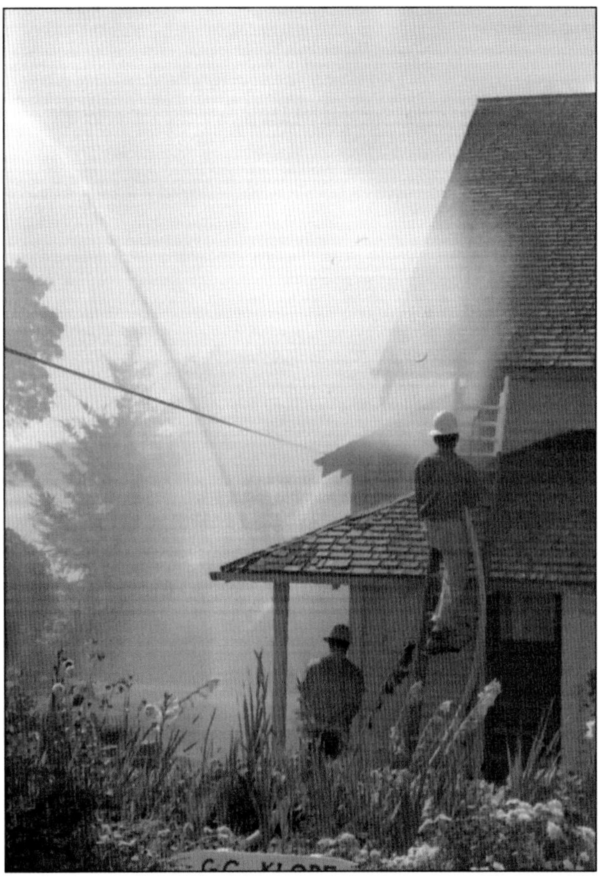

A fire occurred upstairs at residence 104 in the late 1960s and was quickly put out by the fire department. This was a blessing because the home was the original settler home built by the Ward family around 1900, although remodeled extensively. The fire department had paid staff but was manned by trained trustees who were able to go out with supervisors to fight fires on McNeil and elsewhere. (Loren Else.)

Rev. Fr. Francis Prange, the originator of the Self-Improvement Group (SIG), stands on the right. Catholic chaplain at McNeil in the 1950s and 1960s, Prange's inmate-led SIG led to many similar positive groups. Prange was the driving force behind the Chapel of Mt. Tahoma, with support from Warden Paul Madigan and the outside community. This good man led by example and left a large shadow. (Loren Else.)

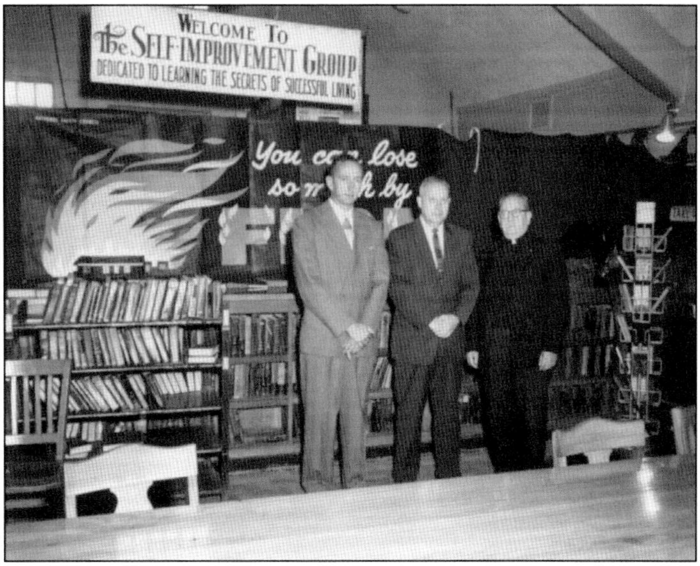

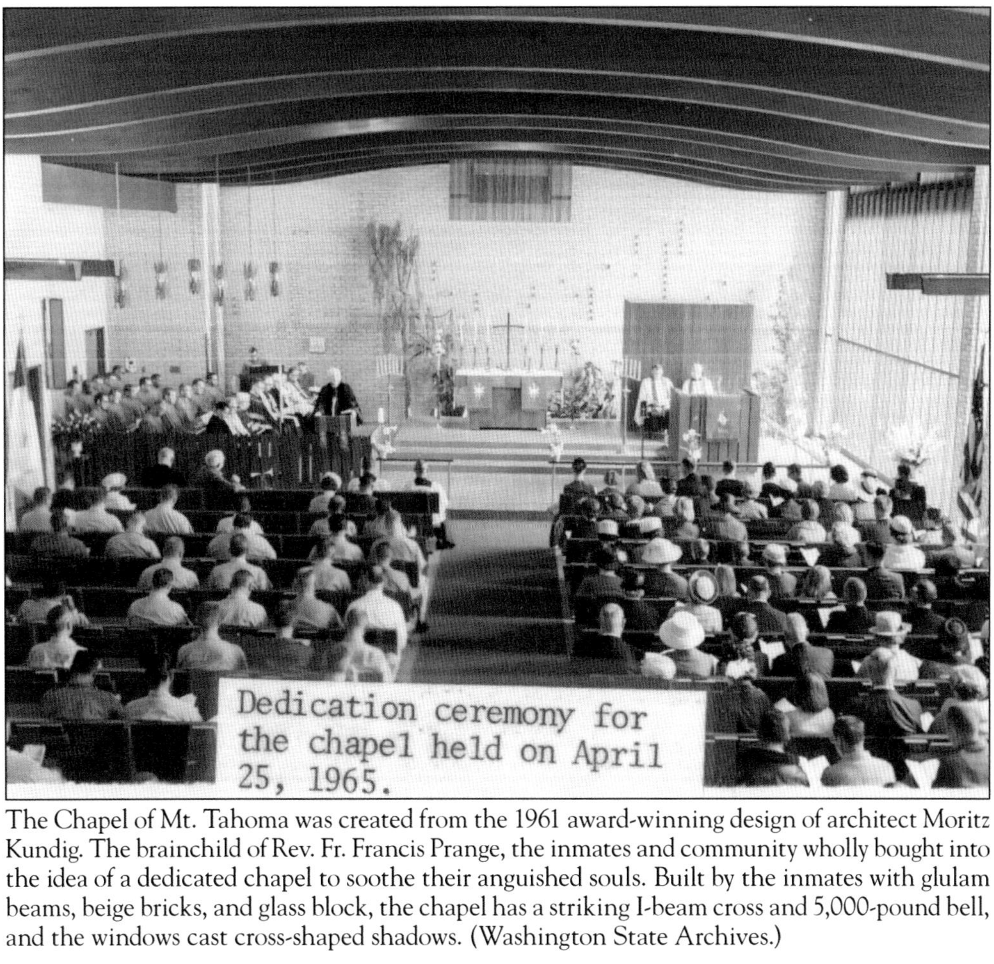

The Chapel of Mt. Tahoma was created from the 1961 award-winning design of architect Moritz Kundig. The brainchild of Rev. Fr. Francis Prange, the inmates and community wholly bought into the idea of a dedicated chapel to soothe their anguished souls. Built by the inmates with glulam beams, beige bricks, and glass block, the chapel has a striking I-beam cross and 5,000-pound bell, and the windows cast cross-shaped shadows. (Washington State Archives.)

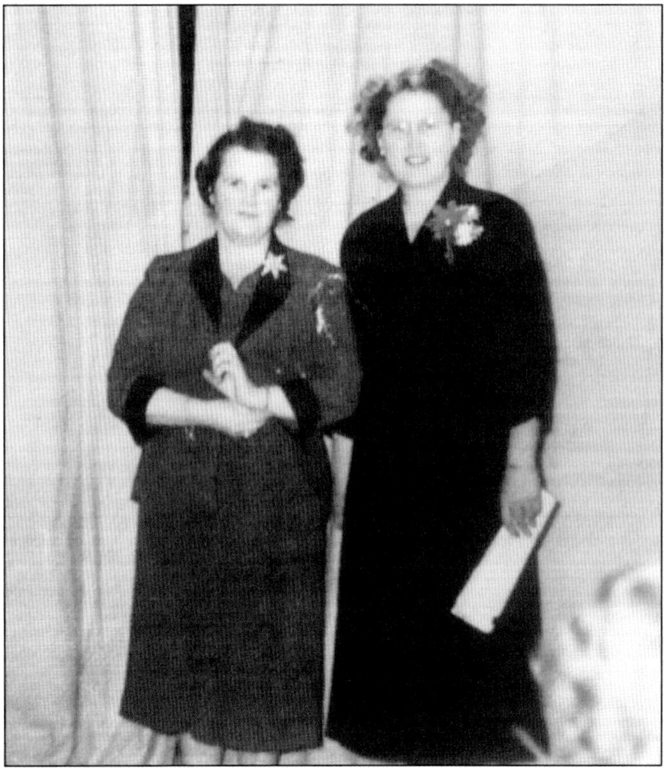

Teachers Doris Taylor (left) and Nellie Heimbecker are on the stage at the community center for a school program in the late 1950s. McNeil children were fortunate to have really capable and caring teachers who expected a lot from them but used professional discretion to err on the side of kindness when offering correction. The teachers ran a tight ship but provided wonderful elementary education. (Loren Else.)

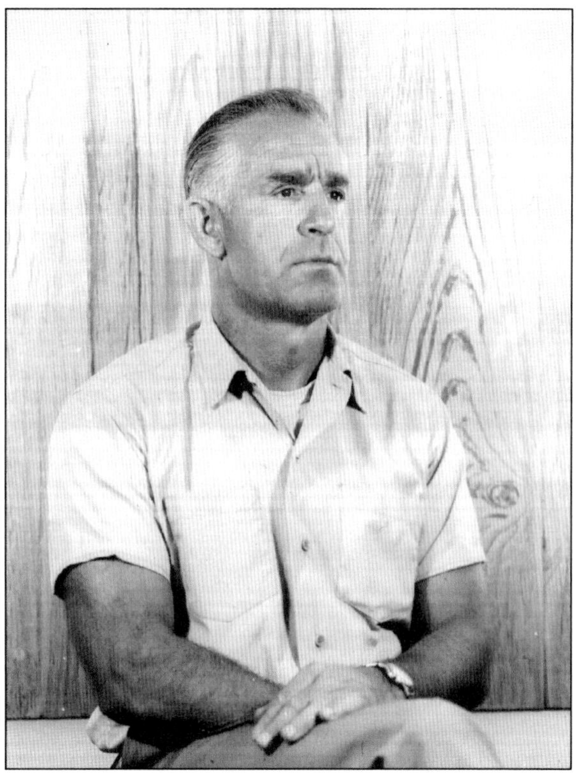

Arthur "Woody" Woodruff and his wife, Sally, were a part of McNeil culture from the late 1940s to 1980. Woody worked as a correctional officer, but his calling was the marine department, where he eventually became manager. He acquired his state ferry captain's license and ran the Anderson Island–Steilacoom ferry for years after retiring from the BOP. Sally passed on, but Woody still lives in Steilacoom. (Washington State Archives.)

McNeil not only held prisoners, but also a Japanese internment camp during World War II. These Japanese American inmates had their own very competitive baseball and athletics teams. They made the most of a tough situation and eventually were awarded reparations. There is also a conscientious objector pictured with them, a scenario that continued through the Vietnam War. Most objectors were released by 1979. (Rubado family.)

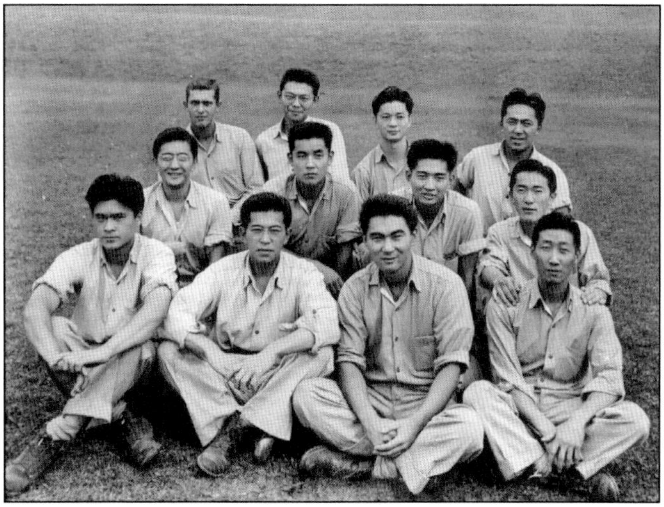

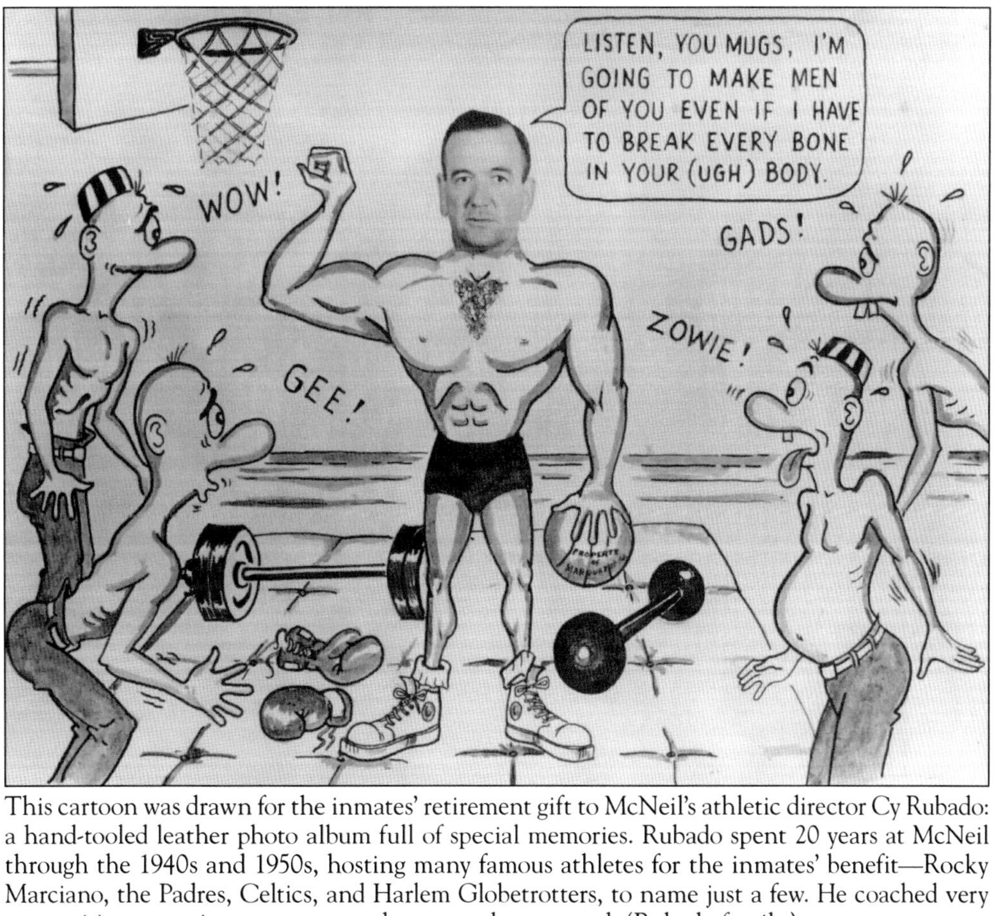

This cartoon was drawn for the inmates' retirement gift to McNeil's athletic director Cy Rubado: a hand-tooled leather photo album full of special memories. Rubado spent 20 years at McNeil through the 1940s and 1950s, hosting many famous athletes for the inmates' benefit—Rocky Marciano, the Padres, Celtics, and Harlem Globetrotters, to name just a few. He coached very competitive teams in every sport and was greatly respected. (Rubado family.)

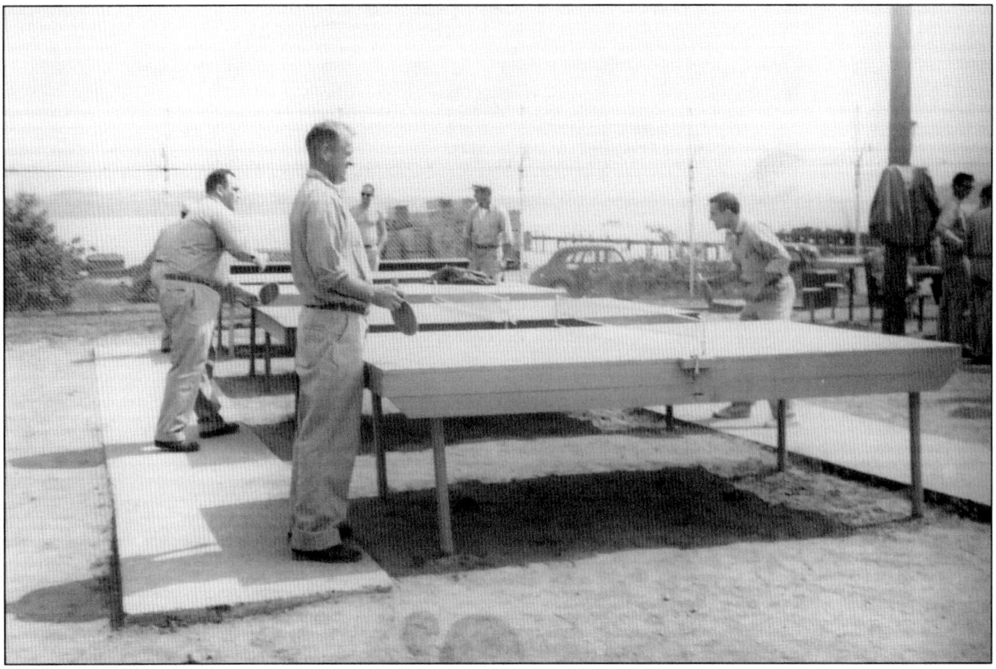

Here, the inmates play ping-pong out in the big yard in the late 1950s, with a gorgeous view of Puget Sound and Mt. Rainier. Pretty intense matches took place, but the yard was set up so weight-lifting and other sports could be enjoyed too. At one time, there was a putt-putt golf course as well. (Courtesy of the Rubado family.)

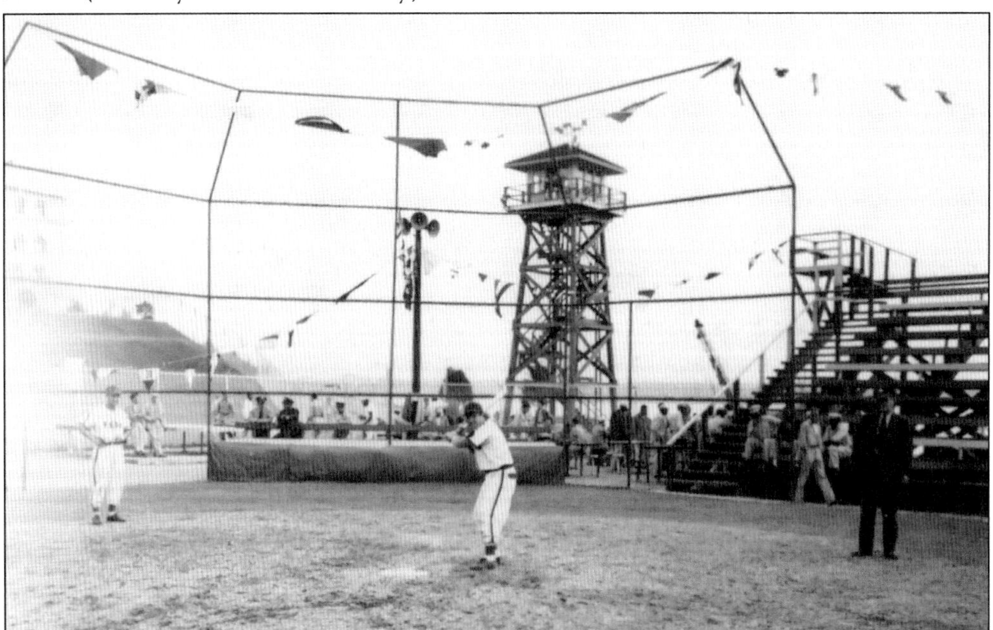

"Wheezer" Montez is at bat on "Babe Ruth" field, striking fear into the Vikings' opponents. McNeil supported intramural teams as well as a prison team that could compete on any level. Many high school and college teams got a surprise when they played McNeil. Before 1950, the McNeil team was called the Federals, but after that, it was called the Vikings. (Rubado family.)

The McNeil Island inmates sponsored a Pee-Wee football team, the Little Giants, who won their conference in 1954. The inmates sold subscriptions for *The Island Lantern* and donated their industries monies to pay the league costs and outfit teams for the Boys Club sports programs. The boys would not have played otherwise. It is heartwarming that the incarcerated recalled what they could have used and provided it for a younger generation. (Rubado family.)

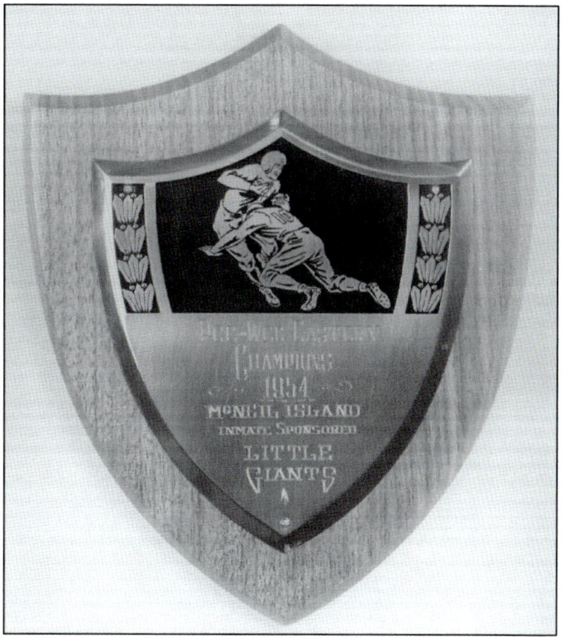

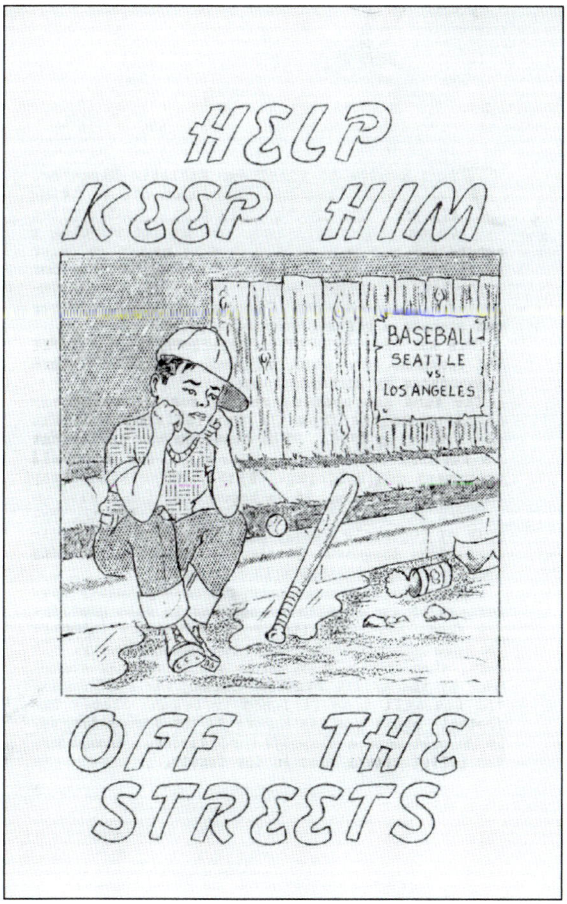

To raise funds to support the Boys Clubs teams in baseball, football, and basketball, the McNeil inmates advertised among themselves via pamphlets, getting cons to contribute donations from their own accounts in the belief that character-building sports would give kids direction and help keep them off the streets. It was a noble endeavor that was successful, owing to the compassion of the inmates. (Rubado family.)

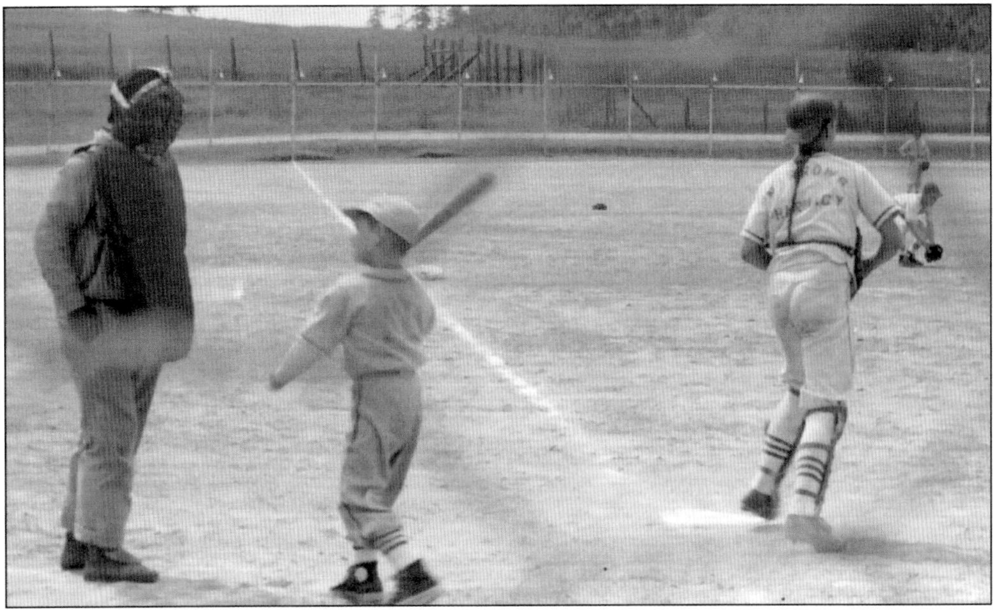

One of the Pee-Wee players takes exception to a call and has a few words to say to the umpire. It was very beneficial to both the boys and the inmates to engage in the normalcy of outdoor sports contests. The more inmates interacted outside their cells, the better they did and the higher their chances for success outside the bars. Likewise for the boys, getting advice from people who had seen some of life would help guide them on the right path. (Rubado family.)

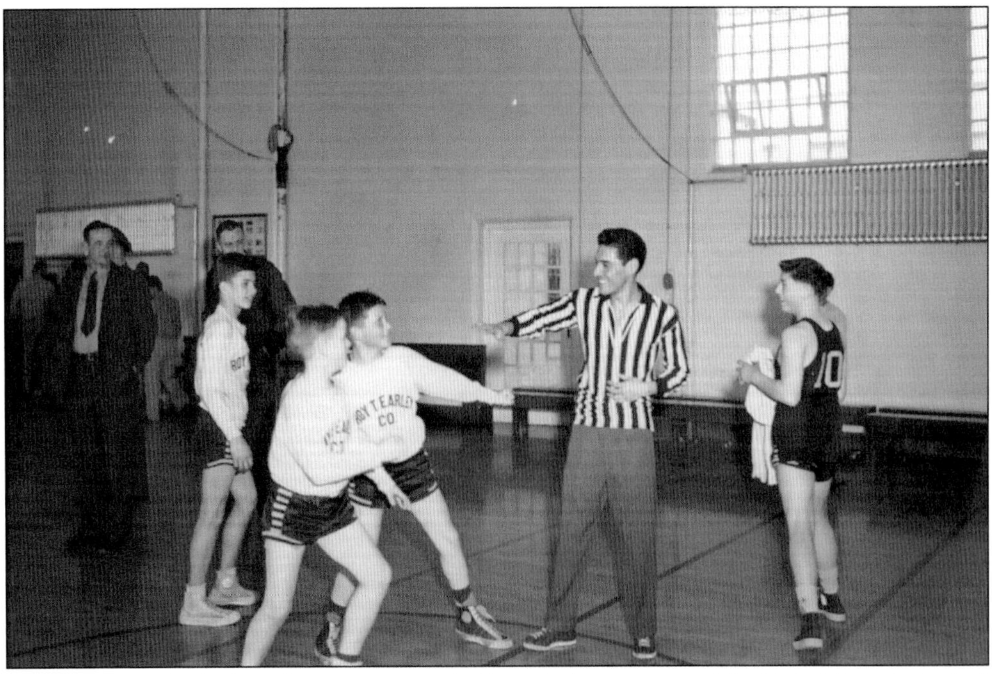

Athletic director Rubado and two correctional officers look on as some of the Little Giants basketball team members gang up on the inmate referee, all in good fun. The happiness evident in this 1950s picture speaks volumes. Sporting events were also held for the kids in boxing and wrestling, and the inmates participated in those sports as well within the institution. (Rubado family.)

Marie-Claude LeGall, a sickly French girl with an ill mother and deceased POW father, was adopted by the McNeil inmates in 1954. Her plight drew the inmates, and they raised funds to provide her with a heavy winter coat, necessities, gifts, and a check for her mother. The inmates exchanged encouraging letters with Marie; their compassion changed her life and showed her the best of humanity. (Tacoma Public Library.)

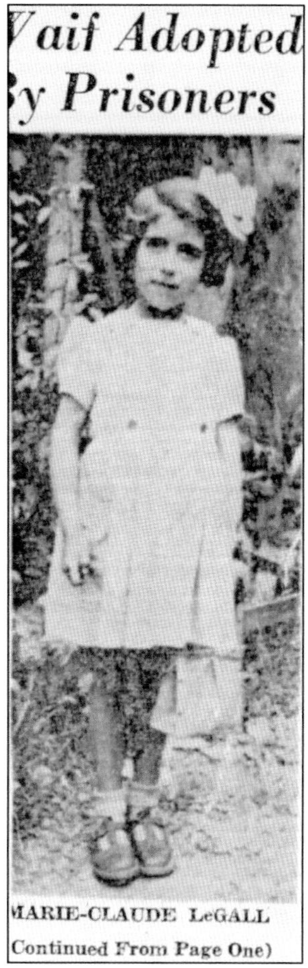

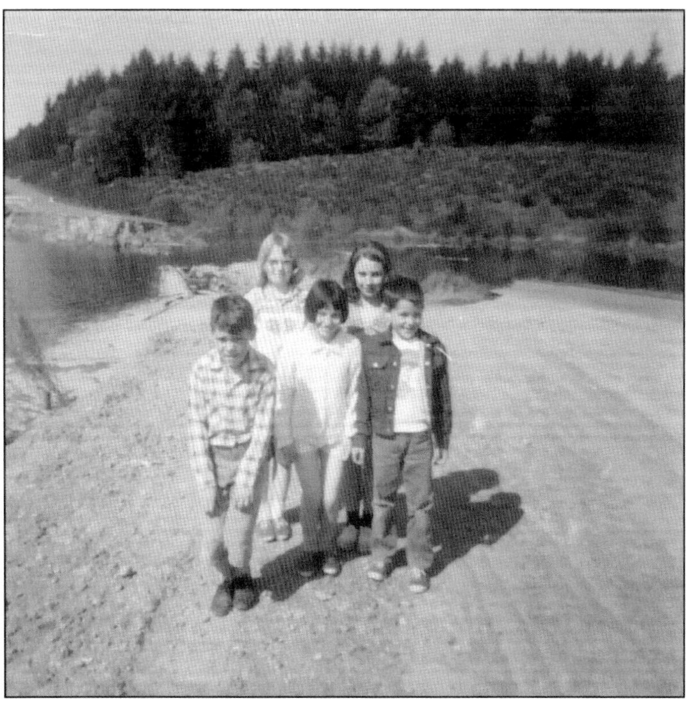

McNeil Island children, with Pat Kane at right rear, stand before the break at Butterworth Dam road, caused by the Puget Sound earthquake on April 29, 1965. Children had an exciting life on McNeil; there was so much natural area to explore and comfort in knowing one was safe on an island. Children interacted with trustees as they completed their tasks, and the exchanges were beneficial to both. (Kane family.)

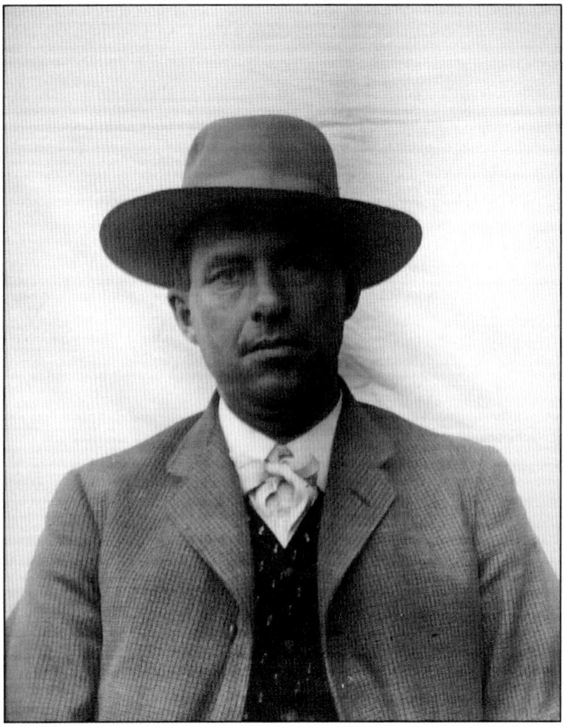

Harry Miller was sentenced to one year of hard labor at McNeil in July 1906. He and his co-conspirator, Frank Kinkart, were confidence men who posed as land brokers. Their scheme bought played-out timber stands and failed claims for basement prices, altered them, and resold them to unsuspecting marks for $60. One of the first timber fraud cases in the country, it marked a change in McNeil's inmate class. (James Miller.)

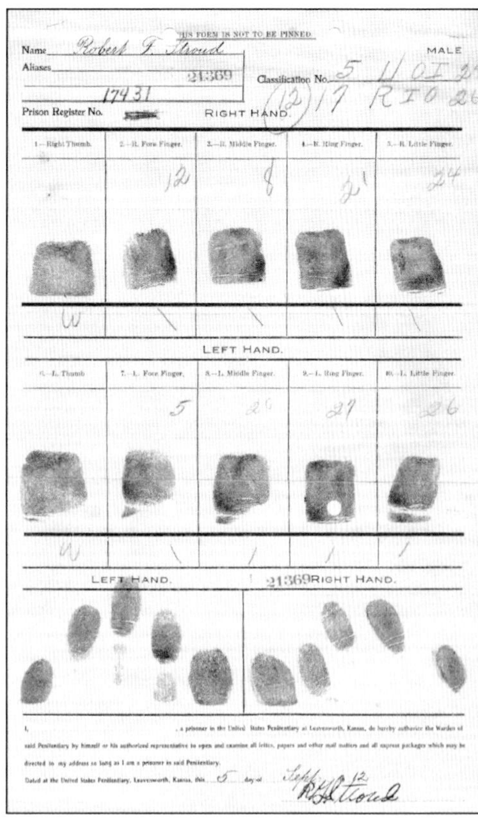

THIS FORM IS NOT TO BE PINNED.

Name Robert F. Stroud MALE

Aliases

21369

17431

Classification No. 5 11 OI 24 (12) 17 RIO 26

Prison Register No.

RIGHT HAND.

1.—Right Thumb.	2.—R. Fore Finger.	3.—R. Middle Finger.	4.—R. Ring Finger.	5.—R. Little Finger.
	12	8	21	24

LEFT HAND.

6.—L. Thumb	7.—L. Fore Finger.	8.—L. Middle Finger.	9.—L. Ring Finger.	10.—L. Little Finger.
	5	26	27	26

LEFT HAND. 21369 RIGHT HAND.

I, , a prisoner in the United States Penitentiary at Leavenworth, Kansas, do hereby authorize the Warden of said Penitentiary by himself or his authorized representative to open and examine all letters, papers and other mail matters and all express packages which may be directed to my address so long as I am a prisoner in said Penitentiary.

Dated at the United States Penitentiary, Leavenworth, Kansas, this 5 day of Sept. 12

R. F. Stroud

Seen here is Robert Stroud's 1912 identification card at Leavenworth, Kansas, after leaving McNeil, where he was sentenced in 1909 for shooting a bartender. At Leavenworth, Stroud killed a guard and was sentenced to life imprisonment in solitary confinement. Although a psychopath, he wrote books about birds while in prison that were smuggled out and published. Stroud later did time at the Rock, where he gained fame as the Birdman of Alcatraz. (National Archives and Records Administration.)

Robert Stroud stabbed a McNeil orderly over seven times because the orderly told the prison staff about Stroud taking drugs. Stroud commented he was sorry that he had not killed the snitch. That sent him to Leavenworth. This form also points out his original crime, killing a man over $8—the difference between what a bartender paid a prostitute Stroud pimped out and the going rate at the time. (National Archives and Records Administration.)

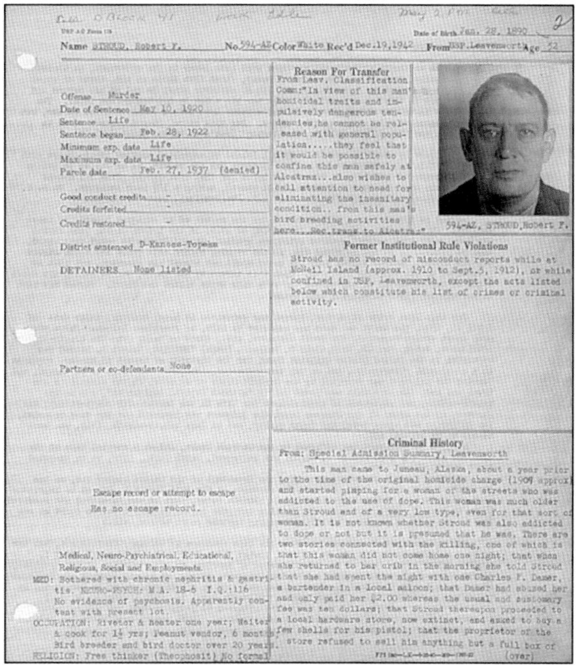

Date of Birth Jan. 28, 1890

Name STROUD, Robert F. No. 594-AZ Color White Rec'd Dec.19,1942 From USP. Leavenworth Age 52

Offense Murder
Date of Sentence May 10, 1920
Sentence Life
Sentence began Feb. 28, 1922
Minimum exp. date Life
Maximum exp. date Life
Parole date Feb. 27, 1937 (denied)

Good conduct credits -
Credits forfeited -
Credits restored -

District sentenced D-Kansas-Topeka

DETAINERS None listed

Partners or co-defendants None

Reason For Transfer

From Leav. Classification Comm:"In view of this man's homicidal traits and impulsively dangerous tendencies, he cannot be released with general population.....they feel that it would be possible to confine this man safely at Alcatraz...also wishes to call attention to need for eliminating the insanitary condition.. from this man's bird breeding activities here...Rec.trans.to Alcatraz."

594-AZ, STROUD, Robert F.

Former Institutional Rule Violations

Stroud has no record of misconduct reports while at McNeil Island (approx. 1910 to Sept.5, 1912), or while confined in USP, Leavenworth, except the acts listed below which constitute his list of crimes or criminal activity.

Escape record or attempt to escape
Has no escape record.

Medical, Neuro-Psychiatrical, Educational, Religious, Social and Employments.

MED: Bothered with chronic nephritis & gastritis. NEURO-PSYCH: M.A. 18-6 I.Q.:116 No evidence of psychosis. Apparently content with present lot.
OCCUPATION: Riveter & heater one year; Waiter & cook for 1½ yrs; Peanut vendor, 6 months; Bird breeder and bird doctor over 20 years.
RELIGION: Free thinker (Theophosit) No formal

Criminal History

From: Special Admission Summary, Leavenworth

This man came to Juneau, Alaska, about a year prior to the time of the original homicide charge (1909 approx) and started pimping for a woman of the streets who was addicted to the use of dope. This woman was much older than Stroud and of a very low type, even for that sort of woman. It is not known whether Stroud was also addicted to dope or not but it is presumed that he was. There are two stories connected with the killing, one of which is that this woman did not come home one night; that when she returned to her crib in the morning she told Stroud that she had spent the night with one Charles F. Damer, a bartender in a local saloon; that Damer had abused her and only paid her $2.00 whereas the usual and customary fee was ten dollars; that Stroud thereupon proceeded to a local hardware store, now extinct, and asked to buy a few shells for his pistol; that the proprietor of the store refused to sell him anything but a full box of

(over)

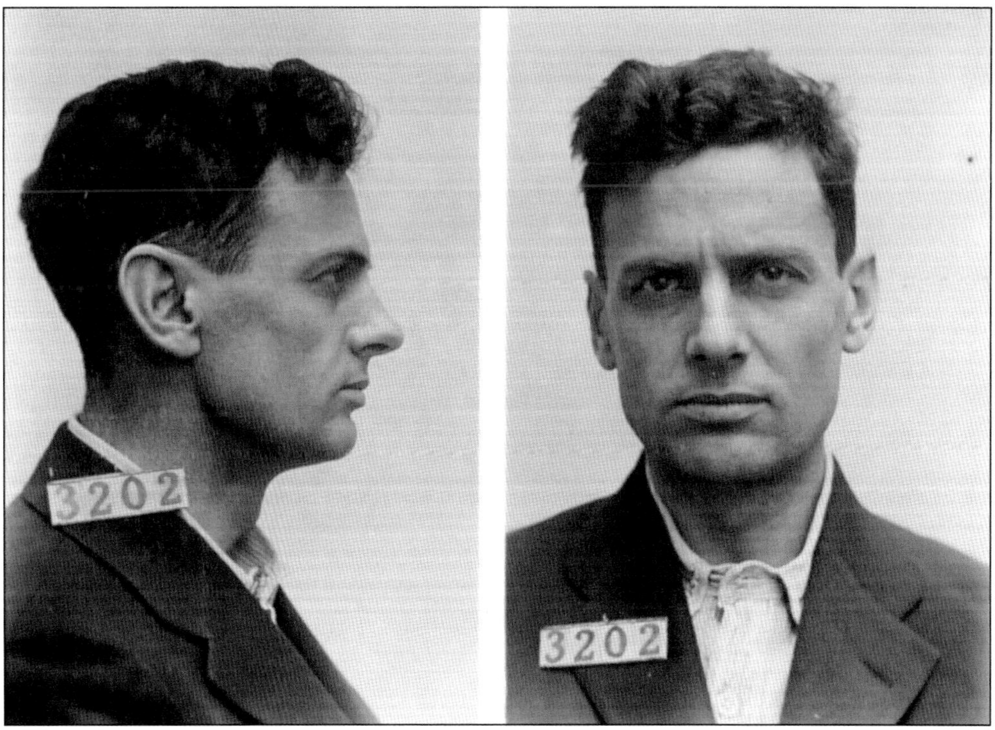

Logan Billingsley's 1963 *New York Times* obituary read, "A real estate developer and authority on American Indian affairs." It did not mention he had been a successful bootlegger who founded the National Bootlegger's Protective Association to protect business profits totaling $200,000 weekly. He was arrested and escaped Seattle jail only to be caught and sentenced to McNeil. He murdered his first father-in-law, but the charge was reduced to manslaughter. (Robert Billingsley.)

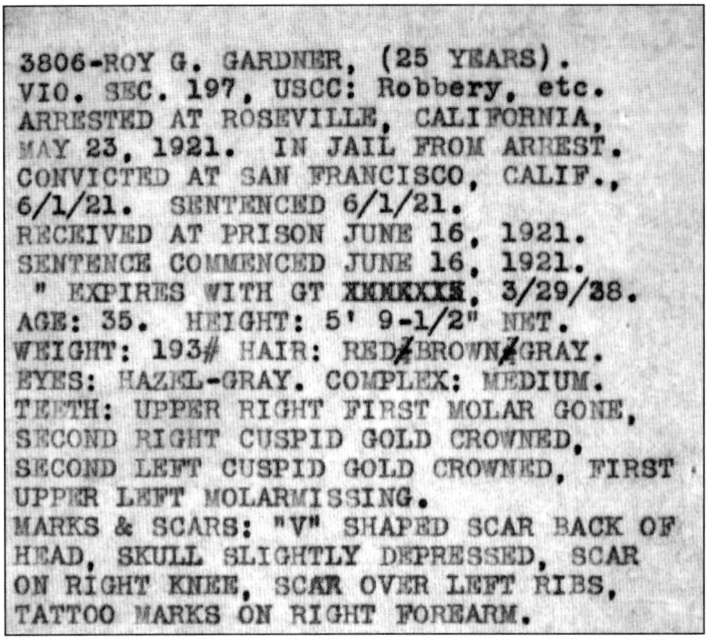

3806-ROY G. GARDNER, (25 YEARS).
VIO. SEC. 197, USCC: Robbery, etc.
ARRESTED AT ROSEVILLE, CALIFORNIA,
MAY 23, 1921. IN JAIL FROM ARREST.
CONVICTED AT SAN FRANCISCO, CALIF.,
6/1/21. SENTENCED 6/1/21.
RECEIVED AT PRISON JUNE 16, 1921.
SENTENCE COMMENCED JUNE 16, 1921.
" EXPIRES WITH GT XXXXXXX, 3/29/38.
AGE: 35. HEIGHT: 5' 9-1/2" NET.
WEIGHT: 193# HAIR: RED/BROWN/GRAY.
EYES: HAZEL-GRAY. COMPLEX: MEDIUM.
TEETH: UPPER RIGHT FIRST MOLAR GONE,
SECOND RIGHT CUSPID GOLD CROWNED,
SECOND LEFT CUSPID GOLD CROWNED, FIRST
UPPER LEFT MOLARMISSING.
MARKS & SCARS: "V" SHAPED SCAR BACK OF
HEAD, SKULL SLIGHTLY DEPRESSED, SCAR
ON RIGHT KNEE, SCAR OVER LEFT RIBS,
TATTOO MARKS ON RIGHT FOREARM.

Roy Gardner, a bank and mail train robber known as the "Gentleman Bandit" and "King of the Escape Artists," escaped McNeil by convincing two inmates the guards would not shoot if they escaped during a baseball game in 1921. Gardner was shot in the leg, but both of his conspirators died—one on the spot. Gardner was captured in Phoenix and sent to Leavenworth. (National Archives and Records Administration.)

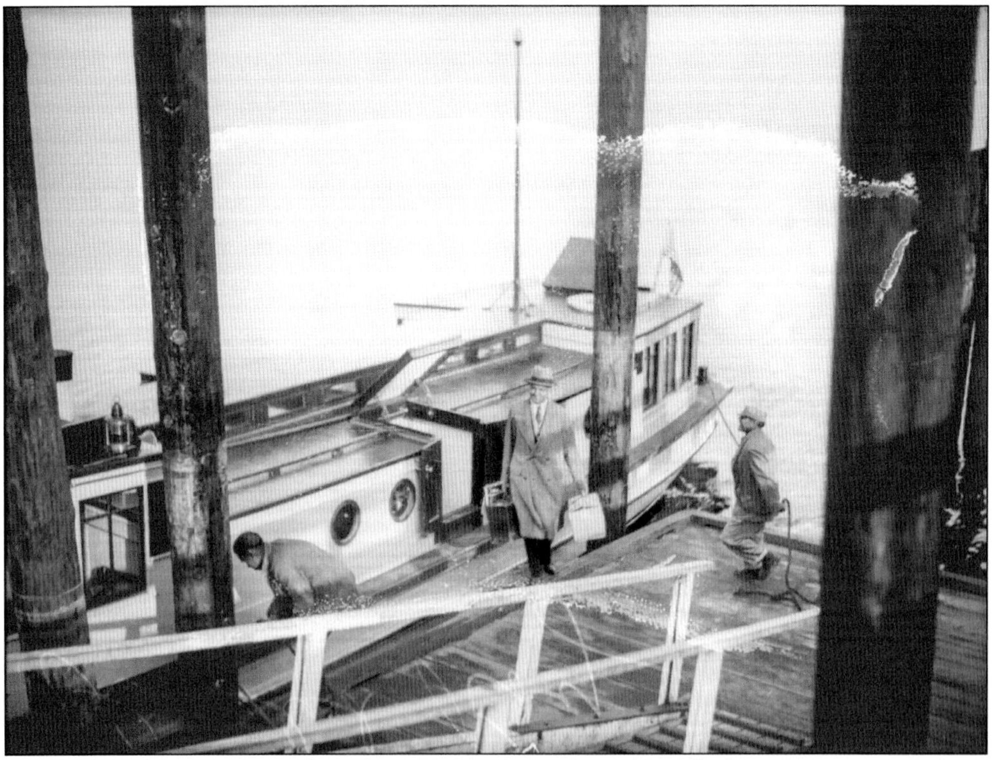

Roy Olmstead departs McNeil on the *A.H. MacCormick* in 1931. The launch was named after a prison expert and was one of inmate Fred Peter's 1930 Navy requisitions. Olmstead, "King of Seattle Bootleggers," bootlegged while a police lieutenant but never let his men carry guns. Sentenced to four years, he found religion and, upon release, preached against alcohol, taught Sunday school, and visited the King County Jail weekly. (Museum of History and Industry.)

Gangster Al Karpis, former public enemy No. 1, spent 26 unrepentant years at Alcatraz, but seven years on McNeil changed his outlook. Befriended by warden Paul Madigan, Karpis became a model trustee, drove the island school bus, and served as a father figure to the young inmates at Summit House. After release in 1969, he went straight. Karpis also taught Charles Manson to play the guitar, leading to the beginning of a tragic tale. (National Archives and Records Administration.)

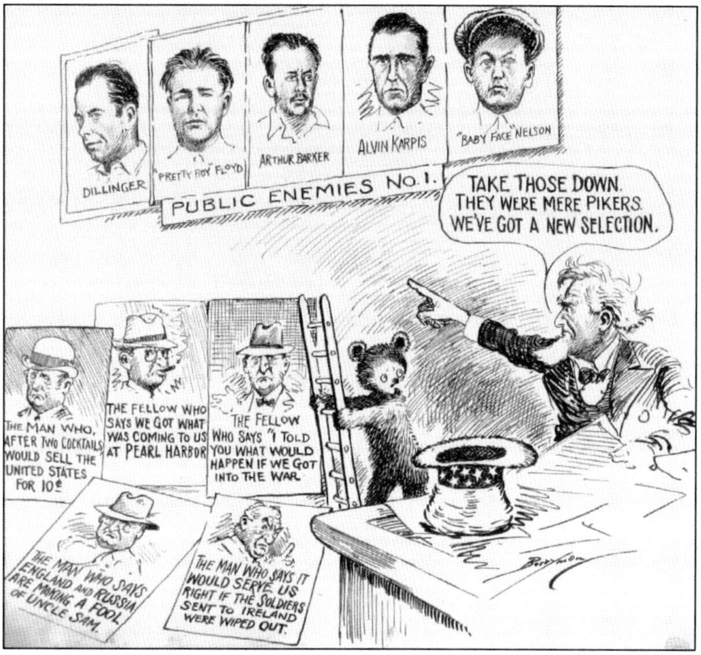

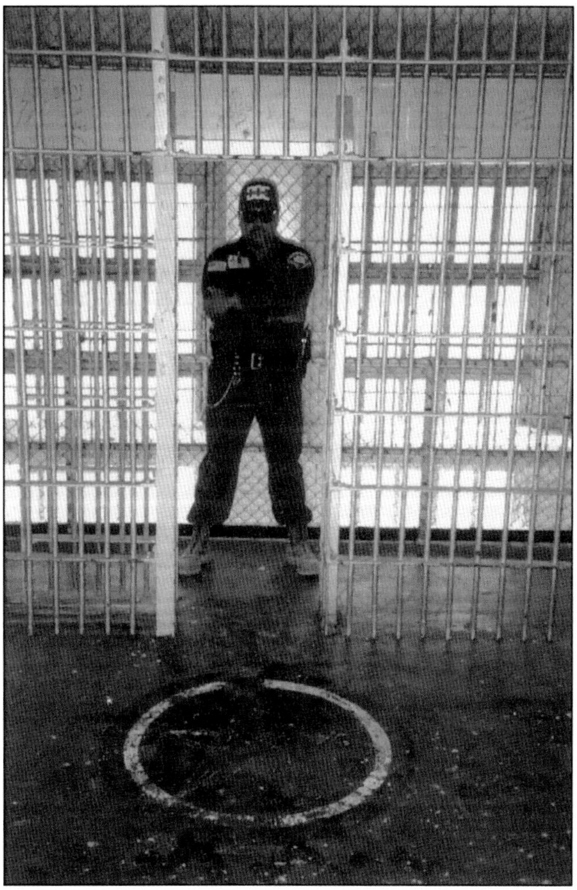

This 1995 photograph shows officer Komo standing before the pentagram painted by Charles Manson with chicken blood stolen from the kitchen, from within Manson's former cell in Three/Four House, before it was torn down. The cellblock had five-man cells that were designed by the architectural firm of Heath, Gove & Bell that then became 10-man cells, thanks to convertible bunks to maximize space. (Washington State Archives.)

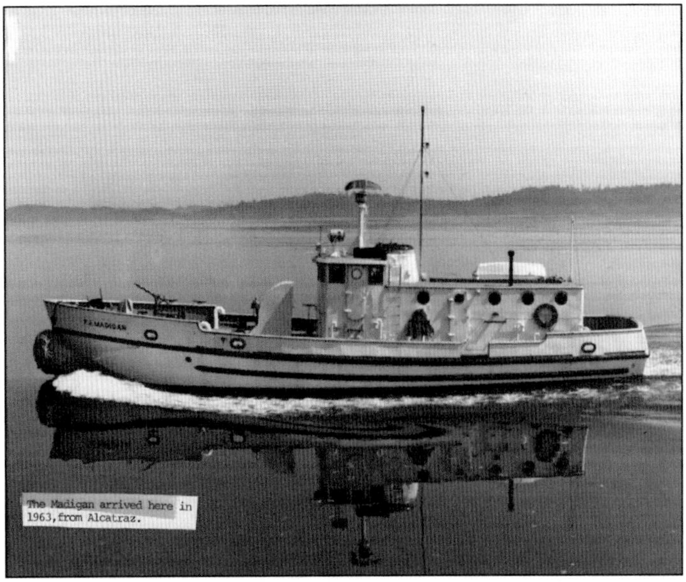

The *P.J. Madigan*, named for Warden Paul Madigan, followed him from Alcatraz. Madigan started out a correctional officer there, where he gained fans by knocking out McNeil's Clem Zukowski, who came to teach self-defense. Madigan talked an Alcatraz hostage-taker out of killing him and others, converted Al Karpis to a clean life, was respected by prisoners and staff, and approved the building of the Chapel of Mt. Tahoma. (Washington State Archives.)

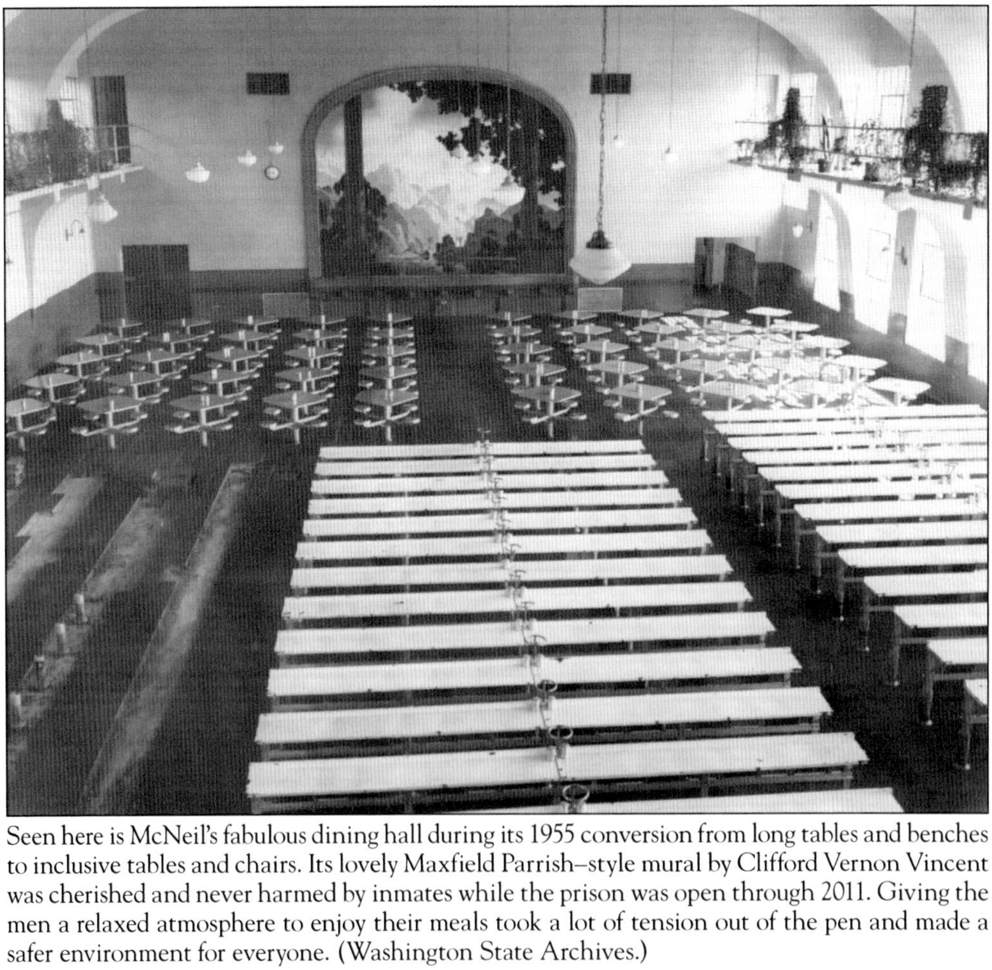

Seen here is McNeil's fabulous dining hall during its 1955 conversion from long tables and benches to inclusive tables and chairs. Its lovely Maxfield Parrish–style mural by Clifford Vernon Vincent was cherished and never harmed by inmates while the prison was open through 2011. Giving the men a relaxed atmosphere to enjoy their meals took a lot of tension out of the pen and made a safer environment for everyone. (Washington State Archives.)

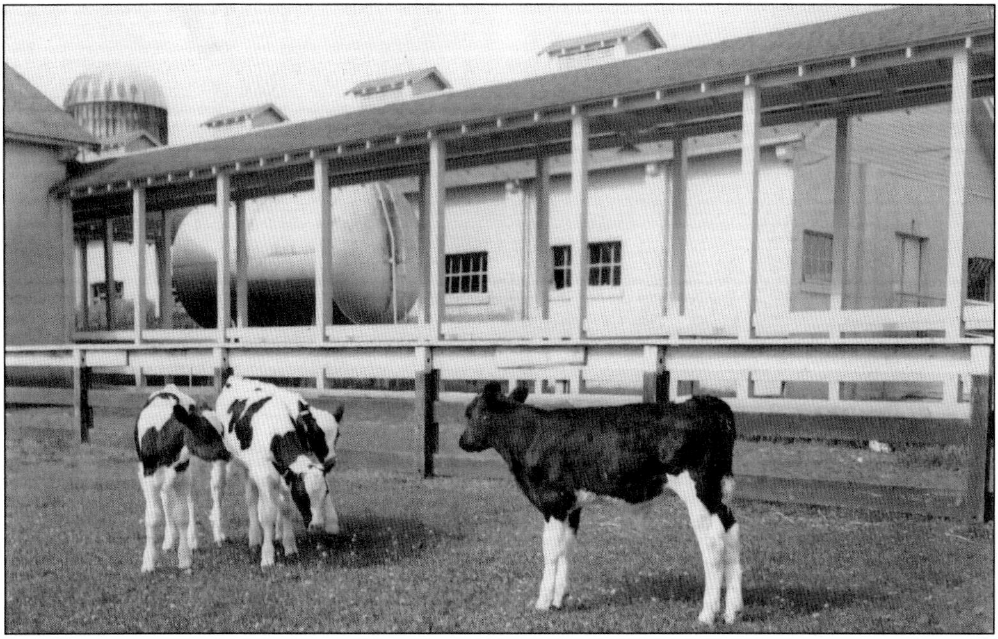

Part of what made McNeil run so smoothly was the great food, and the dairy operation was a large part of it. Here, four Holstein calves eat buttercups in the grass surrounding the dairy in the 1960s. Thousands of gallons of milk were processed at McNeil, and at one time, the prison supplied all the school milk in the western part of the state until private enterprise complained. (Washington State Archives.)

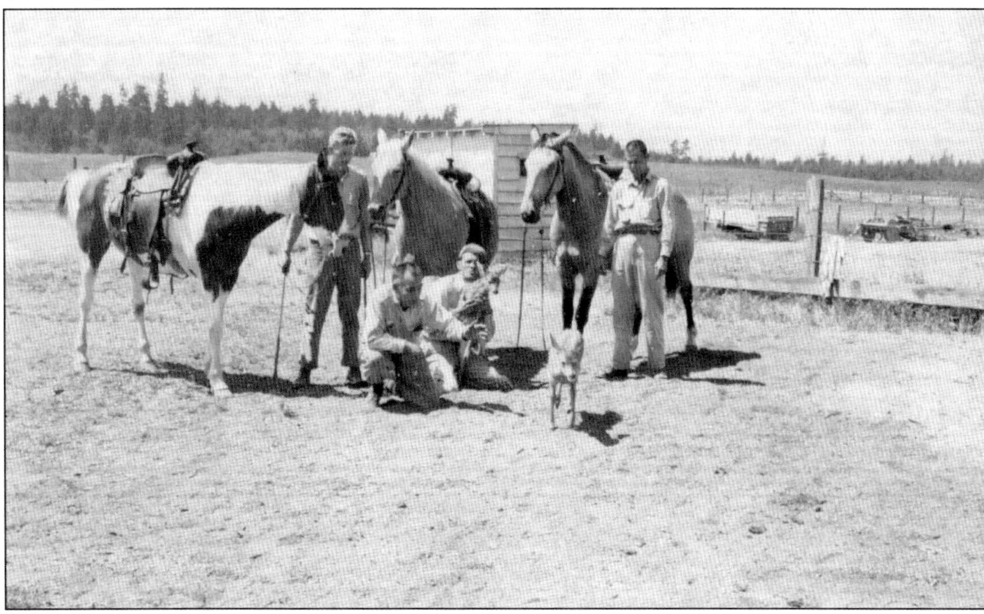

Here, inmate cowboys, including Al Karpis on the right, play with two fawns they have befriended in the late 1960s. Inmates and families on McNeil were always feeding and befriending the wildlife, as it was such a contained environment. Certainly, it was a wonderful exercise in humanity for the inmates to be able to show concern and compassion for living animals. (Washington State Archives.)

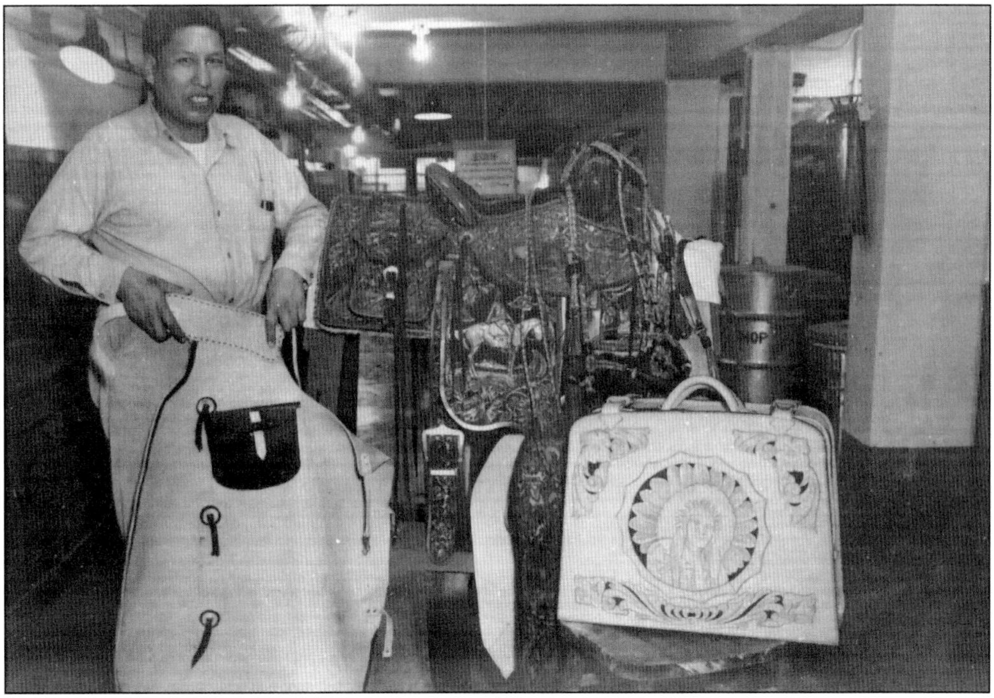

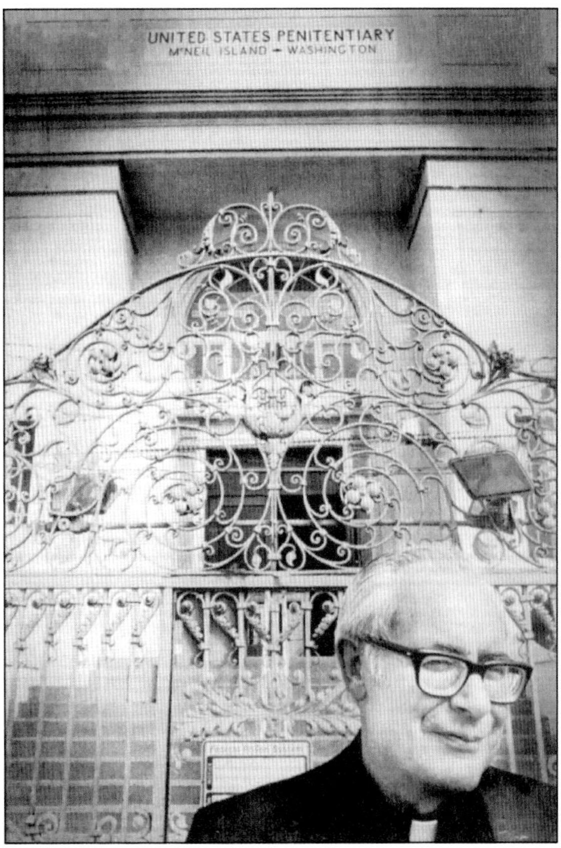

A Native American proudly displays detailed leatherworks he made in McNeil's hobby shop in the 1960s. How wonderful that the loss of time spent in prison could be put to good use, creating skills and producing stunning and practical products. The heavy chaps, deeply carved suitcase, and gorgeous saddle would make anyone proud to own them. Items from the hobby shop were frequently sold at markets the prison organized. (Washington State Archives.)

Rev. Fr. John McBride was part of the 7th Cavalry in World War II and waded into prison riots with calm. He supervised the Prisoner's Assistance Program (PAP), an emergency fund for inmates and their families that raised cash by selling Easter flowers, shoes to prisoners, artwork, and other legitimate enterprises. At the 1981 closure, PAP donated its $6,000 balance to Mount St. Helens victims. McBride led by example with kindness. (Washington State Archives.)

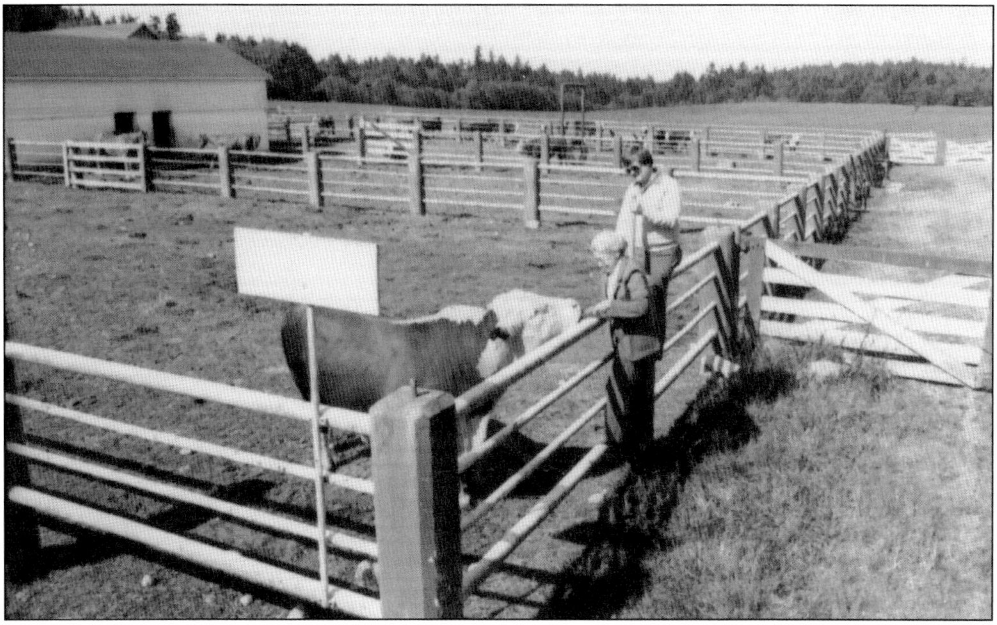

Here, the renowned Anderson Island author Betsey "Bessie" Johnson Cammon feeds a Hereford cow at McNeil's honor farm in 1975 on her last visit to her former island home. Bessie moved to Still Harbor in 1906 and lived there until 1916 before returning to Anderson. She appreciated what the history of a people means to the future; she wrote *Island Memoir*, the classic work on her twin island homes. (Washington State Archives.)

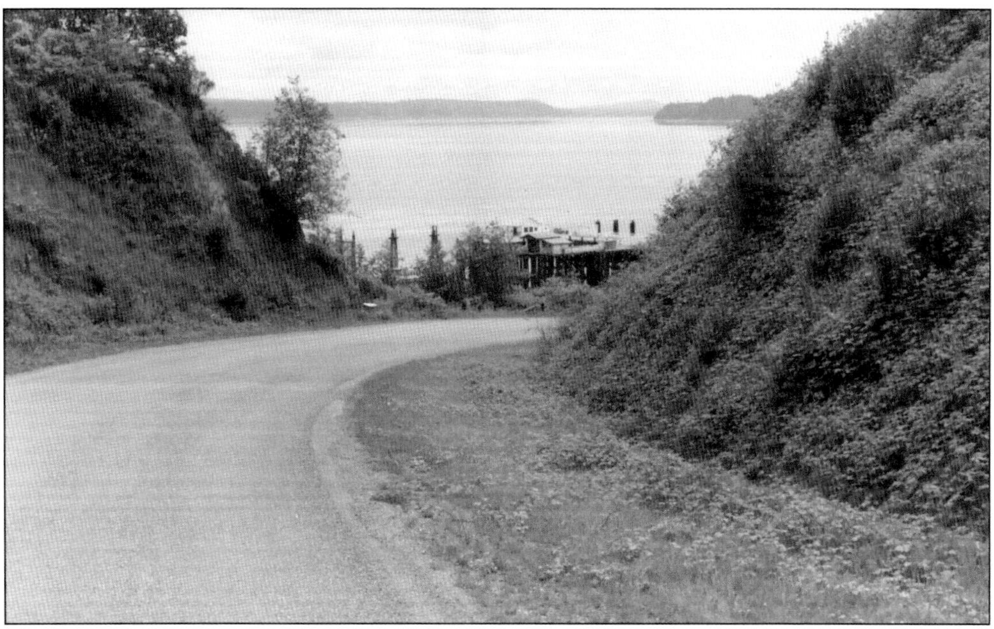

This is the view of McNeil's main dock, the sound, and Ketron Island from Minkema Pass in 2013. Built by engineer Henry Minkema in the late 1940s, the pass cut through a high bluff to better serve staff families. Reaching this point, one knew if they would make the boat or not, which was always a questionable thing. It also is a slice of home, making one appreciate the daily boat ride full of camaraderie. (McNeil Island Historical Society.)

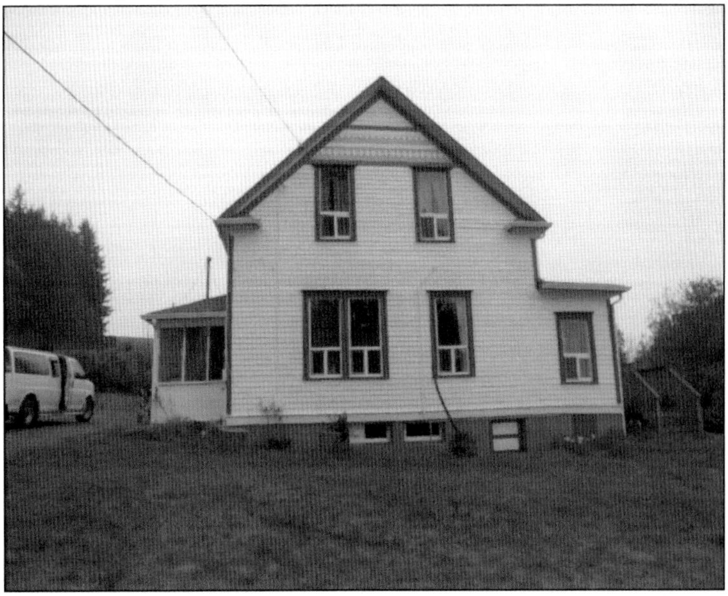

Eden Creek, the home John Eden built in Eden County on McNeil Island in 1885, still stands today, although silent and abandoned. The home had just been refurbished in 2011 when this picture was taken. Overlooking a sandbar on the sound where orca cavort chasing seals or salmon, it was a wonderful place to play as a child, and memories made there will never fade. (Eric Heinitz.)

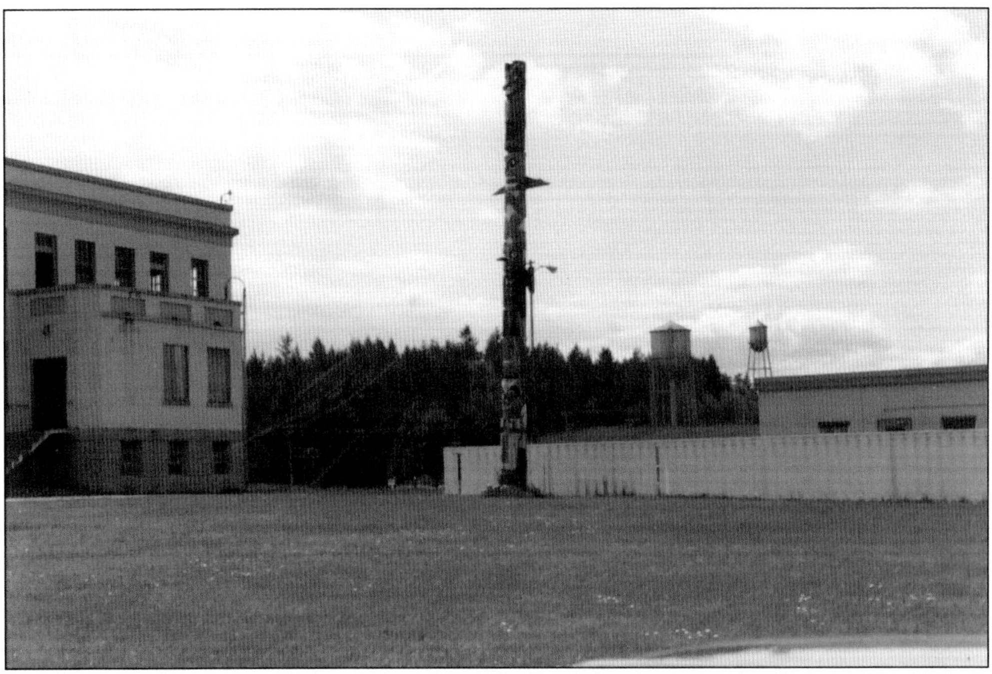

Seen here are the totem pole beside Kingdom Hall and the dormitory building at the old farm camp, where the SCC sits today. There were a decent number of Native Americans and Native Alaskans incarcerated over McNeil's decades, and in the early 1970s, they carved a totem pole to decorate the honor farm facilities. The totem pole and much of the farm are gone now, replaced by SCC's modern buildings. (Washington State Archives.)

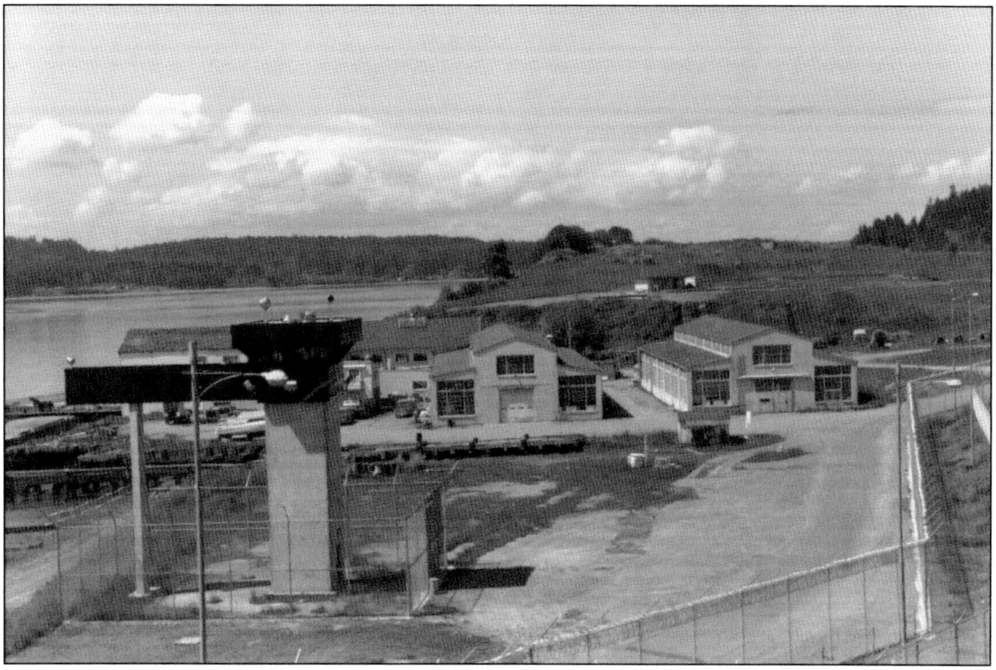

The prison had several towers over the years as technology and designs changed. Tower three was built as a temporary tower in the early 1990s and has sat idle since the prison closed. The buildings in the background housed marine services and the machine and auto shop, comprising Shop Row. (Washington State Archives.)

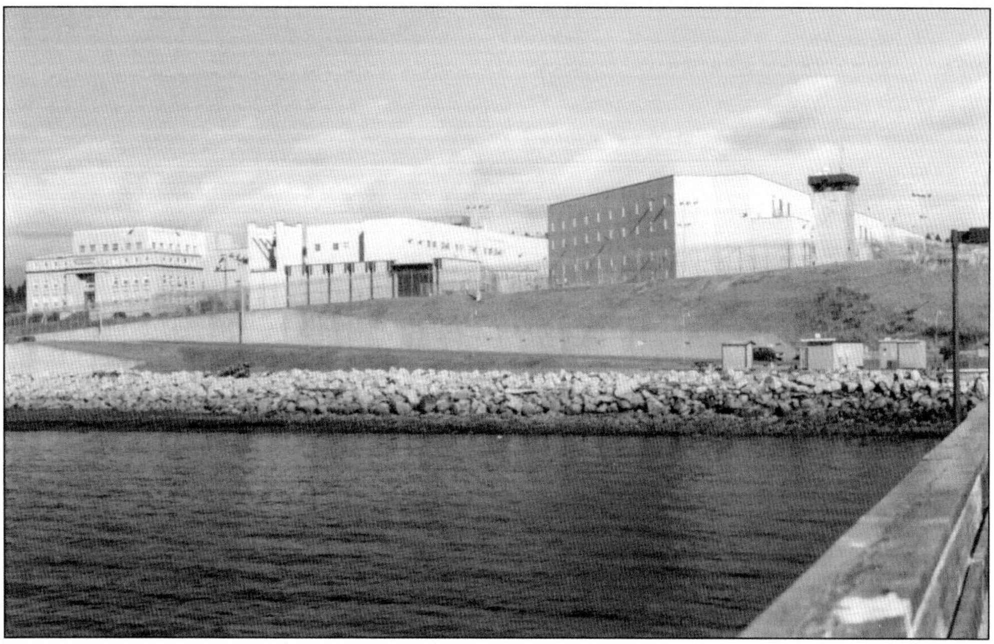

This is the view inmates and visitors had of the prison right after arriving by ferry from Steilacoom. The administration building is on the left, followed by the award-winning Chapel of Mt. Tahoma and cell blocks. The waterfront road leading to the prison runs along the center. (Washington State Archives.)

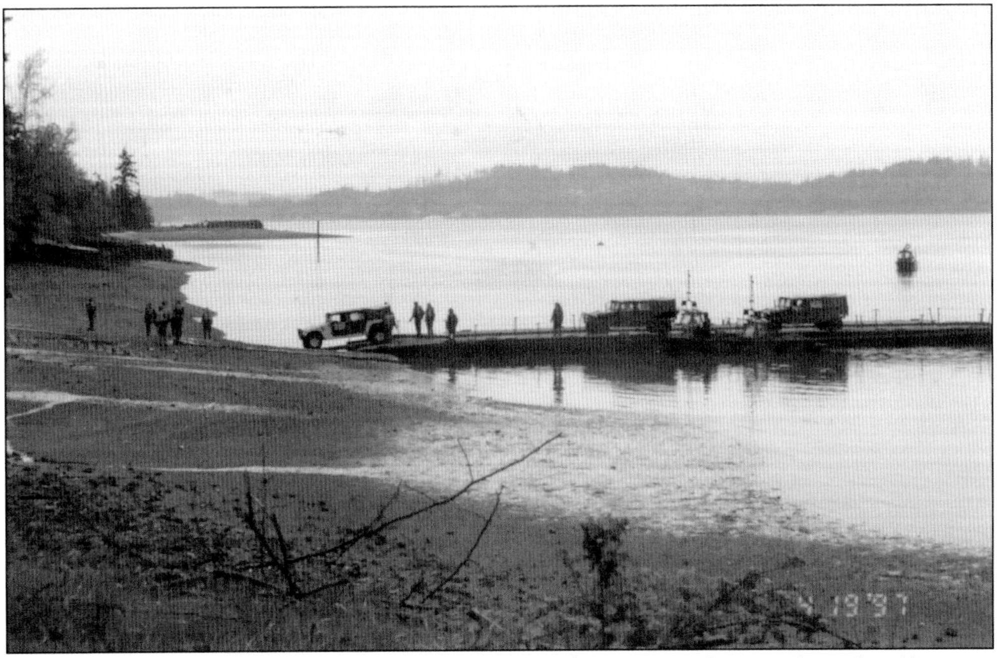

McNeil Island's various size buildings, from cell blocks to houses, away from residential and business areas, along with the best rifle range in the state and miles of shoreline, make it ideal for training exercises by emergency response teams, as seen in this 1997 photograph. Multi-agency teams from around the state still practice interagency training on McNeil. (Washington State Archives.)

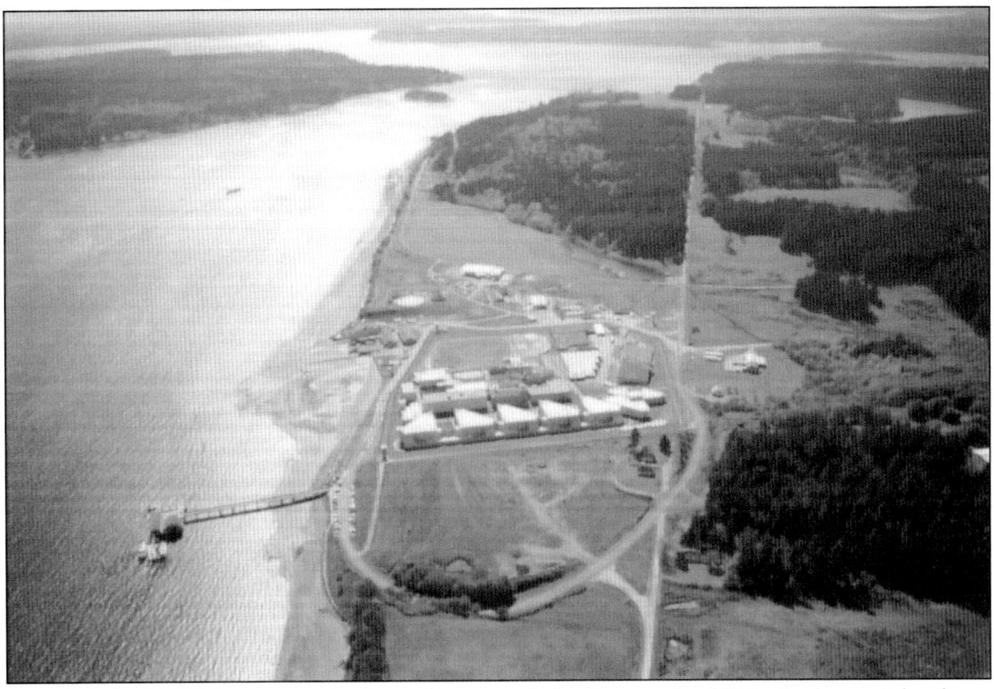

This aerial view of the current facilities shows roads leading to the SCC. Anderson Island can be seen at top, with a patch of Eagle Island between McNeil and Anderson. Note how much of McNeil has never been developed. (Washington State Department of Corrections.)

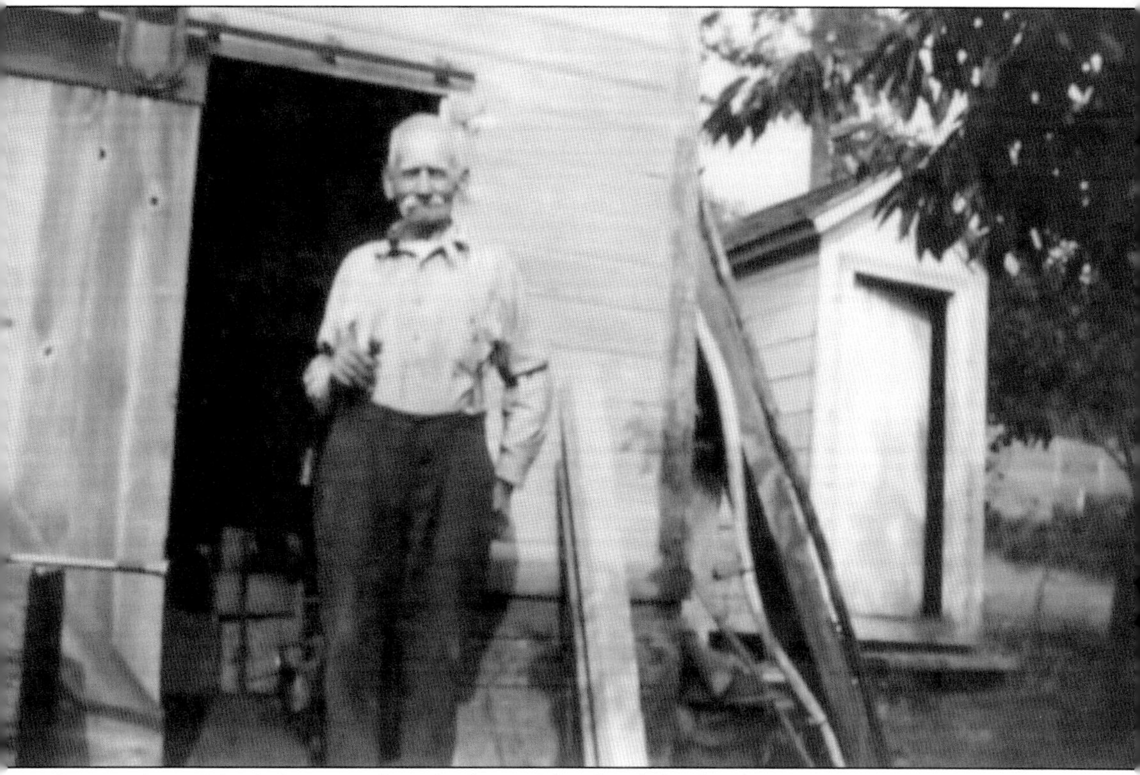

German-born John Luhr arrived on Anderson Island with his brother Ernest in 1899 but spent his adult life on McNeil, raising his family until they had to leave Luhr Creek in 1936 and return to Anderson. Luhr farmed, played the harmonica, and recalled McNeil. He knew that home is where the heart is. Memories of McNeil Island will always be in the hearts of those who lived or worked there. (Luhr and Johnson families.)

Consistent with our mission to preserve history on a local level, this book was printed in South Carolina on American-made paper and manufactured entirely in the United States. Products carrying the accredited Forest Stewardship Council (FSC) label are printed on 100 percent FSC-certified paper.